The Philosophy of
Kierkegaard

Continental European Philosophy

This series provides accessible and stimulating introductions to the ideas of continental thinkers who have shaped the fundamentals of European philosophical thought. Powerful and radical, the ideas of these philosophers have often been contested, but they remain key to understanding current philosophical thinking as well as the current direction of disciplines such as political science, literary theory, comparative literature, art history, and cultural studies. Each book seeks to combine clarity with depth, introducing fresh insights and wider perspectives while also providing a comprehensive survey of each thinker's philosophical ideas.

Published titles

The Philosophy of Gadamer
Jean Grondin

The Philosophy of Merleau-Ponty
Eric Matthews

The Philosophy of Habermas
Andrew Edgar

The Philosophy of Nietzsch
Rex Welshon

The Philosophy of Kierkegaard
George Pattison

The Philosophy of Schopenl
Dale Jacquette

Forthcoming titles include

The Philosophy of Deleuze
Peter Sedgwick

The Philosophy of H
Burt Hopkin

The Philosophy of Derrida
Mark Dooley and Liam Kavanagh

The Philosophy
Jim O'Sl

The Philosophy of Foucault
Todd May

The Philosophy o
Patrick Riley, Sr and

The Philosophy of Hegel
Allen Speight

The Philoso
Anthony

The Philosophy of Heidegger
Jeff Malpas

The Philosophy of Kierkegaard

George Pattison

McGill-Queen's University Press
Montreal & Kingston • Ithaca

ISBN 0-7735-2986-1   (hardcover)
ISBN 0-7735-2987-X   (paperback)

Legal deposit third quarter 2005
Bibliothèque nationale du Québec

Published simultaneously outside North America
by Acumen Publishing Limited

McGill-Queen's University Press acknowledges the financial support of
the Government of Canada through the Book Publishing Development
Program (BPIDP) for its activities.

Library and Archives Canada Cataloguing in Publication

Pattison, George, 1950-
    The philosophy of Kierkegaard / George Pattison.

(Continental European philosophy)
Includes bibliographical references and index.
ISBN 0-7735-2986-1 (bound).—ISBN 0-7735-2987-X (pbk.)

    1. Kierkegaard, Søren, 1813-1855. I. Title. II. Series.

B4377.P37 2005   198'.9   C2005-900997-7

Designed and typeset by Kate Williams, Swansea.
Printed and bound by Biddles Ltd., King's Lynn.

Contents

For students past and present who have wrestled with me over the interpretation of Kierkegaard and to whom I owe many of my best insights into his thought.

Acknowledgements

I am grateful to Acumen Publishing for the invitation to write this book. Working on it has made me bring together and to think through a lot of loose threads that have been floating around in my reading and teaching of Kierkegaard. As the dedication states, I am also grateful to undergraduate and, especially, postgraduate students who have read Kierkegaard with me and have provided me with innumerable insights, angles and questions that I would never have reached on my own. I am particularly indebted to Dan Conway and an anonymous reader who commented on the original outline of the book, and to Ed Mooney, Anthony Rudd, Robert Stern and Merold Westphal, who saw portions of the text in preparation and gave helpful advice and encouraging words. John Lippitt and Jamie Ferreira read the draft for Acumen and their characteristically precise and sharp comments have helped to tighten the book and to make it more accessible, although there will doubtless remain some points on which we shall continue to disagree. Thanks too to Steve Shakespeare, to Helle Møller Jensen for explaining the mysteries of the *"Hopsasa"* and to Matthew Power for helping with the cover illustration.

George Pattison
Christ Church, Oxford

Abbreviations and forms of reference

I have given all references to Kierkegaard's works in the main text, and the translations are my own. References to Kierkegaard's published works are of the form 6 175/CA 87. The first number refers to the volume number in the third Danish edition of Kierkegaard's *Samlede Vaerker* (Copenhagen: Gyldendal, 1962), the second number to the page number in that edition. The letter(s) after the slash refer to the abbreviated title of the English version found in the 26-volume translation *Kierkegaard's Writings* (Princeton, NJ: Princeton University Press, 1978–2002), edited by H. V. Hong and E. H. Hong, and the number to the page number in that edition. A list of the abbreviated titles follows. References to Kierkegaard's unpublished works are given in the form Pap IV A 33/JP 301, where "Pap" refers to Kierkegaard's *Papirer*, P. A. Heiberg, V. Kuhr & E. Torsting (eds) (Copenhagen: Gyldendal, 1909–48), followed by the standard form of reference used in this edition. "JP" refers to the six-volume selection from Kierkegaard's *Journals and Papers* (Bloomington, IN: Indiana University Press, 1967–78), selected, translated and edited by H. V. Hong and E. H. Hong. Entries are numbered consecutively through all six volumes. It should be noted that a definitive and unified edition of both the published and unpublished works is currently in production under the common title *Søren Kierkegaards Skrifter* (Copenhagen: Gad, 1997–). However, this is still incomplete, and the third edition of *Samlede Vaerker* remains the most accessible for students reading Kierkegaard in Danish.

Abbreviations

An asterisk indicates that the work was first published under a pseudonym, which is given in square brackets.

CA*   *The Concept of Anxiety* (1844) [Vigilius Haufniensis]

CI   *The Concept of Irony with Continual Reference to Socrates* (1841)

CUP1* *Concluding Unscientific Postscript to Philosophical Fragments*, Volume 1 (1846) [Johannes Climacus]. Referred to in the text as the *Postscript*.

EE1*   *Either/Or: A Fragment of Life: Part One* (1843) [A, ed. Victor Eremita]. Referred to in the text as *Either/Or 1*.

EE2*   *Either/Or: A Fragment of Life: Part Two* (1843) [B, Assessor William, ed. Victor Eremita]. Referred to in the text as *Either/Or 2*.

EUD   *Eighteen Upbuilding Discourses* (1843–45)

FTR*   *Fear and Trembling* (1843) [Johannes *de silentio*] and *Repetition* (1843) [Constantin Constantius]

M   *The Moment* (1855) and late writings

PC*   *Practice in Christianity* (1850) [Anti-Climacus]

PF*   *Philosophical Fragments, or a Fragment of Philosophy* (1844) [Johannes Climacus] and *Johannes Climacus, or De omnibus dubitandum est. A Narrative* (1842–43, unfinished and published posthumously).

PV   *The Point of View for My Work as an Author* (1848, published posthumously 1859)

SLW*   *Stages On Life's Way* (1845) [William Afham, A Married Man, Frater Taciturnus, ed. Hilarius Bookbinder]

SUD*   *The Sickness Unto Death* (1849) [Anti-Climacus]

TDIO   *Three Discourses on Imagined Occasions* (1845)

UDVS   *Upbuilding Discourses in Various Spirits* (1847). Includes *Purity of Heart*.

WA   *Without Authority*, an editorial collection of minor works (1849–51)

WL   *Works of Love* (1847)

Fear and trembling (cf. Phil. 2.12) is not the *primus motor* in the Christian life, for this is love ...   Kierkegaard

Kierkegaard and philosophy

To speak of "the philosophy of Kierkegaard" is, it may be said, problematic. It is not simply that Kierkegaard did not offer a rounded "philosophy", in the sense of a conceptually grounded and logically consistent worldview. Whether in the analytic or in the continental tradition of philosophy, many of those considered to be leading philosophers of the twentieth century would stand with Kierkegaard in their resistance to the systematic ambitions of some versions of philosophy. Nor is the hesitation about naming Kierkegaard "a philosopher" confined to those from within analytic philosophy who continue to be dubious about the credentials of continental philosophy in general, although there are aspects of Kierkegaard that analytic philosophers may find even more off-putting than what repels them in a Heidegger or a Sartre. Nor is the question even one as to whether Kierkegaard himself was really concerned about philosophy, its history and its problems, in the way that such revolutionary figures as Marx and Nietzsche in the nineteenth century and Heidegger, Wittgenstein and Derrida in the twentieth were. What, then, is the problem?

Before attempting to answer this question, it has to be conceded that there are, undeniably, "fragments of philosophy" in Kierkegaard, including scattered claims about logic, arguments contesting important philosophical positions concerning the limits of knowledge or the nature of ethics, forays into the history of ideas, reflections on aesthetics, adumbrations of phenomenological description and so on. Yet we don't have to read very far in Kierkegaard to find ourselves asking whether these might not turn out to be merely the by-products of an authorship that is essentially non-philosophical. However, while it would seem churlish to legislate against contemporary philosophers taking those fragments of philosophy that can be found in Kierkegaard and using or misusing them as occasion arises (perhaps even using them to illustrate what can go wrong with thinking when it abandons philosophy), it is clearly one thing merely to plunder the literary remains of this or that thinker of the past and another really to engage with his thought in its own sphere and sense. If, then, it turns out to be the case that the real core of Kierkegaard's writing is in some important sense non- or even anti-philosophical, then the best we can hope for is to cherry-pick whatever suits our current purposes and leave the rest to literary historians. However, if the hermeneutical current of modern philosophy has any merit at all, it would seem oddly casual to be totally indifferent to whether what we are taking from this or that thinker is being used in accordance with what it meant in its original text and context. For, on a hermeneutical view, it would only be as and when we knew what Kierkegaard might have meant with such and such an argument or assertion that we could weigh its relevance for philosophy.

Returning Kierkegaard's texts to their own literary and historical contexts might at first seem to offer an opening for a philosophical approach to his thought, for Kierkegaard belonged to an age when all the best young philosophers were rewriting the scripts bequeathed them by the tradition. The brash or sometimes sour young men of the 1840s scattered the worn-out husks of time-honoured questions and approaches in all directions. One could even add that that is what the best young philosophers always do, at least in modernity. From Descartes via A. J. Ayer to Derrida, each new wave of philosophy announces itself by dashing to pieces all previously accepted views and assumptions. Radical philosophy belongs as much to philosophy as any of the great systems and syntheses of calmer times, and if the rhetoric sometimes gets a little overheated, isn't that only to be expected of young firebrands? Can't we allow for the fact that by the time they are forty, such philosophical rebels will have learned to paint in "grey on grey" what the youthful manifesto declaimed in black and white, and to recognize how their own thinking is inevitably dependent on the great tradition that they had once momentarily confused with philosophy as such. As Kierkegaard lived only a couple of years beyond forty, can't we allow a little extra indulgence in his case?

Do such reflections give us a perspective in which to get Kierkegaard into proportion? To an extent, maybe. But it nevertheless seems that Kierkegaard was doing something very different from, say, Feuerbach's translation of the idealist philosophy he inherited into materialist terminology. He went beyond saying that the task of philosophy had been misconceived or misdescribed and therefore needed to be somehow reformulated: he was saying – or he often sounded as if he was saying – that philosophy was downright wrong, and that the task was not to revise it or to transcend it but, simply, to stop doing it. Even worse, he often seems to be saying that philosophy is one of the more damaging illnesses that can from time to time afflict human beings. In this respect, the closest analogy with his contemporaries seems to have been with the Marx who, in his eleventh thesis on Feuerbach, urged his readers to stop philosophizing and to get on with changing the world. And if Kierkegaard's counsel would be aimed more at changing your-*self* rather than the world, the implications for philosophers and their passion for interpreting the world would seem equally catastrophic.

Of course, not everything that philosophers have to be concerned with is itself philosophical. Heidegger, Merleau-Ponty and Derrida – among many others – have done interesting things philosophically with something as unphilosophical as painting – and whatever else painting may or may not do, it does not formulate propositions or make truth-claims in a manner well adapted to the reading habits of philosophers. Kierkegaard was no painter, but, whatever else he was, he was some kind of literary artist and sometimes spoke of himself as a "poet" (or "kind of poet"), and literary art seems even better placed than painting to engage the attention of philosophers. At least, it does its work in philosophy's own favoured medium of language. Should we, then, group Kierkegaard with other philosophically interesting writers and leave it at that? But this doesn't get us very far. The fact that a writer's work has been of interest to philosophy doesn't at all imply that he has any claim, still less any right, to the title "philosopher". Martha Nussbaum has shown how the novels of Henry James can be fruitfully used in deepening moral philosophy, but if this suggests that philosophers should be more open to the kinds of insights to be found from literature it by no means leads to us thinking of James as a philosopher rather than a novelist. Whatever we might be doing for Kierkegaard by having him rub shoulders with Henry James or, it may be, with Shakespeare, G. E. Lessing, Goethe and other poetical thinkers who have undeniably influenced philosophy, we would still not be making him "a philosopher".

In any case, the texts themselves stand in the way of any such easy solution. Certainly his output includes many passages of virtuoso prosody, and at least three of his works (*Either/Or*, *Repetition* and *Stages on Life's Way*) can plausibly be read as versions of the "novels of education" popular in Kierkegaard's literary culture. Even in works that appear more philosophical or theological (*The Concept of Anxiety* or *The Sickness unto Death*, for example), there are literary features that are no mere embellishments but belong to the very integrity of the text. And, quite apart from his own literary practice, it is clear that an extensive preoccupation with issues of art and culture runs almost throughout the authorship. Here, in fact, is an aspect of Kierkegaard's writing where questions of philosophy do seem to appear, if only in the relatively narrow sphere of aesthetics (although even here it could be argued that Kierkegaard is less of a philosophical aesthetician and more of a very penetrating critic). But there is also much in what Kierkegaard had to say about art and literature that makes it as difficult to speak of him simply as a literary figure as it does to speak of him as a philosopher. "The aesthetic", no less than philosophy, seems to be seen by Kierkegaard as an obstacle we need to get rid of if we are to achieve what really has a claim to constitute our chief life-interest. Here we broach the question of the "indirect communication" that pervades both Kierkegaard's primary works (as we might call a large number of both pseudonymous and signed works) and those works, such as *The Point of View for my Work as an Author,* in which he became his own commentator. From these self-commentaries it seems to be clear that Kierkegaard's own identity as a writer served him chiefly as a kind of laboratory within which writing itself could become the object of a constant, nagging enquiry as to its legitimacy and its limits *vis-à-vis* what Kierkegaard really had it in his mind (or was it in his heart?) to say. In this perspective the literary dimension of the work can, at most, be a part of the *in*direct moment of an authorship that was directed at a direct communication. The subordinate role of the literary dimension of his writing in the overall dynamics of indirect communication therefore suggests that, finally, literature and "the poetic" cannot provide a definitive point of view for the interpretation of Kierkegaard's work. He may have been a "kind of poet", but whatever "kind of" poet he was, it wasn't the same kind as a Shakespeare or a Goethe or a Henry James. It is true that Shakespeare, Goethe, James and any number of other writers and artists, especially but not exclusively in modernity and postmodernity, have demonstrated a self-consciousness regarding their own artistic practice that may remind us of Kierkegaard, yet the point here is that he was not merely preoccupied with the inner paradoxes, agonies and ecstasies of being a writer: this is not a case of pure literary irony. Literary irony there certainly is, but Kierkegaard's poetic anxiety rotates around his sense that he has something else to say that can't be said this way, and that (maybe) we *shouldn't* even try to say this way.

Some philosophers might detect an analogy to their own concerns at this point. Hasn't "the raging quarrel between truth and beauty" been a perennial trope of philosophical thinking for nearly 2500 years? Didn't philosophy begin with the attempt to separate out the *logos* of truth from the *logos* of myth? And hasn't the same task been rediscovered in each generation, as when Hegel, with whose writings on aesthetics Kierkegaard was certainly familiar, said that the world of fine art was for us moderns a thing of the past, since "thought and reflection" had "spread their wings over fine art"?[1] However, Kierkegaard's reasons for breaking with art bring us back to the reasons for his breaking also with philosophy. It is not the claims of reason that lie behind the restraining hand placed upon the literary, for his attitude towards the domain of artistic production and enjoyment often seems to go beyond merely wanting to set certain sensible critical limits (such as: that we shouldn't confuse our ability to distinguish between good and evil in a the-atrical performance with a competence for making such distinctions in life as it is lived). In this vein he can, in certain decisive moments, appear to regard everything to do with poetry and art as a sign of a fundamental de-pravity in human beings and, as one commentator put it, he did his best to strangle his own artistic virtuosity in the interminable pages of his last and most ponderous *Bildungsroman, Stages on Life's Way.* Art and philosophy alike, and for similar reasons, reflect – or, at best, entice us towards – some basic misapprehensions or, to put it in Nietzschean terms, some basically erroneous values.

Let me put it as directly as possible. The problem seems to lie in the reli-gious imperatives of Kierkegaard's self-confessed Christian commitment. In other words, the real stumbling-block to a thoroughgoing philosophical in-terpretation of Kierkegaard is that he himself fairly consistently (and plausi-bly) claimed that his authorship was first and foremost religious. This is not of itself a barrier to interpreting a thinker philosophically. Augustine, Aquinas, Joseph Butler and many other important philosophical voices, in-cluding, arguably, Hegel, were all "religious" in various senses of the word and their religious commitments were significant for the aim and tenor of their philosophical work. However, Kierkegaard's particular understanding of religion required him to deny that its claims were open to scrutiny by hu-man understanding. The sphere of religious faith was, as any introduction to Kierkegaard will make clear, the sphere of the paradox, the absurd, and of a "leap of faith" that took faith into a realm beyond any possibility of rational clarification. It is a realm in which reason has no rights and provides no insights. The very attempt to utilize reason to clarify religious questions dem-onstrates that the person who makes such an attempt is religiously incompe-tent. The philosopher's anxiety in the face of such claims is well summarized by Stephen Mulhall in the last sentence of his study *Inheritance and Original-ity,* in which he groups Kierkegaard with such other revisionist thinkers as Stanley Cavell, Wittgenstein and Heidegger. The sentence is, in fact, a question and, I take it, seriously intended as such: "But can philosophy acknowledge religion and still have faith in itself?"[2]

What are philosophers to do about Kierkegaard's intransigent religiosity? One strategy might be to simply ignore it, as (putting it very crudely) the Heidegger of *Being and Time* seems to have done. Here Heidegger appears simply to lift the anthropological material supplied by Kierkegaard and to reuse it, but in a very different way and for very different purposes. Indeed, Heidegger makes it clear that he is using Kierkegaard in a context essentially alien to Kierkegaard's own thought, which he describes as "merely" ontic, *existentiell,* or psychological and therefore, at best, as merely providing materials for the fundamental ontology that Heidegger himself is pursuing.

Thus we hear much in *Being and Time* of such Kierkegaardian categories as idle talk, anxiety, guilt, temporality, the moment, existence, resoluteness and repetition but nothing of the paradox of the God-Man.

But if philosophers are not simply going to ignore Kierkegaard's religious commitments, they could always resort to the expedient of declaring them to be misdescriptions of human states that resist rational scrutiny, but that are not for that reason beyond the scope of other kinds of human evaluation. Sartre, in contrast to Heidegger, directly embraces such religious categories as sin and faith in his Kierkegaard interpretation, but reinterprets them in what he takes to be a non-Christian way, seeing the Kierkegaardian paradox as translatable into the idea of the "singular universal" that each of us potentially is.[3] Although this might be appealing to a secular community of philosophers, it would seem not only to do violence to Kierkegaard's texts but, given the centrality and pervasiveness of his religious commitments, to block any attempt to take these seriously in their own right. In the face of Sartre's almost cavalier short-cut one is tempted to ask the following, perhaps mischievous, question: if the content of Kierkegaard's religious faith can be translated without remainder into anthropology, why should not one equally reverse the process and retranslate the Sartrian model of the existential subject into a religious model? If Kierkegaard's insistence that his words are to be understood religiously can be brushed aside, why should we respect Sartre's insistence that his words are to be understood atheistically? If Kierkegaard's religious self is "really" an – absurd – secular self, then where are the controls that would prevent us from saying that Sartre's secular self is "really" a religious self? And, of course, there have been Christian theologians who would interpret even the most radical expressions of existentialist meaninglessness as a kind of faith.[4] Why interest ourselves in Sartre's protests that no, he is not a believer, if we once decide for reasons of our own that Sartrian nothingness, for example, can be understood in terms of the nothingness and the void of mystics?

Neither ignoring nor translating, then, seems to do justice to the religious dimension of Kierkegaard's thought. Naturally, it does not follow that Kierkegaard's religious claims have to be accepted, but we, as readers, do, I think, have to respect the claims that Kierkegaard is making, to see, as well as we can, just what these claims are and, only then, to accept, to reject or to reinterpret them. Reinterpretation would, however, have to involve making clear just how far we regarded our reinterpretation as transforming the original tendency of Kierkegaard's thought. Unless philosophy is to opt for a totally unhistorical approach to what it has received from the thinkers of the past, there would seem to be a minimum level of attention to the historical and textual sources from which alone we can derive what Kierkegaard (or Hegel or Aquinas) really said. This means at least acknowledging and reckoning with Kierkegaard's religious claims as being integral to his thought as a whole (or, to put it more weakly, to acknowledge and reckon with the *possibility* that Kierkegaard's thought is incoherent unless or until his religious claims are taken into account).

Once more, however, we have to ask why philosophers should put themselves in this difficult position by even trying to read Kierkegaard as a philosopher. If we've once decided that he was essentially a religious thinker of a singularly anti-philosophical attitude, why not just walk away and leave him to the theologians? There are, I suggest, three reasons that stand out from among the possible answers to this question, and these reasons will, intermittently, accompany us throughout this study.

First, we never start philosophizing with a *tabula rasa*. We don't need to be dogmatic about all Western philosophy being reducible to a compilation of footnotes to Plato or to the choice between Plato and Aristotle in order to accept that philosophy as we know it is historically mediated. It would be self-deceiving on the part of anyone trained in academic philosophy to imagine that their understanding of philosophy was contextless. Even if the aim of their philosophizing is progressively to strip away inherited presuppositions or radically to explode the bogus problems that mesmerized our philosophical ancestors, some kind of picture of the past and some kind of relation to that past will be a part at least of their philosophical development – even if it only serves to convince them that such radical measures are indeed the task of any contemporary philosopher worthy of the name.

If some relation to the history of philosophy is integral to philosophy itself, then, whatever Kierkegaard's own intentions may have been, and whatever suspicions we may have about his religious claims – even if we refuse to allow that Kierkegaard was a philosopher in any "normal" sense – he does in some sense clearly belong to the history of philosophy to which we are heirs. Not only are his works regularly catalogued by libraries and booksellers as "philosophy" but, as we shall see at greater length in Chapter 1, there was a period in the twentieth century (more or less the period between the two world wars) when he played a pivotal role in the shaping of mainstream German philosophy, especially in the form of the "philosophy of existence". For a time, at least, everyone who was anyone in philosophy was obliged to take a stand for or against Kierkegaard. The reverberations of that role continue to be heard in such leading contemporary German philosophers as Jürgen Habermas and Michael Theunissen. Via such commentators as Lev Shestov, who "discovered" Kierkegaard in discussions with Martin Buber and Edmund Husserl, Kierkegaard's influence was also carried over into the history of French existentialism, even if this was never quite as "Kierkegaardian" as its German predecessor. Yet here, too, we find that such recent figures as Paul Ricoeur and Jacques Derrida are still obliged to produce their statutory Kierkegaardian essay. Whether or not it was a case of mistaken identity, Kierkegaard was enrolled in the lists of modern European philosophy at one of its most crucial junctures. To the extent that we still stand within the "effective history" of that juncture, Kierkegaard must engage us.

But, secondly, Kierkegaard does not just belong to the history of philosophy. There are areas in which, for all the vehemence of his polemics, he is making points that have a prima facie claim to be considered "philosophical" in some sense. These not only include those "fragments of philosophy" listed at the start of this chapter, but other, more pervasive and fundamental topics. Plainly, much depends on what we mean by philosophy but this is precisely the question. For Kierkegaard knew as well as we do that philosophy is not simply identifiable with the kind of rationalism that he believed he saw in Hegelianism and that he devoted so much energy to attacking. Whether in terms of the Kantian notion of critique or of Wittgensteinian "language-games", much modern philosophy has sought to trace the lines of demarcation between the various human and philosophical discourses rather than to define the content of knowledge, a task best left to the various specialist sciences. Such issues of demarcation might include questions such as: "Where should the line be drawn between the proper domains of metaphysics, cognition and ethics?" and "What are the rules that respectively define the religious and the philosophical or the aesthetic and the ethical language-games?" But these are precisely questions that concern Kierkegaard himself, phrased in terms of what he called the *confinium*: the boundary that, in varying shapes and moods, divides one existence-sphere from another and that also marks the subdivisions of these spheres as well as determining the scope of the scholarly disciplines that deal with them.[5]

Thirdly, some of Kierkegaard's headline categories – subjectivity, the ethical, the self, passion, character and so on – suggest that he had important interests in at least one substantive philosophical question, namely, the question as to what it is to be a self or person. This has recently been remarked on by Alastair Hannay in terms of "personality", which Hannay takes to be a central element in Kierkegaard's project.[6] As Hannay notes, this relates well to Kierkegaard's own intellectual context, in which he especially mentions the Danish philosopher Poul Martin Møller, but one could equally well adduce F. H. Jacobi, the later Schelling and other antecedents of the later nineteenth century's philosophy of personalism. But this also relates to contemporary concerns to understand philosophy as requiring a concern for the virtuous or good life and even "spirituality" as a dimension more or less inseparable from even the most scholarly philosophy.[7] This seems to promise a good stretch along which Kierkegaard and philosophy can, at least, be fellow-travellers. Yet here too, as we shall see, we cannot finally avoid the question as to whether Kierkegaard's depiction of the self is tenable if we are unable to share his religious presuppositions.

I have indicated the desirability of at least trying to read texts such as those of Kierkegaard in terms of their own terms of reference, which means taking into account such factors as their form, their stated intentions and their historical context. However, assuming that a philosophical study is not merely a literary or historical study (even if it cannot ignore literature or history), we have to consider the lines of approach that will, for our time, offer the best access to these particular writings. Merely to reproduce Kierkegaard's own organizational categories, as if his works were school textbooks, cannot be philosophically interesting. Simply to list such topics as the aesthetic, the ethical and the religious (what Kierkegaard called the three existence-spheres), anxiety, repetition, the teleological suspension of the ethical, the paradox, suffering and so on does not of itself help clarify what Kierkegaard's thought can mean to us, although a study that did not mention these would, of course, be incomplete. In any case, there are sufficient introductory works on the shelves of most libraries that provide such guided tours of the main features of the Kierkegaardian landscape. Really to engage with the philosophy of Kierkegaard, then, we have to do so in the light of those questions that concern us in our own contemporary philosophical existence (a comment that perhaps already signals a step towards philosophizing *à la* Kierkegaard). This is not, as should be clear from what has been said above, to abstract from the history of philosophy that, so to speak, delivered Kierkegaard to us, but is the condition of our engaging with that history as philosophy and not just as history. The structure of this study is, then, provided both by Kierkegaard's place in the history of modern European philosophy and by the points of convergence between Kierkegaard's central path of thinking and questions that concern us now. Especially I shall have more or less clearly in view the question as to what, in a Kierkegaardian perspective, it means to be a self and what might be the best form of life for a self thus constituted, as well as the characteristically Kierkegaardian question as to how one might communicate anything essential concerning such a self. In order to maintain this focus I have not dealt with a number of questions that might claim their place within a full study of the philosophy of Kierkegaard. I have said little about Kierkegaard's aesthetics (as opposed to his concept of "the aesthetic" in the sense of an inauthentic form of existence) or his critique of culture, although this is something I have written about extensively elsewhere.[8] Nor have I considered the question as to whether Kierkegaard can in any way be considered a political thinker, nor, if so, what his politics might be like.[9] Although thinking together these two aspects – the poetic and the political – of Kierkegaard's thought has the potential to open up a fresh horizon for our overall assessment of his contribution to the European intellectual heritage,

I have not considered an introductory study such as this the best place to attempt it.

Although the question of Kierkegaard's conception of the self has often been treated in the secondary literature in close connection with his own biography (something one might justify philosophically via Kierkegaard's own concept of subjectivity), I shall refrain from dealing with the standard biographical tropes of Kierkegaard commentary. This is not because they are uninteresting. On the contrary, both the success of and the controversy surrounding the ground-breaking recent biography by Joakim Garff indicate that a biographical approach to Kierkegaard raises important questions for the overall interpretation of his work.[10] It is more because there is enough in the texts themselves to engage us and that, in the present context, the intrusion of biographical material would only confuse and distract. My interest here is not in what "Kierkegaard the man" has to say to us, but more in "Kierkegaard – the matter to be thought". The reader will therefore find nothing or next to nothing about the melancholy father, the broken engagement, the persecution by a satirical newspaper or the falling-out with Bishops Mynster and Martensen.

Another general comment should be made at this point. Contrary to the practice of many contemporary Kierkegaard commentators I shall, frequently, use the name "Kierkegaard" for the author of the various pseudonymous books.[11] Clearly there are some views expressed in some of the pseudonymous works that Kierkegaard elsewhere disowns. Even *within* a work such as *Either/Or* we have one half of the book constituting an argument against the other half. Nevertheless, I think there is important continuity between much that is in the pseudonymous works and what Kierkegaard said in his own voice. If Johannes Climacus does not say all that Kierkegaard has to say, in his own voice or in the guise of a later pseudonym such as Anti-Climacus, he does prepare the way for this more decisive word and the way in which he does so is importantly shaped by what Kierkegaard himself finally wants to get said. That Kierkegaard himself "disowns" Johannes Climacus does not, in fact, mean that Climacus is irrelevant to Kierkegaard or Kierkegaard to Climacus. Basically, I do not regard this as a case where a general rule can be bluntly applied one way or the other. Context – the context of one's own writing as well as Kierkegaard's (but that, too, of course) – must be decisive. This admittedly leaves me exposed to the occasional objection that I have ascribed to Kierkegaard what exclusively belongs to one or other pseudonym, but that danger is, I believe, compensated for by the gains in what we are able to understand of what *Kierkegaard* said.

The questions of how to read Kierkegaard and, more particularly, of how to read him philosophically will continue to dog this study. Perhaps, if we follow Heidegger, and take the very life of philosophy to be bound up with the question concerning philosophy itself – the quest for wisdom as the quest for a right way of thinking philosophically – then this already provides one preliminary hint as to the value of reading Kierkegaard: that it will at the very least provoke us to revisit fundamental questions about our very conception of philosophy, and about its relation to religion and to literature. In this respect we may also come to understand why, from among all the representatives of the history of philosophy, it was Socrates who uniquely provided Kierkegaard with a model for what a thinker could be and achieve and, therefore, as a prototype for his own authorship, even though (as he wrote in his doctoral thesis), "the similarity between Socrates and Christ consists in their dissimilarity". The dissimilarity of the similar, it is tempting to add, is already an important clue to what it is that makes Kierkegaard philosophically interesting, but as we are now beginning to think with Kierkegaard, to think in the proximity of Kierkegaard's own texts, it is clearly time to finish this Introduction and to begin to examine "the philosophy of Kierkegaard".

CHAPTER ONE

Existence

Kierkegaard and the philosophy of *Existenz*

In 1934 the young German philosopher Werner Brock held a series of lectures at the University of London that were published the following year under the title *Contemporary German Philosophy*. The date was significant. Brock, a Jew, had been stripped of his right to function as a university teacher when the National Socialists had come to power in Germany in 1933 and he was now laying the foundations for a new life and career in Britain. No less significant was the fact that, only shortly before the National Socialist revolution, Brock had been given the much-coveted post of teaching assistant to Martin Heidegger, then at the height of his university career and subsequently much criticized for his own involvement with Nazism.[1] Brock was therefore well placed to comment on "contemporary German philosophy", coming from within the inner circle of one of its most eminent, if controversial, representatives. What, then, was the story he had to tell?

Essentially, Brock saw the issue of German twentieth-century philosophy as the struggle between, on the one hand, a positivistic view, in which philosophy served to regulate the manifold practices of the natural, social and human sciences, and, on the other hand, a return to "interpret[ing] existence in a more universal sense and so once more giv[ing] strength and significance to human life, as it did in Greece and in earlier modern times".[2] Heidegger himself is given a decisive role in the shaping of this alternative. For Heidegger, Brock writes, "attempts to raise philosophy again to a height which in the nineteenth century, the age of science, it seemed to have lost for ever."[3] Much of Heidegger's inspiration comes, Brock tells us, from his study of early Greek philosophy. But there are two more recent thinkers who are said to have played a vital role in alerting both Heidegger and German philosophy more generally to the "universal" tasks that had been becoming obscured in philosophy's positivistic turn. These are Nietzsche and Kierkegaard. Although Brock comments that Kierkegaard's influence is past its zenith, he immediately adds that "it is due to his work that the two leading philosophers of the last decade, Jaspers and Heidegger, attained to their most fundamental principle, and thus contemporary philosophy, like Protestant theology, received from Kierkegaard its decisive impulse."[4] It was, he says later, through Nietzsche and, *above all*, Kierkegaard that philosophy regained the possibility of retrieving its "universal tasks" from the centripetal forces of the specialized autonomous sciences.

But how could a thinker who, as Brock emphasizes, was essentially a religious – indeed a *Christian* – thinker, acquire such importance for philosophy? One word stands out from Brock's short account, and that is the word "*Existenz*" (or, as he also puts it, "Existenz of the individual"[5]). Without necessarily dissenting from anything in Brock's brief summary as to what is involved in Kierkegaard's conception of *Existenz*, we shall now turn directly to Kierkegaard himself for the further elucidation of this clearly pivotal term, pivotal, at least, for the reception of Kierkegaard in the history of philosophy, although, naturally, that does not of itself decide whether it is the true centre of Kierkegaard's own thought or what its relevance to *our* contemporary intellectual situation might be. But in turning to Kierkegaard we shall also, at this point, drop the German spelling "*Existenz*" (preserved in English by Brock and, at the time, many others) and switch to the English "existence". This is not because there is anything intrinsically wrong with the German spelling (and it does alert us to the fact that we are dealing with a very specific philosophical usage), but (i) it is not, in any case, how Kierkegaard spelt the word in Danish and (ii) it brings with it the connotations of the "philosophy of *Existenz*" associated with Jaspers and Heidegger, and that cannot be assumed in advance to represent the sole or even a correct development of what is to be found in Kierkegaard himself. The relationship between Kierkegaard, Heidegger and existentialism is, it should be added, both vexed and complicated, and I shall return to it at a number of points; indeed, it could almost be said to constitute the inevitable sub-plot to any consideration of "the philosophy of Kierkegaard".

Existence and the system I: the question of becoming

"Existence" belongs to a complex of terms and themes in Kierkegaard's writing that have an essentially twofold character. On the one hand, they are used in a critical and sometimes even polemical manner, most conspicuously in relation to Kierkegaard's treatment of Hegel and idealist philosophy, but also with regard to his attack on Romantic aestheticism. On the other hand, they initiate what could be seen as a descriptive account of the human condition, that is, of life seen from the point of view of the existing individual. Both the negative and positive senses of existence are, of course, interconnected. In this chapter, however, we shall begin by looking exclusively at Kierkegaard's critical use of the idea of existence as a negative criterion by which to evaluate philosophical positions, before turning in subsequent chapters to see how existence takes shape in the actual contours of human life.

The pre-eminent example of this negative use of existence is to be found in Kierkegaard's critique of Hegel and idealist philosophy, and perhaps the most succinct statement of this critique is to be found in the section of his voluminous *Concluding Unscientific Postscript to Philosophical Fragments* (hereafter *Postscript*), in which he comments on Lessing's saying that, if God held all truth in his right hand and the lifelong pursuit of truth in his left hand, then he, Lessing, would always choose the left, that is, the infinite pursuit of truth over its possession (or supposed possession).[6] *Supposed* possession, because, as Kierkegaard now attempts to show, no actually existing human being can possess "all truth": truth as a whole necessarily transcends our capacities of knowledge. Kierkegaard summarizes his position in two claims: (i) that a logical system is possible; and (ii) that an existential system is impossible.[7]

This section is, famously, typical not only of Kierkegaard's philosophical objections to Hegelianism but also of his witty, ironic, bantering style, quoting indiscriminately from scholarly sources and from popular and classical literature, and maintaining a tone of almost frivolous mockery. Ignoring – for now – these idiosyncratic stylistic features, we begin by looking at the more conventionally philosophical points that Kierkegaard is making.

With regard to the claim that a logical system is possible, Kierkegaard begins with the simple assertion that "If a logical system is to be constructed, it is especially necessary to take care not to include in it anything which is subject to the dialectic of existence, that is, which 'is' in the sense of existing or as having existed and not as simply being" (9 93/CUP1 109). Kierkegaard's point here seems to be that what he is calling a "logical system" is something constituted as a system of purely formal relationships from which nothing can be inferred concerning any existing states of affairs and which are valid in themselves no matter what states of affairs may actually hold in the world. In other words, Kierkegaard is thinking primarily of something like traditional logic and such logical laws as the principle of non-contradiction or the law of the excluded middle, understood as principles for evaluating propositions but not as providing information about the contents of the world. These laws had, in fact, been the focus of intense debate among Danish philosophers and theologians in the 1830s (i.e. in the period of Kierkegaard's undergraduate studies), with the "conservatives", including Kierkegaard's philosophy professor F. C. Sibbern and Bishop J. P. Mynster, defending Aristotle against the Hegelians. That Kierkegaard's own anti-Hegelian arguments seem to continue this line of argument suggests that he should not be seen – as he is in so many introductory studies – as rising up single-handedly against a Hegelian establishment but rather as defending the traditional academic values of the Danish establishment against radical innovation by an upstart Hegelian minority. The Aristotelian timbre of Kierkegaard's approach is underlined when he signals his agreement with the criticisms of Hegel found in the *Logical Investigations* of the Aristotelian scholar F. A. Trendelenburg.[8] Strikingly, the key points of the objections to Hegel here and elsewhere in the *Postscript* are nearly all paralleled in Trendelenburg. The most relevant points concern the question of movement, the hypothetical nature of logic, the problem of the beginning and the idea of immediacy.

The question of movement is the first target of Kierkegaard's attack. Following on from his statement concerning the need to exclude "anything which is subject to the dialectic of existence" from the logical system, he continues: "From this it follows quite simply that Hegel's matchless and matchlessly lauded discovery, that one could introduce movement into logic, is precisely to confuse logic" (9 93/ CUP1 109), to which he adds parenthetically that, as far as he can see, even Hegel makes no pretence anywhere to have proved this. In other words, not only is the idea of movement inappropriate in logic, but even Hegel, who claims to have established such a thing, merely asserts and does not demonstrate this most controversial of claims.

I have mentioned the mocking tone of this passage, and one might naturally ask whether Kierkegaard is, in fact, caricaturing Hegel at this point rather than fairly representing him. Yet Hegel does seem to claim that movement is a legitimate, indeed a fundamental, category of logic. In the first section of *The Science of Logic* published in 1812 and headed "Determinateness (Quality)", Hegel sets out the threefold relationship, as he sees it, between "Being", "Nothing" and "Becoming". "Being", or, as he has already identified it in the Introduction "pure Being", is Being abstracted from all possible specifications, which "in its indeterminate immediacy [...] is equal only to itself. It is also unequal relatively to an other; it has no diversity within itself nor any with a reference outwards."[9] This, in other words, is the most abstract formula of idealism, $A = A$, or the bare predication of an unknown X that "X is" or, perhaps, even more abstractly, the statement "There is", without even the specification of an unknown X. Putting it like this, Hegel suggests, makes it at once apparent that "Being, the indeterminate immediate, is in fact *nothing* and neither more nor less than *nothing*."[10] Why? Because in saying of the unknown X simply that it "is" or in saying "there is" without specifying in any way "what" there is, we are essentially saying nothing; we are applying no category of time or place, no attribute or determination of any kind. "X is" or "There is" is a pure, abstract, content-less affirmation. To say of something that it is, and nothing more, is to say nothing. And "Nothing", as Hegel now goes on to say, is the sheer indeterminacy of abstract Being. In a crucial next step, Hegel then states that neither Being nor Nothing is what it is other than in its identity with its opposite: neither can be regarded in isolation from the other, but each is as it is because it has always already "moved over" or "disappeared" into its opposite. "Their truth is, therefore, this movement of the immediate vanishing of the one into the other: *becoming*, a movement in which both are distinguished, but by a difference which has equally immediately resolved itself."[11] This "Becoming" is itself then redescribed in the conclusion of the first section as "Dasein", as the being-there of something of which we can say that "it is".

We shall not follow Hegel further at this point, other than to note that there is an important connection between this seemingly esoteric piece of logic and the "big picture" of his system as a whole. For this opening section of *The Science of Logic* provides the theoretical underpinning for Hegel's general claim that historical life (i.e. temporally extended existence or "becoming") is a proper object of philosophical understanding and that there can be reason *in* history. Thinking is not limited to the analysis of time-less relations, but can grasp entities in their coming to be and passing away. As Hegel had put it in the Preface to *The Phenomenology of Spirit*, whereas "conventional opinion gets fixated on the antithesis of truth and falsity", genuine philosophical thinking sees "the progressive unfolding of truth". And to illustrate the point, he adds the following example:

> The bud disappears in the bursting-forth of the blossom, and one might say that the former is refuted by the latter; similarly, when the fruit appears, the blossom is shown up as a false manifestation of the plant, and the fruit now emerges as the truth of it instead. These forms are not just distinguished from one another. They also supplant one another as mutually incompatible. Yet at the same time their fluid nature makes them moments of an organic unity in which they not only do not conflict, but in which each is as necessary as the other; and this mutual necessity alone constitutes the life of the whole.[12]

True philosophical thinking, in other words, does not fixate on the isolated parts, but follows the movement of the temporal progression of the phenomena in its successive stages and sees in this an integral whole. This whole, as a unitary phenomenon, is then available for logical analysis. The mutual implication of logic and movement thus cuts both ways: once movement or "becoming" can be allowed in logic, then logic, as the rationale of reason itself, can map or elucidate what we experience in the movement of becoming as history or as "life". Now Kierkegaard too, as we shall see, will also seize on temporality as a decisive and characteristic dimension of human existence and provide a strategy whereby to make temporality meaningful. However, that Kierkegaard is like Hegel in wanting to draw time and movement into the core of human self-understanding does not of itself say anything as to *how* either of them do this, and, as we shall see, their way of treating time is in fact very different. Kierkegaard already serves notice on the nature of this difference when he comments that movement not only cannot be mapped logically but that it is an "unclarifiable presupposition" of both being and thought (9 94/CUP1 110). And as we have already seen, his use of Lessing's saying about the infinite pursuit of truth suggests that for Kierkegaard, in contrast to Hegel, it will never be appropriate to claim that we have achieved a grasp of "the whole".

Whatever Hegel might have meant by it, then, Kierkegaard does seem justified in claiming that Hegel sought, in some sense, to introduce "movement" or "becoming" into logic.[13] And Kierkegaard also seems right to insist that this is no mere footnote: it is essential to the very method of Hegelian philosophy and, therefore, to the coherence of the system as a whole. Sarcastically noting that some Hegelians seem to accept that the introduction of movement into logic has not been carried through in a completely adequate way, Kierkegaard maintains that this is not a point on which there can be any fudging. If the principle of movement in logic is not established, then the system as a whole fails.

It is at this point that Kierkegaard calls for Trendelenburg's back-up. Although he says relatively little about Trendelenburg, other than to praise him for "being content with Aristotle and with himself" (9 94/CUP 110), his own argument, as he acknowledges, closely matches that of the German Aristotelian. The latter addresses the question of "the dialectical method" in the second chapter of his *Logical Investigations*. Of the Hegelian method Trendelenburg writes, "The basic thought of the Hegelian method is that pure thought is without presuppositions and produces and cognizes the moments of Being out of its own necessity."[14] But, he then asks, is this claim to be without presuppositions tenable? Take the case of "becoming": "Pure Being is at rest; Nothing ... is likewise at rest. How then can the movement of becoming emerge from the unity of these two resting ideas?"[15] Trendelenburg's answer is that this can only happen on the basis of a step that is not actually acknowledged by Hegel himself: "But if thinking produces something else out of this unity, it plainly adds this other on and 'movement' is surreptitiously inserted in order to bring Being and Non-Being into the stream of becoming."[16] Thus, he insists, Becoming has its place due to a "concrete intuitive act that surveys life and death."[17] In other words, it is only because we perceive the world as being in a process of becoming that we are able also to represent it mentally as becoming. In Kierkegaard's terminology, the world of becoming (or the world of which becoming is a constant and salient feature) exists as the "unclarifiable background" of thinking and, therefore, of any concept of Being.

Existence and the system II: the nature of logic

Kierkegaard's next move is to address the question of the nature of logic. What soon becomes clear is that his idea as to what logic is or should be is very different from Hegel's. Fundamental to Kierkegaard's view is that logic is hypothetical. This not only involves distinguishing logic from existence, it also (he says) marks logic off from mathematics. What does he mean by this? To begin with, he says that logic must be regarded as "hypothetical" and, in so far as it is that, "it is indifferent to existence in the sense of actuality" (19 94/CUP1 110). Logic, in other words, has the basic form of "if a, then b", without regard to the actual existence of either a or b. In its own terms it is entirely objective, in that it cannot deviate from its own rules and must be internally consistent and exceptionless and it shares these latter characteristics with mathematics, but, Kierkegaard says, mathematics does not have the hypothetical character of logic: mathematical relations are given, not supposed. The mathematician does not say "if $1 + 1$, then 2" but, simply "$1 + 1 = 2$". Mathematics shows what is the case, not what might be the case. Nevertheless, both mathematics and logic are, or Kierkegaard thinks they should be, "indifferent to existence".

Hegel, however, seems to regard logic as applicable to existence and, indeed, to see it as a way of understanding existence. Yet, at the same time (and Hegel's own claims in his logical writings seem to bear this out), the logical system is capable of being deduced in an *a priori* manner from entirely self-evident principles. As Kierkegaard sees it, however, the kind of abstraction that such a deduction requires would mean abstracting from all possible deliverances of experience, memory and prejudice. Kierkegaard and Trendelenburg see such an exclusion of experience as possible so long as we restrict ourselves either to mathematics or to what is purely hypothetical. However, it is impossible, in these disciplines, to say anything about relations among objects of experience. Thus, in so far as Hegel appears to claim that his logic *does* have some purchase on experience, he is indulging in sophistry, surreptitiously smuggling experiences into the realm of logical relations and not acknowledging that these experiences originate in other, non-logical states of affairs.

Now it may be that Kierkegaard has misread the intention of Hegelian logic.[18] Thus, whatever may be the case with the kind of hypothetical logical relations of the "If *a*, then *b*" variety, that is, with the sort of logic represented in Aristotle's *Prior Analytics*, Hegel's logic does not pretend to be of this kind. Rather, it corresponds more closely to the Aristotelian doctrine of categories, and categories, it could be argued, may quite legitimately incorporate a relation to experience that purely analytic relations cannot have. Experience of place is an acknowledged presupposition of having a category of location. Many Aristotelians would, indeed, say that just this is the virtue of Aristotelian thought: that it constructs its categories out of or in the light of lived experience. Perhaps what Hegel is doing in logic is really closer to Aristotle's exposition of the basic categories – substance, being, and so on – in the *Metaphysics*. Yet Hegel does call his logic a logic and not a doctrine of categories and he claims both that he is able to develop a system of logical relations deductively without reference to experience, and that these logical relations are adequate to the task of conceptualizing experience, even saying of this system that it shows us the mind of God before the Creation. Logic is not merely the form of thinking but, for Hegel, the form of Being itself, or, we might say, the form of ontology. In this regard, Kierkegaard's arguments do count against what Hegel appears to be doing, that is, constructing a logic that is something more than a system of hypothetical relations without any point of contact in the "real" world.[19] His (Kierkegaard's) own position is thus clearly defined against that of Hegel by the claims that, first, purely formal logical relations are not abstracted from experience but have an essentially *a priori* character and, secondly, no act of abstraction from experience could, in fact, ever be adequate to establish the kind of certainty required by the principles of logic. This is not to say that Kierkegaard demonstrates or argues for his position in a convincing way – perhaps he does not – but it does indicate that he clearly identified and articulated a fundamental point of divergence between Hegel's project and his own.

On Kierkegaard's view, then, two types of questions may be asked about what happens in the kind of act of abstraction that Hegel seems to describe as a prerequisite to logical thinking. The first concerns the formal impropriety of the move from experience via abstraction to logic, while the second concerns the psychological meaning of this move.

Regarding the formal argument, Kierkegaard and Trendelenburg agree that a key element in the perpetration of what they see as Hegel's sophistry is the use of the term "immediacy". For Hegel, the starting-point of logic is, as we have seen, the category of "'pure Being", "Being" without any further qualification or determination, which he therefore also calls "immediacy": Being that is totally lacking in any form of mediation (or, as we might put it in non-Hegelian terminology, the bare predication of being without any further qualification, such as being a tree, an animal, a colour, a feeling, or anything at all: just Being as Being, and nothing more – "there is"). Kierkegaard, however, wants to know *How does the System begin with the immediate? That is, does it begin with it immediately?"* (9 95/CUP1 111–12, original emphasis), to which he gives the "unconditional" and un-equivocal answer: no.

There seem to be two reasons for this emphatic reply. The first is that, as we have seen, the logical system presupposes a world of experience from which, subjectively speaking, it is abstracted. Even if one could carry this process of abstraction through to the point at which all the "mediations" of Being found in life as it is lived are suspended, logic nevertheless "does not therefore begin immediately with the immediate with which existence began" (9 95/CUP1 112). But, secondly, even this second or more primary imme-diacy, the immediacy of existence itself, cannot be made into the starting-point of anything "since immediacy never simply is, but is transcended as soon as it is" (9 95/CUP1 112). In the very moment in which we become aware of existing at all, our immediacy is no longer that of a merely existing entity in the world (a stone, a plant, or even an animal): we have become *thinking* or *conscious* beings, *beings conscious of their existence in a reflexive way* and not simply *beings*. The immediacy with which the system claims to "begin" is therefore a derived immediacy, an immediacy, Kierkegaard says, that has been *"reached by a process of reflection"* (9 95/CUP1 112, original emphasis).

Now Hegel is not unaware of this. In fact, in the introduction to *The Science of Logic*, where he sets out the relationship between *The Science of Logic* and its precursor, *The Phenomenology of Spirit*, he addresses the ques-tion head-on. If the basic topic of logical thought is taken to be the condi-tions that apply to any possible knowledge (pure knowledge, Hegel says), then the idea of such knowledge itself is something that has only come about in and through the history of human consciousness, a history that Hegel has tracked in *The Phenomenology of Spirit*. In taking the conclusion of the earlier work as the starting-point of his logic, Hegel is therefore quite consciously seeing this starting-point itself as something arrived at by means of reflection: "Simple immediacy is itself an expression of reflection and contains a reference to its distinction from what is mediated," he writes.[20]

Kierkegaard for his part knows that this is acknowledged by the Hegelians, who appear to concede the distinctiveness of their use of the term "imme-diacy" (as Kierkegaard puts it, in the way that Hegel and his followers use the term, "'the immediate' must evidently mean something other than what it means elsewhere" [9 97/CUP1 114]). But, he objects, the Hegelians do not accept the implications of this concession. Why not? Because a process of abstraction such as this has no necessary conclusion. There is something intrinsically arbitrary about deciding just where and when to start or to stop. The process of abstraction itself cannot therefore provide the basis for the beginning of anything: "if it is possible for a human being to abstract from everything in thinking, it is impossible for him to do more, since if it does not transcend human power, this act [of total abstraction] absolutely exhausts it" (9 98/CUP1 114). The process of abstraction is just that: a process of abstraction. It has no intrinsic absolute stopping-point, but it is just this that Hegel claims to have found.

Instead of the supposed immediacy of the deliverances of abstraction, Kierkegaard suggests, perhaps we should talk about "a leap". Rightly or wrongly, this is, of course, one of the words most associated with Kierkegaard. For now, however, he is not talking about any "leap of faith" in a narrowly religious sense,[21] but pointing to what he regards as the unavoidable discontinuity between the process of abstraction and the kind of "beginning" required by logic. For since all logical relations are merely hypothetical, not assertive, logic by no means requires the kind of "absolute beginning" that Hegel seems to think is needed.

However, if it would be a mistake to read too much in the way of religious content into Kierkegaard's use of the term "leap" at this point, it cannot be denied that he is not simply talking about the disjunction between different levels or spheres of discourse, such as logic and experience. He is also appealing to what I previously referred to as the psychological question: to what this all means for the one who is the actual subject of both of these spheres, the one thinking or reflecting. Thus, the leap is said to be "a decision": something more than a line of demarcation between two levels of discourse (9 97/CUP1 113). A logical system, is possible, Kierkegaard seems to be saying, but then we have to ask ourselves *why* we would want to get involved with thinking logically in the first place and whether and how we might apply logic to existence; these are matters of choice that the system itself cannot decide for us. Jon Stewart argues that Hegel too allows that actually to engage in the kind of abstraction from existence that his system requires calls for an act of will on the part of the thinker and that Kierkegaard is at this point only in *apparent* disagreement with Hegel.[22] However, as we have seen, Kierkegaard not only argues that *if* we were to set about constructing a logical system it would require us to make a willed act of abstraction from the daily reality of our lives, he also questions both *whether* such an act of *total* abstraction as Hegel seems to require is possible and – consistent with this doubt – wants to ask more about what there might be in a person's life that would induce them to attempt such a thing. The thinking subject of philosophy cannot be abstracted from the reality of the existing subject in the way that Hegel seems to suppose it can.

Kierkegaard's interest in the psychological background of philosophy had already been developed in several of his previous pseudonymous works, such as *Either/Or* and *The Concept of Anxiety,* and the psychological context of beginning to philosophize had been especially strongly developed in the fragmentary and posthumously published philosophical biography of a young thinker who, intriguingly, bears the same name as the pseudonym to whom the *Postscript* is ascribed, a biography entitled *Johannes Climacus or De Omnibus Dubitandum Est* [*Everything is to be doubted*]. This, however, is only the tip of the iceberg of what is, in fact, a salient feature of his thought as a whole.

Subjectivity and empirical experience

For all their agreement in opposing Hegel, Kierkegaard's psychological interest seems to distinguish his approach from that of Trendelenburg. The latter too was troubled by what he regarded as the sophistry of Hegel's explanation regarding the role of immediacy in the foundations of logic. Trendelenburg's concerns, however, seem to have chiefly focused on the relationship between logic and empirical experience. It is in this regard that he draws attention to what he sees as an ambiguity in the term itself. Aristotle, he notes, called an element of thought "immediate" when it was not deducible from anything else, either because it was something self-evidently true or because it was something quite singular grasped in an act of sensory intuition in which nothing intervened between sensory representation and the object. The sophistry in the Hegelian usage, Trendelenburg suggests, is precisely to do with the fact that the legitimacy of employing the term in logic is argued in terms of its absolute self-evidence, as self-mediated or self-identical, while, in practice, it is used to introduce elements of experience into the logical sphere – where Trendelenburg (like Kierkegaard) thinks they have no place. The curious situation thus arises that with regard to, for example, movement, the Hegelian claim that this is generated by means of the purely logical operation of negation is the opposite of the truth: it is the positive sense of immediacy "the freshness of intuition" that actually sets thought in motion. Logic "with its pure thoughts", says Trendelenburg, "thus falls away from itself, down into the sphere of sensuousness. This is indeed well concealed by the logical term 'immediacy', but once the veil imperceptibly slips the [sensuous] representation hiding behind it reveals itself." Thus "What the logic of pure thought understands by means of the term immediacy is what it simply cannot understand – sensuousness."[23]

Kierkegaard, as we have seen, seems not to have emphasized this particular aspect of Hegelian sophistry at this point, which raises the question as to whether he could have accepted Trendelenburg's criticism, or whether his own appeal to "decision" points to a very different agenda, an agenda that might be called "subjectivist" rather than "empiricist". There can be little doubt that Kierkegaard's primary interest lies in the direction of existence in the sense of the subjective and, as we shall see, the particular modifications of subjectivity found in ethics and in religion. However, it is important for understanding the exact purchase of his concepts of subjectivity and ethics to know whether they are being developed in a way that allows for the legitimacy of what might, crudely, be called knowledge of the external world. It is important, not least, because Kierkegaard has sometimes been interpreted in such a way as to imply that his ethically existing individual is an individual without a world, a kind of gnostic self, devoid of space–time coordinates. We shall, therefore, briefly digress to consider whether Kierkegaard's critique of Hegelian "abstraction" is not itself committed to abstracting from what most people, most of the time, regard as "reality", that is, the reality of flesh and blood and concrete empirical "things".

One well-known statement of the position that Kierkegaard is, in this way, no less abstract than Hegel (albeit stated with due acknowledgement of the possibility of having been tricked by Kierkegaard's own indirectness) is Louis Mackey's provocatively titled "The Loss of the World in Kierkegaard's Ethics". Mackey's argument is, essentially, that Kierkegaard so magnifies the scope of freedom in human subjectivity that "The Kierkegaardian individual is existentially – in his ethical reality – acosmic if not atheistic. He is infinitely free. But because it is without limitations – by the relative objectivity of the world or the absolute objectivity of God – his freedom is empty of everything but indeterminate possibilities."[24]

Kierkegaard himself was, interestingly, aware that this is an objection that will be brought against him. If "to make thought supreme over everything is gnosticism'", he writes, then "to make the ethical reality of the subject the only reality could seem to be acosmism" (10 44/CUP1 341). His reply to this charge is, basically, to dismiss it out of hand. The individual's reality, he says:

> *ought*, ethically speaking, to mean more to him than "heaven and earth and all that therein is," more than the six thousand years of human history, and even more than astrology and the veterinary sciences along with everything that the age demands, which aesthetically and intellectually is a monstrous vulgarity.
>
> (10 44/CUP1 332, emphasis added)

23

This can be read to suggest that when Kierkegaard says that "the individual's own ethical reality *is* the only reality" (10 31/CUP1 327, original emphasis) he is not necessarily to be taken as saying more than "the ethical reality of the individual ought to *mean more* to him than anything else", something that falls far short of acosmism. In fact, he suggests, the charge of acosmism will only occur "to a busy thinker who explains everything, a nimble mind that takes the whole world in at a glance" (10 44/CUP1 341), that is, someone who does not really take the time to stop and think about what it is that is being said here. Whether this is an adequate reply or not, it at least illustrates that Kierkegaard does not regard himself as endorsing acosmism.

If we were to look for evidence that Kierkegaard believed in a world beyond that of the self-centred, wilful subject, then this would have primarily to do with other subjectivities, that is, the existence of other ethical selves to whom and before whom the ethical self is responsible. That other selves play an important role in Kierkegaard's overall view of what it is to be a self is something for which I shall argue when we come to consider Kierkegaard's ethical views but, for now, this particular question must be left open. Instead, we shall pursue the question as to whether Kierkegaard construes the self as having any intrinsic relation to what everyday parlance understands as the "real" world, a world peopled by empirically experienceable persons and objects. Yet, as I have said, the question of the "empirical", of sensuous intuition, scarcely receives any independent comment in his work, and certainly not in the *Postscript*. Nevertheless, this does not of itself banish the question as to whether there is an empirical "moment" in Kierkegaard's modelling of the self. Indeed, from a certain angle this question remains crucially important, since it has significant implications for the kind of shared reality that ethical selves might possess. Kierkegaard's relative disinterest in the question will, perhaps, allow us only to point out a couple of clues that fall short of conclusiveness, although they are, I think, enough to show something of how he might have addressed it.

On the assumption that whatever Kierkegaard says in criticism of the system is something he would wish to avoid in his own thought, we can note that, first, one of the most important of the objections that he makes of "the system" is that it is fundamentally sceptical, a trait it shares, he says, with all forms of idealism.

> When thinking turns upon itself in order to think about itself, this leads to scepticism, as is well-known. How may this scepticism be brought to a halt, when it has its basis in the fact that thinking wants to think about itself instead of serving the purpose of thinking something? When a horse bolts and runs off, we might well hear someone say … "Let it just run, it will soon get tired." But this

> cannot be said of thinking's self-reflection, for it can go on as long as may be, and keep on running.   (10 38/CUP1 335)

At this point Kierkegaard makes one of his occasional references to another philosopher known as an anti-Hegelian, F. J. W. Schelling. I shall consider Kierkegaard's relation to Schelling, and the latter's role in the *Postscript*, at the end of this chapter. Here, as elsewhere, Schelling seems to be used to indicate an alternative to the Hegelian approach, an alternative that Kierkegaard appears to think preferable to that of Hegel, but still not adequate. Thus, Schelling's appeal to intellectual intuition is said to have offered one solution to the problem of the relationship between thinking and Being, although, as Kierkegaard remarks, it was a solution that Hegel expressly rejected, opting instead for the dialectical method of infinite reflection. But, in terms basically identical to those of the earlier section on the possibility of a logical system, Kierkegaard now mocks the claim that such a process of reflection can, of itself, ever lead to any conclusion.

> What, then, does it mean to say "so long – until"? This is, in fact, nothing but specious talk, which deludes the reader into imagining the issue in quantitative terms, as if one could better understand how self-reflection annulled itself by having it happen after a long time. This kind of mental quantification corresponds to the infinitely small angles used by astronomers which, in the end, become so small that one can call them parallel lines. The yarn about self-reflection continuing "so long – until" distracts attention away from what, dialectically, is the main issue: how self-reflection gets annulled.   (10 39/CUP1 336)

The initial act of abstraction is thus seen as placing the philosopher in an implicitly sceptical position from which he is unable to escape, except by changing the terms of his problem formulation. But Kierkegaard's point is precisely that scepticism is a debilitating philosophical position to be in, and that it is one of the salient faults of the system that, although it offers itself as a way out of scepticism, it is inherently sceptical.[25] The "proper task" of thinking is not to think about itself, but to "think other things", and the critique of the system must therefore, in some respects, be about enabling thought to do this, to think "other things". But it cannot do this unless there *are* other things to be thought. Whatever else is to be said about the ethical individual, then, it is clear that he or she is envisaged as inhabiting a world in which there are things other than thought.

In a rather different tone, a similar inference may, secondly, be drawn from the way in which Kierkegaard uses comic elements in his refutation of

Hegelianism, both in the reflections on Lessing's *bon mot* concerning the pursuit versus the possession of truth and in the section of the *Postscript* entitled "The Subjective Thinker" (and, indeed, at many other points). Such a use of ridicule may scarcely seem like a proper philosophical tactic, although it has recently been defended as such by John Lippitt.[26] What does it involve?

In the discussion of the possibility of a logical system, Kierkegaard gives early warning of what will come to be a pervasive feature of the *Postscript*. Considering the problem as to how the process of abstraction can ever come to provide the foundations for a system of logic, Kierkegaard asks, once more, "But with what do I then begin, since I have abstracted from everything?" In answer he imagines that "Ah! At this point, perhaps, a deeply-moved Hegelian would fall upon my breast and blissfully stammer: With nothing" (9 97/CUP1 114). What lies behind this shift to comic mode? Is it because Kierkegaard is unable to follow the argument through on a philosophical level? Or is it perhaps his way of drawing attention to what he, at least, regards as the philosophically fatuous nature of the claim being made by Hegel, a claim that, like the emperor's new clothes, only has to be pointed out in order to be seen in its ludicrous vacuity? Something like this last view would seem to lie behind the remark, several pages later, that "by now a philosopher has become such a fantastic being, that the most extravagant fancy has scarcely invented anything so fabulous" (9 100/CUP1 117).

As Kierkegaard moves into the next section on the impossibility of an existential system, the tone becomes sharper still. For the question now is: who, actually, *is* the philosopher and how does the philosopher himself relate to his philosophy? Kierkegaard allows that, in principle, an existential system, that is, a system of thought that incorporated knowledge of every possible existing being, *is* possible, but it would be possible only for one who had a God's-eye view of the world, one elevated above the human conditions of time and space. The claim to have developed such a system, then, is altogether presumptuous, we might even say blasphemous. However, Kierkegaard does not choose to follow this last idea, preferring to amuse himself at the sheer ridiculousness of the idea that an existing human being could have such a God's-eye view.

> Let us but smile at the ethico-religious fantasies of the Middle Ages with regard to asceticism and suchlike, but let us by no means forget that the vulgarly comic speculative extravagance of becoming an I = I and, at the same time, being such a philistine qua human being, is such that no enthusiast could ever have cared for such a life.
>
> (9 102/CUP1 119)

The possibility of such a confusion is ascribed by Kierkegaard to what he calls distraction or absent-mindedness:

> Someone who exists but forgets that he exists will become more and more *distrait*, and as people sometimes deposit the fruits of their *otium* [leisure] in literary works, so might we venture to expect as the fruits of his distraction the expected existential system – well, perhaps not all of us, but only those who are almost as *distrait* as he is. (9 103/CUP1 121)

The Hegelian philosophy is named as just such a phenomenon of mental distraction, a case of pure, unadulterated fantasy.

> If a dancer could leap very high, then we would marvel at him. But even if he could leap as high as any dancer had ever done, if he then pretended to be able to fly – why, let laughter then have him. For to leap means by definition to belong to the earth and to have to respect the laws of gravity, so that to leap is merely something momentary; but to fly means to be released from tellurian conditions, something which is reserved exclusively for winged creatures and, perhaps, also for moon-dwellers – and perhaps, perhaps it is only there that the system will find its true readers. (9 106/CUP1 124)

And so, "to be a human being has been abolished, and every speculator confuses himself with humanity, whereby he becomes something infinitely great and at the same time nothing at all" (9 106/CUP1 124). In thus drawing attention to the ridiculousness of the speculative philosopher's intellectual claims when these are measured against the philosopher's own more or less averagely mediocre humanity, Kierkegaard would seem, among other things, to be making clear that some kind of roughly common-sense view of reality is a wholesome antidote to the mental illness of idealist philosophy of this kind. Elsewhere, in other contexts, Kierkegaard will have his own sharp words to say about the limitations of such common sense with regard to human beings' ethical possibilities, but here, at least, he seems to be endorsing common sense's view that there is a real world out there inhabited by people who, if only approximately, correspond to the way in which we see them: people, that is, about whom we can assume that we all share a certain pool of common experiences and perceptions.[27]

Kierkegaard's strategic aim, then, may well go beyond exposing, with Trendelenburg, the subterfuge whereby Hegel covertly relies on empirical intuitions to power up a method that, supposedly, generates its concepts and categories out of its own resources. Ultimately, he has the quality of the philosopher's own life in view, something that may or may not count against his own text being counted as philosophical. Nevertheless, even if his long-term aim is directed elsewhere, we can see that a minimal sense of the term "existence" has to do with what is rooted in the real world known to everyday common sense, a world in which thought gets on with its business by thinking about "things" that are not themselves thoughts.

Who is Kierkegaard's "Hegel"?

Two questions remain, however, questions that are, in fact, closely intercon-nected. The first is whether Kierkegaard has adequately represented the Hegelian position he is attacking, and the second is whether he is, in fact, attacking Hegel at all.

This second point may seem, at first, counter-intuitive. After all, Hegel and Hegelians are named repeatedly throughout the *Postscript* as the prime examples of the fantastic self-forgetfulness of speculative philosophy. This does not mean that they are the only examples, and it could well be that, even if Kierkegaard took some inspiration from the later Schelling in devel-oping his critique of Hegel, Schelling too would fall under the axe of Kierkegaard's assertion that "an existential system is impossible", since Schelling's later philosophy could well be construed as just such an "existential system" (see below).[28] However, in a recent and in many respects definitive study, Stewart has argued, with great historical and textual detail, that Hegel is far from being the real target of the *Postscript*. "At best", he says, "Hegel's presence in the *Postscript* is ... secondhand."[29] Who, then, are the real targets of Kierkegaard's polemic? Stewart believes that it is the Danish Hegelians, primarily Kierkegaard's slightly older contemporary, the Hegelianizing theologian (later Bishop) Hans Lassen Martensen, together with the flag-bearer of Danish Hegelianism, the drama-tist and man of letters J. L. Heiberg.[30] Stewart adduces in support of his position the bitter personal tone of Kierkegaard's polemic and the presence of a number of what he regards as "code-words", terms especially associated with Martensen and that would have been recognizable as such to many of Kierkegaard's first readers. These code-words include the following words and phrases: *de omnibus dubitandum est* ("everything is to be doubted"), an expression frequently used by Martensen in his lectures on modern philosophy; "the system", which in a later journal entry Kierkegaard expressly says was linked chiefly to Martensen's name; the motif of "going further" than Hegel; the much-derided figure of the *Privat-docent* (a new form of unsalaried university teacher) who makes frequent appearances in the pages of the *Postscript*; and, lastly, the phrase *sub specie aeternitatis* ("in the view of eternity"), from which, according to Kierkegaard, the speculative philosopher views history and, indeed, himself.

Stewart also argues that, if the *Postscript* is indeed taken as an attack on Hegel, then it has missed its mark. Hegel's concerns are essentially so different from those of Kierkegaard in this work that there is no real point of contact sufficient to serve as a point of disagreement. "The discussions of Hegel and Climacus are at cross purposes since they are clearly discussing two quite different things. Hegel wants to give an analysis in the academic field of the philosophy of religion, whereas Climacus is concerned with religious faith."[31] A number of other supposedly "Hegelian" faults attacked in the *Postscript* similarly turn out to be not Hegelian at all, or only accidentally so. These include the self-forgetfulness of philosophers (of which Stewart remarks that it could equally well apply to any scientific practice whatsoever); the criticism of the claim that the foundations of logic are without presuppositions; the complaint that the systematizer indulges in inappropriate "world-historical perspectives" (inappropriate for existing individuals, that is); the confusion of thought and being; and the fact that the system has no ethics.

These questions, then – whether Kierkegaard has adequately represented Hegel and whether it is really Hegel he is attacking – are closely interconnected. I do not intend at this point to give a full answer to Stewart's claims, but shall simply focus on what has been the guiding thread of our discussion so far, the question of existence.

We have seen that in his attempts to undermine the claims of the system, Kierkegaard has used some fairly unconventional philosophical tactics, most obviously the use of humour to point up the ridiculousness of the (apparently) Hegelian philosopher's case. Yet we have also seen that his criticism of certain claims relating to the foundation of logic both reflect Hegel's own argument as well as the kinds of arguments being brought against Hegel by such contemporary philosophers as Trendelenburg. The way that Kierkegaard makes his case is, undoubtedly, idiosyncratic and definitely not scholarly. Nevertheless, it can be related quite closely to elements, at least, in the scholarly debate about Hegel. In some respects, if not all, Stewart seems implicitly to allow for this point, since the Danish Hegelians he sees Kierkegaard attacking were, after all, scholarly commentators who understood themselves to be correctly interpreting Hegel. What Kierkegaard is attacking is a position that could reasonably be taken to be "Hegelian" in some tangible sense. And some of his points do have a much closer connection to Hegel than this: that "movement" has a place in logic is, as we have seen, a position plainly advocated by Hegel, even if it is also advocated by some other Hegelians. Whether *everything* that Kierkegaard says about

Hegel is accurate is, naturally, another matter, although Merold Westphal for one describes Kierkegaard's summary of Hegel's argument about the foundations of logic as "impeccable".[32] That Kierkegaard's criticism is concretized and given polemical edge by its relation to some individuals whom Kierkegaard personally disliked, does not, of itself, exclude his arguments from counting as philosophical. Schopenhauer, famously, had a prize essay turned down by the University of Copenhagen (almost certainly by some of Kierkegaard's own philosophy professors) on the grounds that it indulged in personal abuse (again, mostly of Hegel) to an extent unacceptable in philosophy.[33] However, *we* seem to have no qualms in reading it today as a text justly belonging to the history of philosophy.

Philosophical forgetfulness has, of course, been a topic of philosophical anecdotes since the story of the maid who laughed at Thales falling down a well because his mind was preoccupied with higher things, a story with which Kierkegaard was certainly familiar. Clearly, he did not think that Hegel or Hegelians were the only philosophers liable to be led astray by the intoxicating powers of abstraction. On the contrary, as we have seen with regard to scepticism, what he found in Hegel and Hegelianism was precisely the particular manifestation of a more general philosophical problem, although (as he understood it) Hegelianism both compounded the problem to an almost unprecedented degree and, confusingly, believed itself to be providing a definitive solution. Hegelianism, then, is not unique in inducing self-forgetfulness but, Kierkegaard seems to be saying, it is unique in the extent to which it does so. With regard to philosophical fantasizing, to get involved with Hegelianism is to place oneself in the high-risk category.

I have said that it is not necessary to regard Kierkegaard's characterization of Hegel as adequate or correct in order to see it as offering a criticism of Hegel and Hegelianism. Philosophers of all schools are, after all, constantly misrepresenting each other, either wilfully or because of genuine misunderstanding. Yet there would seem to be a need for a minimum accuracy, if anything interesting is to come out of a given discussion. Is Kierkegaard's complaint that the Hegelian philosopher is especially prone to the vice of philosophical forgetfulness, and that this vice is already illustrated in the sophistries relating to the foundations of logic, in any sense legitimate?

Much clearly depends on the way in which we read Hegel. One line of Hegel interpretation would value Hegel precisely because of the extent to which he allowed "real life" to influence his philosophical thought. Whether this "real life" be understood in terms of economics and history (thus Georg Lukács[34]), the issue of Christian faith (thus Hans Küng[35]), or the experience of mortality (thus Kojève[36]), Hegel *can* be represented as the philosopher who more than any other forced philosophy to engage with the real world, a kind of proto-existentialist in his own right. Yet Kierkegaard is not alone in his depiction of Hegel as a philosopher more than usually culpable of the philosophical vice of hyper-abstraction. Another contemporary, Feuerbach, made a similar complaint, when he portrayed his own materialism as differing *toto caelo* from Hegel's way of mystifying human questions by turning them into ideal, logical questions. Marx took the argument further and, as in the early *Economic and Philosophical Manuscripts* of 1844, criticized Hegel precisely for the way in which he obscured the real problems of human alienation (i.e. the economic enslavement of the worker) by construing alienation solely as a problem for knowledge.

> For Hegel *human nature, man,* is equivalent to *self-consciousness.* All estrangement of human nature is therefore *nothing* but *estrangement of self-consciousness.* Hegel regards the estrangement of self-consciousness not as the *expression,* reflected in knowledge and in thought, of the *real* estrangement of human nature. On the contrary, *actual* estrangement, estrangement which appears real, is in its innermost hidden nature – which philosophy first brings to light – nothing more than the *appearance* of the estrangement of real human nature, of *self-consciousness.*[37]

If this seems self-contradictory, that is precisely the point: because of Hegel's idealistic privileging of consciousness, what a Hegelian regards as "real" estrangement and "real" human nature are the exact opposite of what a naturalistic point of view will regard as "real" estrangement and "real" human nature. "An objective being acts objectively, and it would not act objectively if objectivity were not an inherent part of its essential nature", Marx comments a couple of pages later,[38] underlining the point that the issue is not the relationship between the ideal sphere of mind and the "objectivity" of the external world (as he understands Hegel to have argued), but simply the concrete ways in which an objective being, namely the human being, experiences its being in a world of similarly objective entities.

As many historians of philosophy have noted, Marx's critique at this point seems to be a kind of equal but opposite complement to that of Kierkegaard.[39] That Hegel can thus be accused from such a very different standpoint of a kind of abstraction from reality that, for all the differences in their respective conceptions of reality, bears some analogy to Kierkegaard's ethically and religiously motivated accusation, by no means endorses the correctness of Kierkegaard's view of Hegel. Indeed, at this point, Marx and Kierkegaard may be representatives of two essentially irreconcilable positions. They can scarcely both be right in their radically divergent accounts of what is truly human in our humanity. Yet they seem united in their view that, whatever else is to be said for or against him, Hegel is caught in a strangely immobilized state of abstraction from what is "real" in humanity. That a thinker of such a different outlook from Kierkegaard could thus offer a parallel critique of Hegel would seem, at the very least, to add some plausibility, if not to Kierkegaard's criticisms then to the view that what he is arguing against is, in some sense, "Hegelian": that he is not shadow-boxing but engaging in an important way with positions that are decisive for the claims of Hegelian reason.

Clearly, it is impossible here to decide between Kierkegaard and Hegel and, for that matter, between Kierkegaard and Marx. The question is, simply, whether Kierkegaard's objections can be regarded as, in any signifi-cant sense, objections to Hegel. The point of citing Marx (and Feuerbach) is therefore to suggest that, even if at least some of Kierkegaard's detailed points against Hegel are misdirected, then the level of misreading involved in his response to Hegel was what might be expected from an intelligent Hegel-reader of his generation. But, interestingly, the possibility of reading Hegel in quite another way, as the philosopher who did most to enrich phi-losophy with the positive data of human life and history, also suggests why the issue should have become so important for such readers as Kierkegaard and Marx. Might it have been precisely the presence of proto-existential elements in Hegel that made Hegelianism so liable to mislead its adherents into self-forgetfulness? A philosopher who devotes himself to exercises in Aristotelian logic or to Kantian reflections on the transcendental possibili-ties of knowledge is not tempted to confuse what he is doing with acquiring an understanding of, say, the laws that determine the rise and fall of empires, the relative superiority of Christianity over Islam or the inner experiences of the anxious individual. A philosophy such as that of Hegel, however, that incorporates the actual forms and patterns of history, culture and religion into its own content is more likely than others to induce a confusion between purely philosophical problems and such "real" problems as the exploitation of workers or the claims of the religious life. And it is not implausible, as Trendelenburg and Kierkegaard both claimed, to see the possibility of such incorporation and such confusion as connected with the claim that logic is capable of representing "becoming", that is, temporal progression and, therewith, history. Absent-mindedness would thus, in a very definite sense, be a particular risk for philosophers in the Hegelian mould.

This does not get rid of Hegel. It may still be that there is a fundamental misreading of Hegel in play here and we shall be returning to the relation-ship between Kierkegaard's and Hegel's views of Christian faith. The point, for now, is merely to defend the view that Kierkegaard's critique of Hegel constitutes just that: a plausible critique of positions that could reasonably be described as Hegelian, whether or not current scholarship would endorse Kierkegaard's reading of Hegel at every point. And, to repeat, the issue for Kierkegaard is very precisely the failure of Hegelianism, as he sees it, adequately to acknowledge the claims of *existence*.

More self-forgetfulness: the aesthetic

Hegelian philosophers are, then, seen by Kierkegaard as pre-eminent among the practitioners (or is it the victims?) of philosophical self-forgetfulness. But they are not the only ones. An important part of Kierkegaard's early work is given over to the critique of what he calls the aesthetic point of view, and it soon transpires that aesthetes, no less than philosophers, are prone to self-forgetfulness: to periodic or chronic absenteeism from existence.

Curiously, Kierkegaard's earliest formulations of this critique of the aesthetic seem to have taken shape under the influence of Hegel. In his master's thesis, *The Concept of Irony*, he attacks Early Romanticism in terms broadly akin to those used by Hegel himself, especially with regard to what he sees as an illegitimate use of irony. A true master of irony knows how to keep irony as a subordinate element (Kierkegaard's examples are chiefly dramatists such as Shakespeare who use irony in one or other scene or character in order to serve the larger purposes of the plot). Early Romanticism, however, let irony off the leash, with the result that every aspect of experience became material for ironic treatment and it became impossible in any given utterance or expression of the self-styled Romantic poet to know whether he was being ironic or serious.

Importantly, Kierkegaard (again following Hegel) sees this as connected with a philosophical error on the part of the Romantics. The root problem is J. G. Fichte's conception of the absolute "I" or Ego, the supreme self-evident principle of I = I, abstracted from all possibly dubitable experience, and from which Fichte and his followers believed it possible to deduce all forms of actual experience. Kierkegaard, however, views this principle in terms that are essentially identical with the complaints that he will later make in the *Postscript* against Hegelian abstraction. In so far as Fichte does achieve an infinite abstraction from experience, this is precisely a purely negative infinity, an abstraction "from" experience but not "to" anything, and it is therefore an infinity without content. Indeed, Kierkegaard freely uses such terms as "docetic" and "acosmic" that will later be used against his own view of the subjective self. Fichte's mistake, however, is largely a simple philosophical mistake. What happens in Early Romanticism is that Friedrich Schlegel and his circle read Fichte without the appropriate philosophical discipline. Where Fichte uses the term "I" in a purely abstract sense, the Romantics take it to apply to their actual empirical "I", and all the powers that Fichte ascribed to his metaphysically constructed "I" were claimed by the Romantics for their own personal egos. In this sense they regarded themselves in their actual individual personality as having what Kierkegaard caustically referred to as "'the power to bind and to loose" (1 288/CI 276), alluding to the words with which Christ gave St Peter plenipotentiary powers relating to the forgiveness of sins. In other words, reality was no longer construed as a field comprising determinate objects, meanings or values but everything, absolutely everything (including religion and personal morality), was up for constant reinterpretation. Nothing meant more than the ironist wanted it to mean. The world had become no more than a playground, denuded of any constant, substantial values. The best life is therefore not a life lived in pursuit of knowledge or in striving for moral perfection, since knowledge is always uncertain and morality is always shifting. The best life is a life lived poetically, a life lived for pleasure and "redeemed" only by the possibilities it offers for the enjoyment of "beautiful" experiences. Note, however, that for this particular form of poetic existence, beauty itself is not regarded as an attribute of things themselves, but as solely a reflection of the creative power of the poetic "I". The sunset is not beautiful because of some intrinsic natural grammar of beautiful forms, but because I choose to see it as beautiful. What Fichte had formulated as an attempt to find an absolute ground or basis for knowledge is thus taken over by the Romantics as the programme for an ironic, that is absolutely libertarian, lifestyle.

Kierkegaard (following Hegel) isn't persuaded. As he sees it, the Romantic project is doomed to failure. Its claims concerning the absolute freedom of the self to be constantly reconstructing its own experience can only be made good by refusing to acknowledge the "given" quality of our experience of the world and of ourselves. The ironist has no *"an sich"*, Kierkegaard writes, that is, no intrinsic characteristics that make him one thing rather than another; he is nothing but a field of empty and undefined possibilities. The Romantic world is thus essentially a fantasy world, a kind of parallel universe lacking any real interaction with the world of common experience. The poetry cultivated by this form of Romanticism may "triumph over the world" but:

> it is through the negation of the imperfect reality that poetry opens up a higher reality, extends and transfigures the imperfect into the perfect, and thereby reconciles the deep pain which seeks to darken all things. Thus far poetry is a kind of reconciliation, but it is not the true reconciliation since it does not reconcile me with the actual

world [*Virkelighed*] in which I live and in this reconciliation there occurs no transubstantiation of the given, actual world but I am reconciled to the given, actual world by being given another actuality, a higher and more perfect one. (1 305–6/CI 297)

The Romantic, like the speculative philosopher, is, then, engaged in a project of active self-forgetfulness. But this has serious as well as comical possibilities. Although the poet believes himself to be exercising a kind of self-sovereignty, the reality is that his complete abandonment of the given, actual reality of common experience means that, in so far as he nevertheless has to go on living in the same world as the rest of us, this mundane aspect of his life is altogether beyond his control. The poet's self-image is in fact the mirror-image of his real situation; far from creating or controlling his inner life, the entire absence of any inner solidity or coherence means that he is, at most, the spectator of his own constantly shifting mood swings, imagining himself to be their creator. But, at bottom, all there really is is boredom.

Throughout this analysis Kierkegaard is – to repeat – carefully aligning himself with Hegel, although (as we have seen) in the end it will turn out that he arraigns Hegel for essentially the same fault of self-forgetful abstraction as that for which the Romantics are currently standing trial. This has led some commentators to question whether Kierkegaard himself is already – ironically – having a dig at the Hegelian position, appearing to share Hegelian perspectives in order to demonstrate their hollowness. Certainly there are some traces of irony – or is it sarcasm? – in his closing remarks about the claims of some contemporary Danish Hegelians to have overcome irony,[40] but this doesn't of itself prove that he did not endorse the arguments he found in Hegel against the Romantics. Again, we might see the problem as being something like this: that Hegel claimed to be representing the interests of actuality over the abstract view of the self found in Romanticism and, thus far, Kierkegaard can go along with him; on closer examination, however, the way in which Hegel claimed to have secured the claims of actuality is found by Kierkegaard to be inadequate and, still worse, to be only verbally, that is, sophistically, different from the argument underlying Romantic philosophy itself; recognition of this generates a demand to place the question of the self and the self's relation to absolute values on a completely different footing from anything found either in Romanticism or in Hegelianism and it is this that Kierkegaard's turn to existence intends to accomplish. Putting it in these terms also shows why the attack on Hegel had to be as bitter philosophically as it was bitter personally. Precisely because Hegel appeared to offer a solution to the problem that was, in fact, no solution, his presence was all the more dangerous, since it obstructed a true perception of the philosophical and human challenge of contemporary nihilism. The apparent similarity of his (Hegel's) response to that of Kierkegaard, his apparent incorporation of "reality" or "existence" into philosophy, was just what made it so necessary to get rid of him, at all costs.

In his so-called "aesthetic works" (chiefly *Either/Or*, *Repetition* and *Stages on Life's Way*), Kierkegaard offered many further explorations of how the fundamental idealism of Romantic philosophy leads to the shipwreck of those existing individuals who try to base their lives on such Romantic values as art, poetry and free love. Sooner or later all such individuals turn out to be reality-poor and to be lacking solidity. If, unlike Hegelians, they do not confuse themselves with humanity in general or some abstract principle, if they still remember that, in some sense, they are individual human beings, their sense of what that means is so vitiated, so empty, that they too, like the philosophers, can be said to have forgotten what it is to be. In a formulation that, as we shall see, is crucial in the constructive aspect of Kierkegaard's view of existence, they exist merely as possibility, not actuality.

In *Either/Or 2*, the fictional Assessor Wilhelm writes two long letters to a young aesthetic friend (referred to only as "A"), whom he regards as suffering from an excess of Romanticism. Characteristic of Wilhelm's criticism of his friend's ailment is the charge that "You are constantly hovering above yourself", a point he makes twice (3 16, 185/EE2 11, 198): that the poet necessarily lacks a secure foothold in reality. He can thus be anything and everything, mythicizing and mystifying the most everyday situations, but he can thus be and thus do, only because he is nothing, because he has turned his back on the world of real, actual, "given" relationships. The supreme epitome of A's life-view is *The Diary of the Seducer*, included in *Either/Or 1*, but we are never quite sure whether it is a document that A himself simply found (as he claims in its Introduction) or whether he wrote it himself and, if so, whether it is meant by A as a fiction or as a confession of what he did not dare to write openly. This uncertainty is, I believe, deliberately revealing of what it is we are being led to see in the Seducer. As A himself puts it in the introduction to the diary:

> Behind the world in which we live, far away in the background, lies another world, which stands in approximately the same relation to this world as the scene one sometimes sees in the theatre in the background of the main scene stands in relation to the latter. Through a thin gauze one sees, as it were, a world of gauze, lighter, more ethereal, of a different quality from the actual world. Many people who are physically present in the actual world do not actually belong to it but to this other world. (2 283–4/EE1 306)

And, as A goes on to add, "that a man can thus fade away, indeed almost vanish from the actual world, can have its basis either in health or in sickness. This latter was the case with this man" (2 284/EE1 306). These comments, I think, provide an important key to the diary. Although the apparent realism of its style suggests that we are indeed dealing with the story of an actual seduction of an actual girl in contemporary Copenhagen, there is a sense in which the whole action really takes place only in the Seducer's own mind. Essentially, he does not live in the real world, but in the kind of gauzy "other world" of which the introduction to the diary speaks. The climax of the seductive process is, therefore, appropriately described not so much in terms of dishevelled bedclothes and panting bodies but in terms of ideas, of thought: what the Seducer does, essentially, is to give the girl his "idea", to intoxicate her not so much with his physical presence as with the idea of himself. Correspondingly it is essentially only in thought that he himself "enjoys" her: "I have made her light, light as a thought," he writes, "and now, should not this thought belong to me!" (2 404/EE1 438). The whole "seduction" is, fundamentally, nothing more than an event in thought, an idea, and the Seducer, we might add, is therefore fundamentally nothing more than a spiritual onanist. The girl simply doesn't exist for him as an "other": as a real, actually existing human being. And even if it is implied that a sexual act does take place, it has no significance. All that matters in it, in his, the Seducer's, understanding, is his *idea*. But in construing the situation thus, he is precisely a man who has forgotten what it is *really* to exist.

Both in A's comment on the "sickness" revealed in the Seducer's other-worldliness and in an earlier citation from *The Concept of Irony*, where Kierkegaard talks about poetry attempting to reconcile "the deep pain that darkens all things", we see hints of what is an important deepening of the critique of Romanticism and Hegelianism as forms of non-existence, which I shall call the genealogical theme in Kierkegaard. That is to say, Kierkegaard does not simply condemn these differing versions of idealism as having forgotten what it is to exist. He also offers an account of why and how they came to forget existence that depicts them as attempts to avoid becoming aware of a deep pain inherent in the condition of subjective existence. Self-forgetting is not an arbitrary happenstance; it is the outcome of a motivated strategy of survival, but, Kierkegaard believes, the strategy itself is entirely misconceived and, therefore, doomed to failure. We shall come to other aspects of Kierkegaard's use of a genealogical method in Chapter 2, but now we shall look, briefly, at how Kierkegaard does not merely use existence as a negative criterion with which to expose the self-forgetfulness of various kinds of idealists, but also sets about constructing existence as the locus of a positive source of human meaning and value.

Subjectivity and existence

In Part 2 of the *Postscript* Kierkegaard starts to set out his own counter-proposals to the speculative philosophy whose claims to systematic comprehensiveness he has been attacking in Part 1.[41] These centre on the claim that "truth is subjectivity" (9 157/CUP1 189) or, as Kierkegaard also puts it, that becoming truly subjective is "the highest task facing a human being" (9 107/CUP1 129). In saying this he makes it clear that, for him, this claim is intimately connected with the cause of Christianity. Christianity, he says, requires us to emphasize the principle of subjectivity to such an extent that all traces of objectivity are to be eliminated from our reflections on the truth-claims that Christianity makes on us. "Thus Christianity protests against all [forms of] objectivity; it wants the subject to be infinitely concerned about himself. What it asks about is subjectivity, for Christianity's truth consists only in this, if it exists at all, [and] objectively it isn't anything at all" (9 108/CUP1 130). Is this, then, solely a matter of interest for religious types? Certainly, Kierkegaard's presentation of Christianity will raise issues that seem either to defy any purely philosophical approach or that any purely rational philosophy might find itself having to reject, but the distinction between subjective and objective forms of truth does not seem to be an issue of this kind. Defining for the subjective approach is, in the first instance, simply the individual's manner of relating to himself, to his own life. Although Christianity *requires* the individual to take a subjective stance towards truth, the possibility of taking such a stance is itself pretheological. As Kierkegaard puts it, Christianity assumes "that subjectivity exists as the possibility of appropriating this good [i.e. the good of an eternal happiness offered by Christian preaching], the possibility of accepting it ..." (9 107/CUP1 130). In the language of traditional theology, whether or not the human being is *capax dei,* "capable of God", he or she is being regarded here as capable of receiving the salvation that God wills to bestow. Whether or not any actual individuals ever come to believe and to receive this salvation, human beings as such are orientated towards the goal for which God has created them.[42] However, subjectivity is not a capacity we simply possess. In order to be subjective, we have to become subjective, and we can only become subjective by actively engaging ourselves in the process subjectively, which, as Kierkegaard also emphasizes, can occur only by our doing so freely. And this, in Kierkegaard's terms, is to say that the issue is an essentially ethical one.

What has this to do with the question of existence? Quite simply that, for Kierkegaard, becoming subjective is the *only* way in which human beings can truthfully relate to themselves as existing beings: the only way in which their existence can become an issue for them. In other words, whatever may be the case for other types of beings (rocks, vegetables, shellfish, other mammals), human existence is existence characterized by subjectivity. Unless or until we activate our capacity for being subjective we are not living a fully human life: we are not *existing*.

The relationship between subjectivity and existence is especially sharply expressed in the *Postscript*, Part 2, Chapter 3, entitled "Actual Subjectivity, the Ethical: the Subjective Thinker". Once again, the limitations of speculative thought with regard to thinking existence are adduced, serving as a foil to the more positive approach now being ventured. "Precisely because abstract thought is *sub specie aeterni,* it looks away from the concrete, the temporal, the process of existence ..." (10 9/CUP1 301) and, again, Trendelenburg is alluded to in support of the claim that, in so far as Hegel does prove capable of saying something significant about the real world, he does so by breaking the rules of his own logic and smuggling in intuitions and perceptions derived from non-logical sources. Abstract thought, we are told, deals with "questions concerning existence" by simply ignoring what is existential in them. So (this is Kierkegaard's example), it deals with the question of immortality by leaving out the individual who is anxiously concerned as to his own prospects for immortality and, instead, it asks about immortality in general. Again, the comical aspect of this oversight is emphasized and, again, Kierkegaard points to the way in which certain logical confusions help sustain the Hegelian blindness to existence (this time it is the Hegelians' supposed breaking with the law of non-contradiction[43]). But where abstract thought privileges a disinterested approach to truth, the subjective thinker is not ashamed to think passionately and to acknowledge his infinite interest in the matter of his own existence. "To exist, if this is not to be understood as merely existing, cannot be done without passion," Kierkegaard writes (10 18/CUP1 311). Moreover, existence involves precisely what speculative logic ought to have omitted: movement, which is to say, temporality. This constitutes a critical issue for the idea of selfhood, since, if we once take seriously what it is to be temporal through-and-through, how can we then speak of a stable, coherent self at all? How can we say "I", if tomorrow I must be different from what I am today and if today I am already different from what I was yesterday? This is not just a logical question, Kierkegaard insists, it is a question that, here and now, must concern me as just this particular individual I am. His solution to the dilemma (stated, it has to be said, rather than argued), is that:

> For an existing person the goal of movement is decision and repetition. The eternal is what gives continuity to movement, but an abstract eternity is beyond [the realm of] movement, and a concrete eternity in the existing person is passion's maximum [focus].

> All idealizing passion anticipates the eternal, *in* existence, *for* an existing person, *in order that* he might exist … But passion's anticipation of the eternal for an existing person still does not provide absolute continuity but [only] the possibility of approaching the one true [state] there can be for an existing person. Here again one might recall my thesis that subjectivity is truth, since, for an existing person, objective truth is like the eternity of abstraction.
>
> (10 19/CUP1 312–13, original emphasis)

This, like so much in this section of the *Postscript,* is so highly compressed, so dependent on undeveloped cross-references to other Kierkegaardian texts (as in the appeal to decision and repetition), that it is hard to grasp every detail on a single reading or without taking into account the whole context. Nevertheless, the picture that is being painted does start to emerge: that existence is what comes into view when and as an individual begins to take seriously their paradoxical identity as entirely permeated by temporality or becoming, and yet also sensing that, in their humanity, they have a claim to be acknowledged as persons, as free, spiritual beings who are not reducible to a mere chain of temporally conditioned causes. Thus, as Kierkegaard immediately adds, "Abstraction is disinterested, but for an existing person existence is the highest interest" (10 20/CUP1 313). And, a little further on, "For the existing person existence is the highest interest, and being interested in existence is actuality" (10 21/CUP1 314).

At this point we need to make a small but important comment about terminology. The last-quoted sentence appears in the older translation of the *Postscript* as "Existence constitutes the highest interest of the existing individual, and his interest in his existence constitutes his reality."[44] Choosing "reality" as a translation of the Danish *Virkelighed* (cf. German *Wirklichkeit*) is not intrinsically incorrect. However, it not only lends credence to the view that Kierkegaard's individual is acosmic, lacking a base in what common sense calls "reality"; it also obscures aspects of the philosophical implications of the term. Both for Kierkegaard and for his German and Danish predecessors, "actuality" is crucially to be understood in relation to "possibility", as in the medieval Latin translation of the Aristotelian *dynamis* (possibility) and *energeia* (actuality). "Actuality", therefore, does not simply apply to a world of facts, of objects that may or may not exist or may or may not have any purported attributes ascribed to them (as in "Does the tree exist?" or "Is the apple green?"). Instead "actuality" points to a mode of being or existing: young Tom has the potential to become a great rugby player, but whether he "actualizes" (or, as we also say, "realizes") this potential is another matter. However, in the passage just quoted, Kierkegaard raises the stakes somewhat higher than simply the actualization of one or other of our potentialities (being a rugby player, violinist, political leader, etc.). For it is indeed possible that Tom does become the great rugby player his coach believes he has it in him to be. If he does, we can then say of him that Tom "is" a great rugby player. Being a human being, however, is not, according to Kierkegaard, something we can ever finally actualize in this way. I can never turn around and say of myself, "Now I have become the human being I had it in me to become". Why not? Because, as long as we live in time (and that, effectively, means for the whole of our lives), who or what we are is still open to revision and change. I may "be" the great leader of a nation but then, in my dying breath, betray that nation to its enemies. Our end can never be had other than in what Kierkegaard calls the mode of "anticipation". My "actuality" then, is not the actuality of a fully realized potential. It is itself a process of actualization whose end is not yet given. Or, as Kierkegaard puts it:

> Actuality is an *inter-esse* between the hypothetical unity of thought and being offered by abstraction ... Actuality, existence is the dialectical moment in a trilogy whose beginning and end cannot exist for the existing person, who *qua* existing is in the dialectical moment. (10 21/CUP1 314)

For the existing individual, then, this dialectical moment can never be resolved into a stable outcome. The hope that I might, actually, become the person I believe myself to be can only exist for me as a possibility, that is, as something that I *might* become but don't have to. To say of a human being that he is or has an eternal soul can, therefore, only be appropriated by an actually existing human being as one possibility among others, a possibility that can only be "owned" in the manner of anticipation and infinite uncertainty. This recalls one of Kierkegaard's various formulations of truth as subjectivity found earlier in the book: that *"objective uncertainty, held fast in the most passionate act of inward appropriation is truth*, the highest truth there is for an *existing person"* (9 169–70/CUP1 203).

Here we might add that, if one prong of Kierkegaard's attack on the system was to do with what he regarded as the failure of the arguments offered in support of its logical foundations, he was no less scathing about claims that the system could achieve some kind of completeness, that is, that it could establish a completely adequate framework for the explanation and interpretation of all possible phenomena. His remarks here are doubly pointed. On the one hand he mocks the claim concerning systematic completeness as such. On the other he sarcastically notes how one or other Hegelian is publishing a contribution towards the completion of the system, and yet the last part never arrives. With regard to this second point, we may agree with Stewart that there are particular Danish Hegelians in view. Yet Hegel himself does seem to have made the kind of claim regarding finality – what has been called the "eschatological" aspect of his thought – that Kierkegaard thinks cannot, on principle, be made good as long as the system is to be constructed by human beings who are positioned in the midst of the open-ended temporal flow in which thought and being are always separated by existence.

Kierkegaard's use of the terminological pair possibility–actuality can, admittedly, be confusing. Sometimes, for example, he uses "possibility" to describe the kind of abstraction from reality that is encountered both in poetry and in metaphysics, in the sense in which Aristotle remarked that poetry was "higher" than history, that is, that poetry and metaphysics do not show facts or what is the case, but what might be: forms and conditions of possible existence. Against this form of "possibility", Kierkegaard asserts that "Ethically regarded, actuality is higher than possibility. For the ethical aims precisely at annihilating the disinterestedness of possibility by making the matter of existence its infinite interest" (10 25/CUP1 320). "Possibility" in this sense can cover both the hypothetical world of the logical system but also the malaise of the aesthete who merely plays with the possibilities that life has given him and fails decisively to choose any of them. Yet Kierkegaard can also say that, in another sense, possibility is higher than actuality. Quoting his own *Stages on Life's Way*, he asserts the priority of possibility over actuality: "In *Stages on Life's Way* it was said: 'Spirit therefore asks about two things: 1) Is what is said possible? 2) Can I do it? But it is spiritless to ask two things: 1) Is it actual? 2) Has my neighbour Christopherson done it, has he actually done it?'" (10 27/CUP1 322). Why are these last two questions "spiritless"? Because they regard ethical questions as matters of disinterested, objective truth. A genuinely ethical interest, however, will always only be interested in what is presented as a real possibility for the subject's own action. An ethical task, an "ought", has to become present as a possibility before it can be actualized. A world without possibilities would therefore be a world without the possibility of living ethically, of living in and through the exercise of freedom. Possibility in this sense signals the openness and indeterminacy of the future. Much later in his authorship, in *The Sickness unto Death*, Kierkegaard will say even of God that "God is that all things are possible", a formulation that underwrites his conviction that, from the standpoint of Christian faith, the world appears as a field of free and responsible action.

It is worth observing that it is characteristic of Kierkegaard's use of language not merely to accept the fluidity of words but actively to deploy the ambiguities that this fluidity opens up. Language, as Kierkegaard understands it, cannot be abstracted from its context and this context itself always includes the intentions of the speaker. In the present context, in the discussion of the subjective thinker, this point appropriately underlines the impossibility of speaking of subjectivity, freedom or existence in an "objective" manner. It is not as if there is a "correct" or "scientific" vocabulary waiting to be discovered or employed. What subjectivity *means* for an existing subject can only be teased out in descriptions whose vocabulary and syntax reflect or even set in motion the instability and open-endedness of subjective existence itself. The term "unscientific" in the title is to be taken seriously, as well as satirically; for all Kierkegaard's own occasional use of scholarly conventions throughout the book, it is fundamentally not a "scientific" book in the sense that it aims at what might be called an objective depiction of the subjective individual, as, for example, a reader might expect to get from the section on "Subjective Spirit" in Hegel's *Encyclopedia of the Philosophical Sciences*. This does not mean that "anything goes", but that the very peculiar nature of Kierkegaard's task projects both writer and reader into an unexplored space. Of objective and subjective truth Kierkegaard wrote that objectively one must ask about *what* is being said, whereas subjectively one asks about *how* it is said. I have written extensively elsewhere about various aspects of Kierkegaard's strategy of indirect communication, and I do not intend to say too much about it here.[45] However, it would be untrue and unfair to Kierkegaard to overlook his own passionate and painstaking concern with "how" to communicate the demands that a subjective (and, in the last resort, Christian) view of the human condition makes upon us. The peculiar form of the *Postscript* itself bears witness to that. It often reads *like* a philosophical text, but scarcely like any familiar philosophical textbook. Even in the midst of this, often regarded as his most philosophical work, Kierkegaard is struggling with the question as to philosophy's ability appropriately to handle the question that he is posing.

Elizabeth's child

Kierkegaard's relation to Hegel has been one of the guiding threads of this chapter, but we should also note that (in addition to its Aristotelian associations) the term "actuality" puts him into the orbit of the thinker who was, arguably, Hegel's most significant contemporary opponent: Schelling. It is well known that one of the things that excited Kierkegaard about his trip to Berlin in 1841–42 was the prospect of hearing Schelling, a philosopher who, it might be said, had become a legend in his own lifetime. Schelling's lecture course on "The Philosophy of Revelation" began in late November, and, after the second lecture, Kierkegaard wrote:

> I am so happy to have heard Schelling's second lecture – indescribably ... The embryonic child of thought leapt for joy within me as in Elizabeth, when he mentioned the word 'actuality' in connection with the relation of possibility to actuality. I remember almost every word he said after that. Here perhaps clarity can be achieved.
>
> (CI xxi–xxii).

The rhetoric could scarcely be bolder, since Kierkegaard is referring to the moment in the gospel story when Elizabeth, pregnant with John the Baptist, is visited by Mary, herself pregnant with Jesus. According to St Matthew's gospel, Elizabeth reports that the moment she heard Mary's voice, the baby in her womb leapt for joy. Is Schelling then the philosophical Messiah whose prophet Kierkegaard perhaps imagines himself becoming? It is a tantalizing thought, but, unfortunately, the clarity he hoped for didn't come. By February 1842 he is writing back to his brother that "Schelling talks the most insufferable nonsense" (CI xxiii) and to a friend in Copenhagen that "Schelling talks endless nonsense both in an extensive and intensive sense" (CI xxiv).

What were the reasons for this cycle of enthusiasm and disillusionment? Kierkegaard's lecture notes do not offer too much assistance, since they are the fairly typically patchy notes of a bright student who is having trouble making sense of what he is hearing. Yet there are intriguing and suggestive hints. For a start the key words "possibility" and "actuality" are central to Schelling's philosophical vocabulary in a way that they are not to Hegel's. Furthermore, in Schelling's description of his own philosophy as a "positive" philosophy (in opposition to the mere "negativity" of Hegel) and his category of an *unvordenkliche Seyn* ("unprethinkable Being"), he seems to adumbrate the grounding of philosophy in the revelation of existing Being rather than in the kind of abstraction for which Kierkegaard criticizes Hegel. And whereas Trendelenburg's reference to thinking's "unclarifiable background" related more to the realm of sensuous experience, Schelling's idea seems to point more to the inexplicability of some kind of primal act of will, something we might assume would be closer to Kierkegaard's own thought. Indeed Schelling too discusses aspects of the foundations of the Hegelian system in a way that has some overlap with the discussion in the *Postscript*. The central Kierkegaardian concept of anxiety is also found in Schelling, and there would seem to be at least some analogy in their uses. Yet Schelling's lectures lead through grandiose and rambling speculations about theogonic processes and the Eleusinian mysteries that would have been essentially alien to Kierkegaard's interest in the ethically existing individual. If there are intriguing points of possible convergence, Kierkegaard and Schelling were, ultimately, thinkers of quite different interests and styles. Thus it is possible to argue that, behind or along with the polemic against Hegel in the *Postscript*, there is also a critical, if somewhat submerged, dialogue going on with Schelling. For Schelling too would have to be counted "guilty" of attempting to construct what Kierkegaard calls an "existential system".

That Kierkegaard received some kind of creative impulse from Schelling seems likely. But if Schelling helped in the crystallization of some of Kierkegaard's ideas, it does not now seem likely that the key to his own development and use of these ideas is going to be found in the genial but tangled undergrowth of Schellingian philosophy. Something of the ambivalence of Kierkegaard's attitude to Schelling emerges in a footnote to *The Concept of Anxiety*, where he writes that "Schelling himself often talks about anxiety, wrath, pain, suffering, etc. But one should always remain somewhat suspicious of such expressions if one is not to confuse the consequences of sin in the created world with what Schelling uses them to refer to, namely states and moods in God" (6 151/CA 59). Yet in the same footnote he dissociates himself from some of the attacks made on Schelling in this connection by commenting that "a powerful and red-blooded anthropomorphism is distinctly valuable" (6 151/CA 59). Nor does the historical fate of this philosophy suggest that the Kierkegaard–Schelling axis will ever have the same significance for subsequent philosophy as the Kierkegaard–Hegel axis. Yet these lectures (also attended by Engels, Bakunin and Burckhardt), together with the vast idiosyncratic project of the later Schelling, remain a historically fascinating moment in the history of ideas, and they remain interesting, if not decisive, for the discussion of Kierkegaard's affiliation to German Idealism.[46]

CHAPTER TWO

Anxiety

The concept of anxiety

Existence, actuality, subjectivity, passion: we have seen how these terms are used by Kierkegaard to designate an experience of life in which I, as this particular individual that I am, become aware of the uniqueness and fragility of my life, as it moves ineluctably into an unknown future. Does this future contain possibilities for creative self-transformation? Might it even open out onto an eternal happiness? Or, perhaps, eternal damnation? Or just extinction? The questions seem unanswerable, yet how can I know who I myself really am if I cannot answer them? For there would seem to be all the difference in the world between an existing being destined for eternal happiness and one destined for extinction, but caught as I am in the midst of time I have no independent knowledge as to which of these beings I myself am.

If this is indeed my predicament – *our* human predicament – then it is well described by another key Kierkegaardian term: anxiety. In now turning to Kierkegaard's treatment of anxiety and to a range of related themes and concepts, we shall find ourselves extending and elaborating the idea of the self established in a preliminary way by the analysis of "existence". In other words, the concept of anxiety is not engaging a different subject-matter from the concept of existence, for in each case this subject-matter is fundamentally nothing but the self that is *my* self, the self shaped by the passionate, subjective question concerning who I am, how I came here and where I'm bound for.

Nevertheless, when we come to the book entitled *The Concept of Anxiety*, we find a very different approach from that which we have so far seen in the *Postscript*. There, Kierkegaard appeared to be primarily engaged in what could be called conceptual clarification and definition, in constant polemical dialogue with Hegel or, at least, Hegelianism.[1] Kierkegaard's own subtitle to the *Postscript* referred to it as "mimetic-pathetic-dialectical". The subtitle to *The Concept of Anxiety*, however, describes the book as "A simple psychologically orienting consideration", in which (for now) the key term is "psychological". "Psychological" and "psychology" are significant terms in Kierkegaard's authorship, occurring in the subtitles of two other important works, *Repetition* and *The Sickness unto Death*. What exactly Kierkegaardian psychology means for the philosophical interpretation of his work is a question to which we shall return, especially with regard to the claim made by a number of commentators (but implicitly rejected by Heidegger) that Kierkegaard can be read as a kind of proto-phenomenologist. In his own context, "psychology" was still a discipline within philosophy. In Hegelian terms it belonged to the section of the system dealing with "subjective spirit". Since both of these terms were central in Kierkegaard's account of the human person, we can see how "psychology" might appeal to him as a field where, if anywhere, it might be appropriate to conduct a theoretical examination of human existence. And, as many commentators have noted, there are striking affinities between *The Concept of Anxiety* and such contemporary works as the *Psychology* of the Hegelian philosopher Karl Rosenkranz, a text that Kierkegaard quotes and discusses at several points in *The Concept of Anxiety* itself, and other parallels with contemporary philosophical psychology can also be drawn.[2] Here, then, rather than from the kind of conceptual or dialectical discussion we found in the *Postscript* and *The Concept of Irony*, we might expect to learn something more tangible of Kierkegaard's actual view of the human person and of those structures of human personality that are definitive not just of this or that individual but of human beings in general.

However, before we allow ourselves to settle down to read *The Concept of Anxiety* as if it were a straightforward textbook of philosophical psychology, there is a further feature of the subtitle that calls for comment, namely, that Kierkegaard also describes it as orientated towards "the dogmatic problem of original sin". This curious juxtaposition of psychological method and theological problem is addressed in the Introduction, which is largely devoted to the question as to which, if any, academic discipline might be capable of dealing with the question of sin and, in particular, of the respective competences of dogmatics and psychology.[3] Bearing in mind the critique of Hegel in the *Postscript,* it is striking that Kierkegaard's initial illustration of the need to observe disciplinary boundaries concerns the illegitimacy of treating "actuality" in logic. Kierkegaard, perhaps bafflingly on the part of one apparently setting out to deal with sin as a psychological problem, argues that in so far as sin can be treated "scientifically", that is, as the subject of scholarly enquiry, the only science capable of dealing with it is dogmatics. Yet this is only a temporary respite for "science", since, given the nature of sin, it is not possible to observe or to analyse it if one is not also engaged in opposing it. Sin is not something that permits the scientific stance of neutral observation. Sin calls for decision. When it comes to the actuality of sin, that is, when I am actually tempted by some actual sin, then no science can save me. I need simply to resist. It might, then, seem that neither psychology nor any other science has business here, and if dogmatics is allowed to say something, it is only because Kierkegaard clearly presupposes that dogmatics itself is not neutral but allows itself to be shaped by its Christian presuppositions. This clearly sets a limit to anything that psychology might have to offer on the subject but, Kierkegaard suggests, that does not mean that it has nothing to say. Recalling that "actuality" is only one half of the dialectical polarity of possibility and actuality, Kierkegaard finally concedes to psychology the limited but legitimate task of investigating the *possibility* of sin, or, in other words, asking what it is in the structure of the human person that makes it possible for something like sin (whatever sin is like) to become a reality in human life. It is this possibility that he defines as the specific subject-matter of *The Concept of Anxiety*. It is not about sin as such, but about the structures of human psychology that make it possible to see the human being in terms of sin. Psychology itself, *qua* academic discipline, could never determine whether human beings actually are to be described in terms of sin, still less whether any given individual was a "sinner".

It has recently been suggested that *The Concept of Anxiety* is, in fact, far from being the "psychological" work it claims to be and that it is better read as a "parody" of the kind of textbook represented by Rosenkranz's *Psychology*.[4] Irony being what it is, there is, perhaps, no way of finally answering such a claim. However, the picture of the self that emerges in *The Concept of Anxiety* is not unique in Kierkegaard's writings. On the contrary, it is very much of a piece with a large body of descriptive psychological studies that can be found in just about every genre within his authorship. As already indicated, this includes *Repetition* and *The Sickness unto Death*, but also passages from just about any of the major pseudonymous works as well as from the religious treatises that accompanied them, published under Kierkegaard's own name. Indeed, recent work on the manuscript indicates that Kierkegaard had originally planned to publish the work under his own name, only switching to the pseudonym Vigilius Haufniensis at the very last minute. We shall return to the question as to the philosophical status of Kierkegaard's psychology as a whole at the end of this chapter. Now, however, beginning with *The Concept of Anxiety* itself and broadening out into Kierkegaard's other psychological studies, I shall attempt to sketch something of what the Kierkegaardian self looks like.

The self we have encountered thus far – actual, subjective, passionate, existing, temporal – is also a conscious and self-conscious self. This is not yet to say what level or kind of self-consciousness it has, but it could not be concerned about its own existence in the way that it is – passionately, for example – if it were not to some extent aware of itself. In a sense it is precisely this as yet undefined awareness that is the primary object of much of Kierkegaard's psychological writing. What sort of awareness is it? What possibilities of existence does it open up? What possibilities does it foreclose on? But even before we attempt to answer such questions we are stopped in our tracks by a simple reflection. This is that it is characteristic for our common experience of existing in time that, whatever degree of self-awareness we have of ourselves now, it is very different from the kind of self-awareness we had as infants or children. Similarly, when we look around at the other beings with which we share the empirical world we sense a gradation in levels or kinds of consciousness among them: stones, we assume, have no consciousness at all, chimpanzees appear to have a very high level of consciousness, and, in between these extremes, there is just about every possible nuance. Yet, with the possible exception of the higher apes, our ordinary idea of even the animal world is that although some kind of sentience can scarcely be denied to many animals, there is a kind of self-awareness that adult human beings are capable of that is denied even the most sensitive animal. Animals, we imagine, are governed by instinct, and even the cunning of a predator is, finally, instinctive. The animal is what it is. As Nietzsche commented, the bird of prey is not evilly disposed towards the lambs it devours; its nature is simply to prey upon them, just as it is the lambs' nature to fear the bird of prey.[5] We do not therefore hold the kite morally accountable for its feeding habits as we do a human being. As well as the difference between infants and adults, then, there is also a kind of consciousness, a kind of *self*-consciousness we spontaneously attribute to human beings that is different in kind from whatever consciousness we also attribute to animals.[6] Coleridge, for example, spoke of this as the difference between being "scious", or merely aware, and "*con*scious", an awareness in which we are aware of ourselves as well as of the object to which our awareness is directed.[7] Yet, at some point, we were all infants and we are all animal beings, subject to the same physical and biological conditions as all other animals. How, then, did we become different, and in what does our difference consist?

This is, in a sense, one of the key questions of *The Concept of Anxiety*. Kierkegaard's interest, however, is not so much in the when and where of this differentiation as in its *how*, which he sees as the key to its *meaning*, a meaning, of course, that is first and foremost its meaning for the conscious subject itself. As has been noted, *The Concept of Anxiety* takes its orientation from the doctrine of original sin, and Kierkegaard's account of the transition from the unconscious or preconscious life of the child or animal to the self-conscious existence of human adulthood turns out to be largely patterned on the familiar story of the Fall found in the Bible's Genesis 3. Here the Bible tells how, having created Adam and Eve, the first human beings, God places them in the Garden of Eden, where they have everything they need for a happy and contented life. They are allowed to eat from any of the plants of the garden except for one, the tree of the knowledge of good and evil. If they eat of that, then, God says, they will die. But a mysterious serpent persuades Eve that eating of this tree will in fact make them like gods. Eve succumbs to these beguiling words, eats the fruit herself and then persuades Adam to do the same. They become immediately ashamed of their nakedness, they are driven from the garden and condemned to earn their food by work, childbirth becomes painful and, in short, every possible evil is let loose in the world. Classical Christian theology had indulged in considerable speculation about the nature of Adam and Eve, who were often said to have been the most perfect possible human beings before the Fall. These theories compounded the problem as to how such gifted creatures could possibly have fallen for the serpent's rather superficial flattery. Kierkegaard takes note of this line of thinking only to dismiss it. Instead – and closely in line with Hegel and a range of other revisionist theologians of the period – he effectively treats the biblical story as an allegory of each individual's passage from the preconscious, animal-like life of infancy to self-conscious adulthood. Freedom and reason are no longer being conceived simply as attributes that can be assigned to human being, as if they were part of some timeless essence of humanity. Instead, and in a dramatic shift of intellectual sensibility, they are themselves redrawn in terms of process and emergence. Yet if Kierkegaard, broadly speaking, accepts this newly historicized paradigm associated with Hegel, he develops it in his own idiosyncratic way. How, then, does he retell the story of the Fall as a story of the universal self?

The state of Adam and Eve in the Garden prior to the Fall is described by Kierkegaard as one of innocence and ignorance. "In innocence," he adds, "the human being does not have the attributes of spirit but has the attributes only of 'soulishness' in immediate unity with nature" (6 135/CA 41). By "soul" (or "psyche") Kierkegaard here follows contemporary and traditional usage in referring to that part of the self which has affections and sentience but not self-consciousness, that is, the kind of self-awareness that everyday usage ascribes to animals. In these terms, then, the human being starts out from nature, as a part of nature and in complete continuity with it. Yet, at the same time, Kierkegaard takes it as axiomatic that the human being is also *qua* human destined to become spirit. He has not yet defined spirit, but – again in broad agreement with contemporary idealist philosophy – to exist as spirit would mean (minimally) to be characterized by self-consciousness and self-directing freedom, to be capable of action in a decisive sense and, therefore, responsible. In this Edenic childhood phase, however, such a spiritual life has not yet emerged; it is still "dreaming", as Kierkegaard puts it (6 135/CA 41). But this means that it is not entirely absent, for, even if I have not yet awoken to my own possibilities for existing as a self-conscious agent, these are, nevertheless, still my possibilities. The child is, after all, a human child and not an animal. But its very humanness is, on this account, dependent on a capability that it does not yet have. How can one make sense of this? It is not easy, and Kierkegaard is soon driven to paradoxical formulations in his attempt to explain it.

> In this state there is peace and rest, but at the same time there is something else, which does not disturb the peace or engender conflict, for there is nothing to be in conflict with. What is there then? Nothing. But what effect does nothing have? It gives birth to anxiety. This is the deep secret of innocence, that at the same time it is anxiety. Dreaming, spirit projects its own actuality: this actuality is nothing, but innocence always sees this nothing outside itself.
>
> (6 136/CA 41)

Anxiety, then, is the child's dream of its own possibility for acquiring a kind of existence of which it cannot yet conceive. This existence is "nothing" in that it has no definite place in its life, yet is also precisely what makes it what it is, human and not animal. At one and the same time it is repelled by the incomprehensibility of this "nothing", yet, at the same time, it is drawn towards it by an inarticulate sense that this "nothing" contains the secret of its own existence. Thus, Kierkegaard can say, "Anxiety is *a sympathetic antipathy* and *an antipathetic sympathy*" (6 136/CA 42, original emphasis). It is not at all the same as simple fear, he says, nor should it be seen in terms of guilt. It is, he insists, a proper part of a child's psychological constitution.

> If one observes children, one will find this anxiety more precisely manifested as seeking after what is adventurous, monstrous, or mysterious. That there are children who do not have this trait means nothing, for neither do animals have it, and the less spirit, the less anxiety. This anxiety belongs so essentially to the child that he does not want to avoid it: even if it causes him anxiety, it entraps him with its sweet anxiousness. (6 136–7/CA 42)

Anxiety is not fear, but what Kierkegaard is describing here is illustrated by the very familiar childhood allure of "being frightened" – hearing a

51

frightening story, looking at a scary picture, peeking over the parapet of a high building – a "wanting-to-be-frightened" that is very different from the actual fear experienced when the same child is confronted by an aggressive dog or a hostile gang. The actual fear is measurable and focused, but what is alluring in the frightening story is precisely the sense of there being incomprehensible dangers and unimaginable frightfulnesses such as one has never experienced. It is the excessive and ungraspable that both fascinates and repels. In his unpublished essay on how to tell children stories (Pap II A 12/ JP 265), Kierkegaard is careful to stress that the story-teller should not demythologize the scary bits by assuring the child that it's only a story or offering some prosaic explanation. The whole enjoyment depends on arousing the sense for the inexplicable. When the first English translator of *The Concept of Anxiety* opted to translate the Danish "*Angest*" (cf. German "*Angst*") as "dread", it gave a good expression to this aspect of what Kierkegaard is talking about. Yet if anxiety is to be affirmed as a normal and proper part of childhood development it is also dangerous. In an early journal entry Kierkegaard wrote that:

> A certain presentiment seems to precede everything which is to happen ... But just as it can have a deterring effect, it can also tempt a person to think that he is, as it were, predestined; he sees himself carried on to something as though by consequences beyond his control. Therefore one ought to be very careful with children, never believe the worst and by untimely suspicion or by a chance remark (a flame of hell which ignites the tinder which is in every soul) occasion an anxious consciousness in which innocent but fragile souls can easily be tempted to believe themselves guilty, to despair, and thereby to make the first step towards the goal foreshadowed by the unsettling presentiment – a remark which gives the kingdom of evil, with its stupefying, snakelike eye, an occasion for reducing them to a kind of spiritual paralysis. Of this too it may be said: Woe unto him by whom the offence comes.   (Pap II A 18/JP 91)

Something similar seems to be reflected in the story of the Fall, when God prohibits Adam from eating of the tree of the knowledge of good and evil. Naturally, innocence cannot understand this word, but anxiety has, as it were, its first prey: instead of nothing, it has an enigmatic word (6 138/CA 44). What does this "enigmatic word" do to Adam?

> What passed innocence by as the nothing of anxiety has now entered into his own self, and here again it is a nothing, the anxious possibility of *being able*. He has no idea of what it is he can do, for that

would mean presupposing what indeed mostly happens but which comes later, the difference between good and evil. There is only the possibility of being able as a higher form of not-knowing, as a higher expression of anxiety, because, in a higher sense, it both is and is not, because, in a higher sense, he both loves it and flees it.

(6 138/CA 44–5)

Kierkegaard's emphasis is thus on two aspects of this kind of anxiety: the enigmatic nature of the prohibition and its subjective reference. He rejects the view that the prohibition simply generated the desire for the object, as in the popular psychology according to which saying "No!" is the surest way to make a child desire some object or other. There is no direct causal relation between the negative commandment and the positive counter-action (the desire). A direct "No" by no means invariably inspires either desire or anxiety. What is more likely to do so is when the prohibition relates to the child's own subjective possibilities. Imagine a parent and child in a newsagent where there is a particularly lurid display of pornographic magazines. If the parent says, with appropriate seriousness, "Don't look at those horrid magazines", the child may well simply accept the prohibition. But if the parent says, "Now, don't let me catch you looking at those", then, in Kierkegaard's terms, this is far more likely to engender anxiety and, through anxiety, to increase the desire exponentially. For a prohibition couched in these terms relates not so much to the object (the forbidden magazines) as to the child's own capacity *to look,* and what it awakens is not simply *desire* for the prohibited object, but, more precisely, awareness of the *possibility of desiring.*[8] It is in this possibility that anxiety is found, insinuating itself *between* the prohibition and the desire. If desire is conceived of primarily in terms of its object, then anxiety is primarily to do with the subject's sense of self and its own intrinsic possibilities. The thought of anxiety is not so much, "Now *that* might be something desirable" as "*I* could become the sort of person who would desire that."

Crucial to the whole logic both of the book and of the concept of anxiety itself is that since what is thus awoken in anxiety is an (ambiguous) possibility of the self, there can be no question of any simple mechanism of desire. It is not a matter of a simple, centred subject desiring some external object, but rather of an internally differentiated subject discovering the diverse possibilities of relating to its world made available by this internal differentiation. In a formula that anticipates the yet more complex definition of the self with which *The Sickness unto Death* opens (and which we shall shortly be examining), Kierkegaard writes, "Everything hinges on anxiety becoming manifest. The human being is a synthesis of soul and body. But a synthesis is unthinkable if the two parts are not united in a third. This third is spirit" (6 137/CA 43). Anxiety is therefore the form that spirit takes in its emergence as the explicit, self-conscious, self-directing force of personal life. It is the form of the possibility of spirit, and, as such, can only become actual in and as an act of self-conscious freedom, which, as Kierkegaard will say, is and must be as a "qualitative leap". It is this freedom itself which both attracts and repels in anxiety, not the forbidden fruit or the pornography or any other merely external object of desire.

All of this, Kierkegaard reminds us, is the legitimate sphere of psychology. Once the self chooses itself as spirit, once it defines itself in terms of one or other desire or complex of desires, it is removed from the realm of any observational science into the sphere of ethics and, if the issue is – as it ultimately is – sin, dogmatics. Psychology, in other words, has no remit to consider whether any particular action or orientation of the self is right or wrong, it has only to consider what makes it possible for the self to choose to act in such a way.

Yet is it simply an accident resulting from taking the story of the Fall as his starting-point that makes Kierkegaard focus so consistently on scenarios in which, once the leap into freedom is made, it is made in a wrong way or, somehow or other, fails? The Protestant theologian Paul Tillich, strongly influenced by both Kierkegaard and Schelling, argued that a radical understanding of the human condition in terms of finite freedom means that creation is, in effect, identical with the Fall; we cannot come to exist as finite, free individuals without losing our deep bond to the source and origin of our being. To exist is to exist as estranged or separated from the ground of being. It is to be cast out of paradise into the terror of history.[9] Although Kierkegaard himself does not rule out the possibility of the experience of anxiety issuing in a positive outcome, of becoming what, in the final chapter, he calls "saving through faith", he typically portrays anxiety as the occasion of our falling away from the very possibility of free subjectivity that anxiety itself reveals. In the actuality of human lives, the essential ambiguity of anxiety resolves itself again and again in favour of the subordination of freedom to lower levels of selfhood, as we fail to become the personal and responsible beings we potentially are. But, for Kierkegaard as for Kant (and as opposed to Schelling and Tillich), there can be no general ontological entrenchment of the "evil" inclination of human beings, since there would then be no scope either for a psychological or for an ethical approach to human subjectivity. There would be only dogmatics or metaphysics.

This becomes clear in the way that, although the story of the Fall is Kierkegaard's explicit starting-point and the doctrine of original sin his constant foil, he makes it clear that, in so far as it is properly psychological, the investigation is not as such dependent on any particular religious narratives or doctrines. Thus, he quietly indicates that the classical Augustinian doctrine of original sin, according to which we are all encompassed by Adam's sin and rightly punished for it, is psychologically worthless. He writes:

> To want to deny that every later individual has or may be assumed to have had a time of innocence analogous to that of Adam would be as disturbing as it would be thoughtless, For then there would have been one individual who was not an individual, but only an exemplar of his species who was yet, at the same time, being viewed in terms of the individual attribute of being guilty.
>
> (6 152/CA 60–61)

Adam's sin has no causal impact on subsequent human beings, and the phenomenon of anxiety in each subsequent human being is an original psychological phenomenon and its course from the awakening to the loss of freedom is equally original in all. The story begins again with each new life. In a passage that contains one of his most celebrated images of anxiety (an image taken up by Sartre, among others[10]), Kierkegaard writes:

> One can compare anxiety with vertigo. One whose eye looks down into the swirling depths experiences vertigo – but why? The reason has as much to do with his eye as with the abyss. For what if he hadn't looked down? It is in this way that anxiety is the vertigo of freedom, occurring when the spirit wants to posit the synthesis and freedom looks down into its own possibility, and then grasps at finitude as something to hold on to. In this vertigo, freedom faints.
>
> (6 152–3/CA 61)

The universality of the failure to exist in and as Spirit, that is, that freedom repeatedly "faints" at the prospect of its own infinite possibilities, is not a "result" of original sin. For even if it is described as an *almost* inevitable outcome of the awakening of freedom in the life of the individual who, in the very same moment, proves incapable of taking responsibility for this new possibility and "grasps at finitude", as Kierkegaard puts it (or, in Kantian terms, subordinates moral to non-moral incentives[11]), this failure is not described in causal terms.

Anxiety, youth and the aesthetic

We have been looking at anxiety in terms of the transition from the preconscious life of the animal or the child to a life of awakened self-consciousness and freedom. As such, it is a transition that did not take place only once, long ago in the Garden of Eden (or, in a more Darwinian perspective, at that moment in the past when humanity emerged from the last prehuman ape), but is a process repeated ontogenetically in every human life. Now Kierkegaard does not offer the kind of diagrammatic plan for psychological development that we find in, for example, Erik Eriksen's *Childhood and Society*,[12] nor does he develop any very sophisticated schema for the various transitional phases such as we find in Freudian theory (pre-oedipal, oedipal, latency, etc.). If the transition for which anxiety serves as the defining characteristic is seen, broadly, as the transition from childhood to adult life, this leaves wide open the further, more precise specification of exactly when anxiety might be expected to reach its peak, as it were. What, then, is the decisive moment in this transition?

From one angle it might be argued that the question is not so important. There is no reason why anxiety should not manifest itself at a variety of moments in life, if we once regard human freedom and consciousness in terms of process and emergence rather than as attributes fixed once and for all in the human essence. Each time there is a development within the life of spirit there will be the possibility of anxiety, whether as help, hindrance or accompaniment to that development. Kierkegaard would not, I think, dispute this. Yet it is clear that he was especially preoccupied by the particular connection between anxiety and what might, very loosely, be called adolescence. In this connection he shows himself aware that the experience of anxiety is therefore always gendered and in complex ways entwined with the awakening of sexuality. But here too – as we have seen was also the case with his treatment of the dogma of original sin – sexuality cannot be seen as a *cause* of anxiety, for it is only freedom itself and not any external biological force that drives it to experience vertigo or to grasp at finitude. However, this involvement of anxiety with gender and sexuality means that our experience of freedom is never merely an interior experience but is always, *in some way,* shaped by the encounter with the other. And if, in the first instance, this other is not the other of moral responsibility but, rather, the sexually other, a psychological relationship of this kind lays a preliminary psychological foundation for an ethical view of freedom as "always already" in a situation of obligation or other-relatedness.[13]

It is therefore far from coincidental that Kierkegaard's works are littered with stories of a young person's stepping out into the world of adult society and illustrations of the kinds of experiences that he or she (but mostly he) is likely to encounter. We might, for example, think of the sketches for a quasi-autobiographical novel that Kierkegaard wrote when he was 22, in which he describes a moody young thinker walking the lakes and cliff-tops of Northern Sjaelland and brooding upon what he is to do with his life, moving between experiences of deep communion with nature and moments of absolute isolation. This is, so to speak, "classic Kierkegaard", the Kierkegaard who, ever since, has spoken to those undergoing this most painful of transitions. This is not condescendingly to imply that only adolescents are likely to get anything out of reading Kierkegaard or that those who read Kierkegaard show themselves never to have resolved the crisis of adolescence. If the crisis of adolescence is indeed one of the principal foci of Kierkegaardian psychology, the very importance of that crisis in every life and *for the whole* of every life, means that it potentially has a much larger significance than merely providing a mirror to the anguish of alienated youth. What comes to a pitch in adolescence is, in some degree or variation, reflected or repeated in many subsequent life changes.

One place where the connection between adolescence and anxiety is particularly clearly expressed is the encomium on theatrical art delivered by Constantin Constantius, the pseudonymous author of *Repetition*. He writes:

> There is surely no young man of any imagination who has not at some time felt himself caught up by the magic of the theatre and desired himself to be transported into that fictitious reality, so that like a doppelgänger he can see and hear himself, to split himself up into all manner of possible differentiations of himself from himself so that each differentiation is in turn a single self.   (5 135/FTR 154)

Constantin identifies the time when this magic is most likely to work its power as the moment when, in a botanical analogy, what he calls the "cryptic" life of childhood is about to give way to the mature life.

> It is naturally only at a very young age that such a desire expresses itself. Only the fantasy is awake in this dream of personality; every other faculty is still sound asleep. In such a fantastic self-contemplation the individual has no actual form, but is only a shadow, or rather, the actual form is invisibly present, and is therefore not content with casting one shadow, but the individual has a multiplicity of shadows, which all resemble him, and for each moment have an equal claim to be himself. The personality is not yet discovered; its energy announces itself only in the passion of possibility.
>
>   (5 135ff./FTR 154 ff.)

The analogy with the account of anxiety's "dreaming innocence" is too close to miss, and there are no less unmistakable affinities with the "nebulous ... dream-world" of the Seducer, "where every moment one is scared by one's own shadow" (2 287/EE1 310). And, if we are also alive – as

Kierkegaard certainly was – to the etymological connections between the terms for "wind" and "spirit" and recall that the "dream" of anxiety is the dream of its own future existence as spirit, then we will not overlook the implications of the word picture which Kierkegaard goes on to paint:

> If, in a mountain region, one hears the wind expounding the same theme, immoveably, unchangingly, day in and day out, then one is perhaps tempted for a moment to abstract from the imperfection of the image and to take pleasure from its figuration of the constancy and sureness of human freedom. Perhaps one does not think that there was a time when the wind that has now dwelt amongst these mountains for many years came as a stranger to these parts, tumbling down wildly and meaninglessly among the fissures and down into the caves, now whining in such a way as almost to make it stumble over itself, now giving a hollow roar that it itself fled from, now a lament, of which it itself did not know the source, now a sigh from the abyss of anxiety, so deep that the wind itself grew afraid and, for a moment, doubted whether it would dare to dwell in these parts, now a lyrically abandoned polka, until, having got to know its instrument, all of this is made to co-operate in the melody that it expounds from day to day without alteration. Thus the individual's possibility wanders wildly about in its own possibility, now discovering one thing, now another.
> (5 136/FTR 155)

According to Constantin, the theatre provides a perfect environment in which this indulgence in free fantasy can take on a form that is both inno-cent (i.e. not morally accountable) and educative, in that the individual comes to learn which human possibilities most engage him. As a spectator, I can identify myself with the criminality of a Richard III (Constantin's example is a robber chief) or the heroism of a Henry V or the cunning of an Odysseus, and through freely exercising my freedom of choice in this "play of shadows" I prepare myself – playfully – for the exercise of freedom in actuality or "real life". "The main point," Constantin says, "is that everything takes place at the right time. Everything has its time in youth, and what has had its time then has it again in later life" (5 136/FTR 155). This kind of playful self-discovery is entirely positive, as long as we under-stand that it is just a play and that a moment comes when we have to move from possibility to actuality. "At the very same moment the cock crows and the twilight flees away, the voices of the night fall silent. If they continue, then we are in a quite different domain, where all this goes on under the disquieting eye of responsibility, then we are on the border of the demonic" (5 137/FTR 156). Why? Because we are in danger of responding to the demands of actuality by allowing ourselves to atrophy in the domain of possibility. We resist "getting real" and want to remain perpetual adolescents, unable to take responsibility, unable to commit to a clear and consistent existential task, unable, in the last resort, to *be* anything. Yet, to repeat, Constantin is not writing here in order primarily to add to the volumes of Kierkegaardian pathology. What he is describing is in the first instance a normal and healthy part of maturation. As such, and not only in its pathological distortion, it is a part appropriately described as "anxious" in the specifically Kierkegaardian sense.

Yet, as we have just seen, such aesthetic play can, Kierkegaard seems to think, easily become pathological if the step into actuality and the ethical responsibility that comes with actuality is ducked. It is thus of the essence of the aesthetic life described by Kierkegaard that it is a life frozen in possibility, a life that, so to speak, remains in the theatre – remains the life of a spectator – when it should be getting out into the world of action. In this connection too we can see how Kierkegaard several times suggests that the aesthetic life is also a cult of perpetual youth, with the implication that it is accompanied by the shadow of self-deception that attends any such inherently doomed project. Assessor Wilhelm notes that he consistently refers to A, the aesthete of *Either/Or 1* as "my young friend", but then stops to comment that, in actual fact, there is no great age gap between them. The problem is simply that A has never grown up.

It may seem something of a moral leap from the kind of immaturity exemplified in the rather effete, affected and somewhat whimsical personality of A himself to a psychopathic tyrant such as Nero, but this is precisely the illustration to which the Assessor turns to show the consequences of an aesthetic existence as a "perpetual youth". Nero precisely exemplifies the problem of someone who, although adult in years, has not developed a correspondingly adult attitude towards his own freedom and responsibility.

> [D]espite all his experience, he is still a child or a youth. The spirit's immediacy cannot break through, and yet it demands a breakthrough, it demands a higher form of existence. But if this is to happen, then there will come a moment when the splendour of the throne, his power and dominion, will grow pale, and he does not have the courage for this. Now he catches at pleasure, all the cunning of the world must be used to devise new pleasures for him, for he can only find rest in the moment of pleasure, and when it is over he gasps with weariness ... Then the spirit within him gathers itself like a dark cloud, its wrath broods over his soul and it becomes anxious, and its anxiety does not cease, even in the moment of enjoyment. See, therefore his eye is so dark that none can bear to

look at it, his glance flashes so angrily that it causes anxiety, because behind his eye lies the soul, which is like a deep shadow. One calls the glance "royal", and the whole world goes in awe of it, and yet his innermost being is anxiety ... he is a riddle to himself, and anxiety is his essence. (3 174f./EE2 186–7)

Nero perfectly illustrates Constantin's dictum that everything has to happen at the right time. The problem with Nero is not that he is anxious, but that he has not used – has not had the *courage* to use, Wilhelm says – his anxiety in the right way. He remains an actor, even though, of all men, he, as Emperor, carries the heaviest burden of responsibility. The point is precisely not to remain in anxiety, for to remain in anxiety is to surrender to an atrophy of the spirit, it is never to enjoy the freedom that anxiety anticipates but always to fall away from it, opting for spectatorship over engagement and pleasure over responsibility. And there is a further point here that should not be overlooked. The example of Nero – although he is seemingly a "monster" of a very different kind than A or even the Seducer – illustrates what is a potentially important link for Kierkegaard between the aesthetic character of contemporary society and its propensity for violence. A culture of aesthetic spectatorship, he several times suggests, is also inherently a culture greedy for images of violence. It scarcely needs to be pointed out that the complex of aesthetic narcissism, spectatorship and violence continues to haunt our own contemporary world.[14]

Kierkegaard's account of the aesthetic is genealogical in a very Nietzschean sense. It is a hermeneutics of suspicion that reveals the reality of the aesthetic life to be quite different from what the aesthete himself imagines it to be. In their own imaginations the Kierkegaardian aesthetes are brilliant, audacious, poised, interesting and free from all the pettiness of bourgeois life. At one moment in *Stages on Life's Way*, however, we see a group of these aesthetes emerge from an all-night banquet at which they have been eating the finest foods, drinking the rarest wines and delivering the most eloquent speeches. To a third-person observer, they present a very different spectacle from their self-presentation at the banquet:

They made a fantastic impression on me: a nocturnal society, seen in the morning light in a pleasant natural surrounding, has an effect which is almost *unheimlich*. One might think of ghosts, surprised by the dawn; of subterranean beings, who cannot find the cracks through which they must vanish, because they are only visible in the dark; of unhappy creatures, for whom the difference between day and night has vanished in the uniformity of suffering. (7 76/SLW 81–2)

Such figures, like that of Nero, seem to have crossed a line separating the normal, creative function of anxiety, from a chronic, pathological anxiety that we scarcely hesitate to call despair. Assessor Wilhelm, indeed, warns A that his attitude to life is fundamentally one of despair and that he refuses to leave the enchanted world of a prolonged aesthetic childhood because he is incapable of believing that the world outside will be favourable to the fulfilment of his aspirations and desire for creative self-fulfilment. In this perspective, the fallen Adam is precisely the prototypical aesthete.

From anxiety to despair

In principle anxiety need not lead to despair. Precisely as a phase, as a category of pure transition, as *movement,* it is to be accepted and affirmed, for it is the doorway into life. Yet, as we have seen, there seems to be something about the entanglement of freedom's best possibilities in finitude that virtually condemns each of us to fail to be the selves we might be and, consequently, to an existence in unmitigated despair. Kierkegaard himself seems to imply something like this when, five years after *The Concept of Anxiety,* he writes the following in *The Sickness unto Death*:

> As a doctor might well say that there lives scarcely a single human being who is entirely healthy, so, if one really knows human beings, one might well say that there lives scarcely a single human being who is not a little bit despairing, in whose inmost parts there does not dwell a restlessness, a lack of peace, a disharmony, an anxiety concerning an unknown something, or concerning something he dare not become acquainted with, an anxiety concerning a possibility of existence or an anxiety concerning himself. Thus, as the doctor talks about walking about with a sickness in the body, so too he goes about carrying a sickness of the spirit, which just once in a while can be glimpsed in and as an anxiety that he himself cannot explain, an anxiety that lets it be shown that [the sickness] is in there. And, in any case, there has never lived a human being and there does not live a human being outside Christendom, who is not in despair, nor within Christendom, insofar as the human being is not a true Christian – and insofar as he is not entirely this, he is still somewhat despairing. (15 81/SUD 22)

Anxiety seems to be being treated here more as a symptom of despair than as a state or phenomenon in its own right. What has happened to anxiety as a part of the healthy transition from childhood to adulthood or the possibility of anxiety as "saving through faith"?

Before addressing that question, let us pause to note other features of *The Sickness unto Death* that echo but also appear to transform the analyses of the self found in *The Concept of Anxiety*. I have already alluded to the famous definition of the triadic self with which the book's first part opens:

> The human being is spirit. But what is spirit? Spirit is the self. But what is the self? The self is a relationship that relates itself to itself or is that in the relationship that the relationship relates itself to itself; the self is not the relationship but that the relationship relates itself to itself ... In the relationship between two, the relationship is the third as [their] negative unity, and the two relate themselves to the relationship and in the relationship to the relationship; thus, in terms of the attribute of "soul", the relationship between soul and body is a relationship. If, however, the relationship relates itself to itself, this relationship is the positive third, and this is the self.
>
> (15 73/SUD 13)

For a thinker who is known as a critic of Hegelian abstraction, this all sounds suspiciously like Hegelian abstraction. And, of course, in many ways it is. For what is decisive for both Hegel and Kierkegaard is that spirit, the self, is not to be construed in terms of some pre-existent essence or nature but as the free and active process whereby the differentiated structures of the self are brought into a unity. This is not a unity that simply emerges out of some kind of organic process; it is a unity that exists only as the free synthesizing action of the self, as a constantly repeated event. Once again, however, Kierkegaard is careful to make a distinction that separates him from the kind of idealism found in Fichte and his Romantic interpreters. The self, according to Kierkegaard, does not and cannot create itself out of nothing. Already in *Either/Or 2*, Assessor Wilhelm, the fictional representative of the ethical point of view in that work, insisted that the self only exists in a radical sense by choosing itself, thus emphasizing the centrality of the self's own free involvement in its self-constitution, but also drawing attention to the fact that the very nature of "choice" precluded absolute self-creation: the self that *chooses* itself chooses itself as something given to it. For the Assessor this is to be ultimately understood in a religious sense: that we choose ourselves "from the hand of God". So too in *Sickness unto Death*, the relationship that freely brings about a synthesis between the polarities of its being also brings its self into existence, "is yet again a relationship, relating itself to what has established the entire relationship" (15 73/SUD 13), a dynamic that finds its conclusion only when "in relating itself to itself and in willing to be itself, the self is transparently grounded in the power that established it" (15 74/SUD 14).

When this last state is not achieved – and we have seen that, for Kierkegaard, it rarely, if ever, is achieved – then the various polarities of the self, losing their ground and centre, split up and fragment in a variety of ways. In some lines that I omitted from the foregoing definition of the self, Kierkegaard details the key polarities as being the infinite–finite, the eternal–temporal, and freedom–necessity. When these are not drawn together into the concrete fullness of a willed and grounded synthesis, then, he explains, one or other will come to dominate the self. The poetic personality is thus one that loses itself in infinitude, while the petit-bourgeois outlook is more typically characterized by a loss of all horizons except for the crudely finite horizons of day-to-day life and mediocre ordinariness. Again, the speculative philosopher is alluded to as Kierkegaard offers a brief comment on how knowledge that loses its grip on the finite "becomes fantastic" (15 89/SUD 31) and loses itself in vacuously infinite generalities. In other works, Kierkegaard gives further examples of this fragmentation. Especially striking is the account of what he calls "double-mindedness" in the first part of the collection of religious discourses entitled *Upbuilding Discourses in Various Spirits*. This part, published separately in English as *Purity of Heart*,[15] contrasts the purity of heart that wills one thing and in doing so brings the self itself into a willed unity, with those who, in failing to will one thing inevitably end up double-mindedly willing a multiplicity of things. Typical of these is the worldly minded man who wills the good, but only up to a point, only so long as willing the good also serves the achievement of some other aim, such as economic or social advantage. But while such a both-and approach may be typical of how things go in the world, it betrays the inability of the person concerned to be the self they could be or to exist as spirit.[16]

But despair can also be analysed according to whether the one who despairs is conscious of doing so or not. Clearly, some kind of minimal self-consciousness must be assumed in every human being, but, as Kierkegaard says, there is a broad spectrum of possibilities stretched out between this minimum and a maximum consciousness that still falls short of the desired synthesis. Given that there is a clear interdependence between the intensity of self-consciousness and the ability to be cognizant of the manifold elements that belong to the fully synthesized self, a self that has fallen under the domination of one or other polarity will be unable to know its own possibilities for wholeness and may therefore be largely unaware that it has a problem. And this applies as much to petit-bourgeois materialists as it does to idealist philosophers:

[Example 1] If one thinks of a house with a basement, first floor, and second floor occupied, or designed, so that there was or was meant to be a distinction of class between the occupants of the various floors, and, if one compares what it means to be a human being with such a house, then, alas, what is sad and laughable about most people's lives is that they prefer to live in the basement in their own house. Every human being is a synthesis of soul and body intended to be spirit – this is the building – but each prefers to live in the basement, that is, in the determinations of sensuousness. And it is not just that they prefer to live in the basement – no, they love it so much that they get angry if anyone recommends move to the upper floor that is vacant and available ... [Example 2] A thinker raises a huge building, a system, a system that embraces the whole of existence, the history of the world, etc. Yet if one looks at his private life, one is astonished by the alarming and laughable situation that he himself does not personally occupy this huge, domed palace but a shed alongside it, or a kennel, or at most the caretaker's apartment.

(15 100/SUD 43–4)

Such characters are, largely, unaware that they are in despair. But there are others who are conscious of their despair, and these are divided by Kierkegaard into two classes: those whose despair takes the form of not willing to be themselves, which he calls the despair of weakness or "feminine" despair; and those whose despair takes the form of choosing themselves without reference to God or to any power other than their own will-power. This is the despair of defiance or "masculine" despair: the despair of a Prometheus, of a Byron or of militant atheism.

Kierkegaard is at pains to point out that all of these taxonomic categorizations comprise a vast multitude of actual variations and that deciding the dividing-line between them or, perhaps, deciding the exact mix in any given case, is always going to be difficult: "multiply nuanced" (15 104/SUD 48), he writes. "To a certain extent [the person who is unconscious of being in despair] notices in himself that he is in despair, in the way that a person does who walks around with a bodily sickness but does not really want to admit what the sickness is" (15 104/SUD 48). Further nuances emerge when Kierkegaard considers the Socratic alternative to the Christian doctrine of sin: that no one knowingly does what is wrong. Christianity, however, teaches that a person can know what is right but nevertheless be betrayed into doing the opposite (or simply doing nothing) by a corruption of the will. Typically, as Kierkegaard describes it, this corruption shows itself when the individual postpones the demanding imperatives of the ethical, allowing the clarity of his moral principles to be obscured by distance, qualifications and practicalities, "And thus, perhaps, live a great multitude of people – they work away so minutely at dimming their ethical and ethico-religious awareness, which leads them to decisions and conclusions that the lower element in them does not desire" (15 146–7/SUD 94). At any point, then, it is going to be hard to say just how much self-knowledge any given individual really possesses. It may be less, but it may also be more, than appears. Not only will a third-person observer always have difficulty in penetrating the inwardness inform-ing another's actions, but even as agents we are dogged by constant possibilities of self-deception.

But, to whatever extent its inhabitants are blanketed by a fog of wilful ignorance, the world depicted by *The Sickness unto Death* is a grim one, for it is a world in which human beings are universally and chronically failing to be the beings they could be, failing, in short, to be truly human. Kierkegaard, we could easily imagine, would share Zarathustra's great cry of lament:

> Truly, my friends, I walk among men as among the fragments and limbs of men!
>
> The terrible thing to my eye is to find men shattered in pieces and scattered as if over a battle-field of slaughter.
>
> And when my eye flees from the present to the past, it always discovers the same thing: fragments and limbs and dreadful chances – but no men![17]

But how does such a vision of all-encompassing despair relate back to the starting-point of *The Concept of Anxiety*? Has "anxiety" proved to be no more than a symptom of despair or, to put the question differently, if we once accept the view of the self that is required by the concept of anxiety, are we committing ourselves to a programme that ends, inevitably, with the scenario of universal despair set out in *The Sickness unto Death*? Can one have anxiety without despair?

We have already noted that Kierkegaard himself insists that anxiety can be "saving through faith" and, in fact, even *The Sickness unto Death* holds open the possibility of a redemption from despair for those who put their faith in the forgiveness of sins in Jesus Christ. We shall return to the ques-tion of Kierkegaardian faith and its implications for a philosophical read-ing of Kierkegaard in Chapters 3 and 4, but, in a preliminary way, it would seem that to offer religious faith as the only way out from what is otherwise a universal destiny of despair leaves nothing for a non-religious humanistic philosophy to hold on to, unless it is prepared, with Sartre, to affirm that despair is indeed the only legitimate basis for modern philosophy. But, the non-Sartrean humanist might say, this is simply to accept the sleight of hand that Kierkegaard is playing. For, such a humanist might argue, it is far from being the case that Kierkegaard's anthropology is constructed on the basis of a general psychological observation to which the religious superstructure is added as a kind of optional extra. On the contrary, the religious conclusion, that life is nothing unless rooted and grounded in God, is what determines the negative anthropology. If one does not accept the religious conclusion, then the whole structure of the anthropology falls away, including the evaluation of human life in terms of despair.

We shall return to consider the implications of this objection in Chapter 4, but there are further features of Kierkegaard's discussion of anxiety that merit some attention: chiefly the relationship between anxiety and time and anxiety and language. Consideration of these will help us to see to what extent, within the limits of a purely psychological approach, we can regard anxiety as a positive and not merely a negative phenomenon.

Anxiety and time

In the discussion of existence we saw that Kierkegaard rejected what he regarded as the philosophical pretension of regarding the human being *sub specie aeternitatis*. In the actuality of existence we have no access to such a view from nowhere. Nor should we be misled by the term "actuality" itself to think of existence as arriving at some finished state. Rather, existence itself is a *process* of actualization; it is in constant transition, constant movement, and, therefore, is essentially temporal. That anxiety is also described by Kierkegaard in terms of the transition from the possibility of freedom to its actualization suggests that anxiety too will prove to be an essentially temporal phenomenon. The anxious self is a self caught up in a process of development, poised vertiginously in the moment of transition from innocent ignorance to free self-consciousness. But, although Kierkegaard himself describes – and insists upon describing – anxiety as a "state", the very instability of this state, its vertiginous ambiguity, suggests that it would be misleading to think of it as anything static. Perhaps it would only be proper to speak of a "state" of anxiety once anxiety has atrophied into the still life of despair, but even such a still life would be a maximum that might be more theoretical than existential. Anyone still in existence must, one way or another, be in movement, in time.

Yet, whether for Kierkegaard or for anyone wishing to promote a non-nihilistic account of human life, it would seem that the acceptance of such a temporalized view of the self is highly problematic. How, if all is flux, can we affirm such transtemporal values as truth and goodness? How, indeed, can we even speak of "a self" at all, since, surely, a thoroughly temporalized self is a self that has been dissolved into pure process? Nietzsche and Buddhism might counsel us simply to accept that that is how it is, but Kierkegaard – along with the mainstream of Western thinking – doesn't find it that easy. And here the anxiety of the Kierkegaardian aesthete reveals another aspect. For the aesthete's dread of committing himself to life, of courageously embracing existence, is also dread of the self-loss that existence necessarily involves, since existence, it would seem, means time, change and, in the end, death.

That such is the case emerges quite explicitly from the pens of several of the aesthetes themselves. *Either/Or 1* introduces us to a society of such characters called the "symparanekromenoi", an invented Greek name that, etymologically, suggests a conscious proximity to death.[18] In a speech to this company, A declaims the following confession of faith:

> Certainly men say that the voice of the deity is not in the rushing wind, but in the gentle breeze; our ears, however, are not formed to catch gentle breezes, but rather to drink in the roaring of the elements. And why should they not break forth more powerfully still and make an end to life and the world and this brief talk, which has the advantage over all the rest that is soon ended? Yea, let the vortex that is the world's innermost principle, even though men do not acknowledge it but eat and drink and marry and multiply in busy carelessness, let it break loose and display its inner wrath, shaking the mountains from their places along with the nations and all that has been produced by culture and all the cunning inventions of mankind, let it break loose with that final terrible shriek that, more surely than the last trump, declares the downfall of everything; let it stir itself and sweep away this exposed cliff on which we stand, as it were a speck of dust blown away on the breath ...
>
> (2 156/EE1 168)

Note the deliberate rejection of a Christian view of the end of time as fulfilment (the expression "the last trump" refers to the angelic trumpet calling the living and the dead to the final judgement of God) and the postulation of everything ending simply in one last, meaningless dissolution. It is a vision of sheer flux and, therewith, the total relativization of all human values and goals.

A similar outlook is expressed by Constantin Constantius when, having failed to achieve the repetition that would bring meaning into his life, he composes a eulogy to the post-horn, declaring this musically unreliable instrument a fit symbol of life in general, since one never knows what note it is going to sound and it never seems to sound exactly the same note twice. "One does not need to move from the spot in order to be convinced that there is no repetition," he writes. "No, when all is vanity and passes away one travels faster than a railway train when one is sitting quietly in one's room, although one is sitting still" (5 153/FTR 175). And so he concludes with a series of "farewells" to all the experiences and possibilities that might have meant something to him in his life but that all, inexorably, fall prey to time's all-devouring rush into annihilation.

> Speed on, you drama of life, which no one calls a comedy, no one a tragedy, because no one ever saw the end! Speed on, you drama of existence, where life cannot be spent again any more than money! Why did no one ever return from the dead? Because life does not know how to trap one as death does, because life has no persuasive powers like those of death.   (5 154/FTR 176)

If this, then, is the fear that underlies the chronic anxiety of the aesthete, how can it be countered? One well-worn response would be to say that, powerful as such a vision may be, it is not, finally, the whole truth: that the human being does have certain intrinsically transtemporal attributes or capacities or, through religious faith or devotion, access to the supratemporal life of the divinity. Over against the sheer flux of the nihilist stand the eternal values of the humanist and the eternal life of the believer.

This would seem to be the strategy adopted by Kierkegaard himself. As he puts it in a characteristic passage from his religious discourses:

> How should we go to meet the future? When the seafarer is out at sea and everything is changing all around him, when the waves rise and fall, he does not stare down into them, for they are changing. He looks up to the stars. Why? Because they are reliable, as they are now, so they were in the time of one's ancestors and will be in the time of those to come. How, then, does he overcome change? By means of the eternal. By means of the eternal one can overcome the future, because the eternal is the ground of the future, therefore one can use it to provide a basis for the future. What is the eternal power in the human being? It is faith. And what is the expectation of faith? It is victory, or, as Scripture so seriously and feelingly teaches us, that all things work together for good for those who love God.   (4 26/EUD 19)

In such passages – and there are many of them – Kierkegaard appears to subscribe to a somewhat conventional and even simplistic religious dualism of time and eternity for which a prototype is already found in the biblical psalms, and according to which the uncertainty, suffering and transience of all things earthly is matched by the certainty, joy and eternity of God's power, a power available for those who, through faith, have access to it. Of course, there are considerable variations within the religious tradition itself concerning whether the divine eternal truth is in some way an attribute of humanity itself (an indwelling divine spark or the image of God in which human beings were created) or whether it is solely available to us on the basis of external divine assistance (as grace or redemption). The question is, however, whether Kierkegaard's response to the nihilistic vision of life in time as sheer flux is simply and solely to appeal to an atemporal "eternity" or whether, in terms of the psychological analysis of anxiety there is anything within the flow of human life itself that provides a preliminary foothold for a non-despairing response to time.

We shall return to *The Concept of Anxiety* itself shortly. However, it is worth noting that the religious discourses themselves collectively offer a somewhat more complex picture of the mutual entwining of self and time than the last quotation might suggest. Importantly, although Kierkegaard assumes that the readers of these discourses will be open to a religious interpretation of the world, he does not assume that they will necessarily think in terms of such dogmatic Christian concepts as revelation, incarnation or redemption. The appeal of the discourses is therefore developed through what Kierkegaard hopes will prove to be psychologically persuasive scenarios, which readers are constantly invited to evaluate on the basis of their own experience of life. "Is it not so, my listeners ..." and "Has your experience not shown you ..." are characteristic phrases that recur throughout the discourses.

As does *The Concept of Anxiety,* the discourses offer a depiction of the self as emerging into self-conscious freedom out of a state of nature that is also described as a simple flow of temporal becoming. In what could be a description of life in Eden, Kierkegaard writes of those living such a preconscious life:

> Without knowing how, they are carried along by life, one link in the chain that joins past and future; [they are] unconcerned as to how it happens, they are carried along on the wave of the present. Reposing in that law of nature that permits a man to develop himself in the world in the same way that it spreads a carpet of flowers over the earth, they live happily and contentedly amidst the changes of life. Not for one moment do they wish to tear themselves loose, they give credit where credit is due, thanks to the one to whom they ascribe the good gifts [they have received], help to the one they think needs it, according as to what they believe will be most helpful for him. That

there are good and perfect gifts they know well, and they know from whence they come; for the earth gives its increase and the heavens give the former and the latter rains and their families and friends are concerned as to what is best for them, and, naturally enough, their plans, wise and reasonable as they are, succeed, since they are [indeed] wise and reasonable. For them, life contains no riddles, and yet their life is a riddle, a dream … (4 36/EUD 33)

Of course, it is disputable whether anyone actually lives like that, although some, including Kierkegaardian aesthetes and 1960s' flower children, might claim to do so. But such a life lived in the moment is, Kierkegaard suggests, unsustainable. Few of us would really wish to recognize in it a life corresponding to the claims of human reason, responsibility and freedom. So, Kierkegaard tells us, there comes a moment when, rather than just being carried along on the stream of natural becoming, a person starts to ask "what the world means to him and he to the world, what all that within him by which he himself belongs to the world means to him, and, on this basis, what his life means for the world …" and it is "only then that the inner being announces itself in this concern" (4 83/EUD 86). This "concern", which becomes a technical term in the religious discourses, is, I suggest, a near neighbour of anxiety, and is, indeed, several times qualified by the adjective "anxious". Like anxiety it is an awakening to possibilities that reach beyond the self's given natural condition, a questioning of the self's own relation to itself and its world. Like anxiety it can become the occasion for the self to fall into an inappropriate multitude of distractions that serve as a strategy of avoidance *vis-à-vis* the decisive possibility of taking responsibility for its own existence, and Kierkegaard's several volumes of religious discourses are as rich in descriptions of such states of distraction and fallenness as his better-known pseudonymous works (often, unsurprisingly, many images recur in both sets of texts[19]). But, like anxiety, concern is also a rite of passage that must be lived through if we are to realize the possibilities that it opens up. For what concern gives us, Kierkegaard says, is the possibility to become "older than the moment" (4 83/EUD 86). In becoming concerned about what the world means to us and what our lives mean for the world we establish a focus or nexus of selfhood that outlasts the moment. This question, once asked, can be asked again today, tomorrow, the next day. Concern is our stake in the future and, as such, the possibility of becoming what might seriously be called "a self":

[T]he complaint that people have neglected the present in favour of the future is, perhaps, well-founded. We shall not deny that it has been the case in the world, not least in our own time, but we shall still

70

not omit to recall that what is great about the human being, the proof of his divine origin, is that he can occupy himself with it. For if there were no future, then there would be no past, and if there were no future and no past then the human being would be in a state of thraldom like the animal – his head bowed towards the earth, his soul caught in the service of the moment ... To be able to occupy oneself with the future is a sign of a human being's nobility, to strive against the future is the most ennobling strife ... [For] he who struggles with the future ... struggles with himself, [since] the future does not exist, it borrows its strength from the self, and when it has taken this [strength] from him, it shows it to him as if it were an external enemy he is to encounter.   (4 23–4/EUD 17–18)

The question concerning the meaning of my life becomes a question, a struggle, concerning the future and, as such, it gives a coherence and unity to my life, even if, by definition, the "answer" is indefinitely deferred, to be discovered only "in" the future, and, as such, unknowable in the present. In a striking parallel to the use Kierkegaard makes in the *Postscript* of Lessing's saying that if God held all truth in his right hand and the infinite pursuit of it in his left then he, Lessing, would always choose the left, he now writes that if God held an eternal happiness in his right hand and the concern for it in his left then he, Kierkegaard, would wish always to choose the left (4 243–4/EUD 272). Just asking the question, just being concerned, is already to be on the way to finding coherence and unity in life.

Kierkegaard sees the phenomenon of concern as the manifestation of the eternal in the self or as that in the self which makes it capable of having a relation to the eternal. Yet concern itself, whether or not it finds fulfilment in faith, is in the first instance a recognizable psychological phenomenon that offers the human subject the prospect of something more than a life in mere flux, a life more ordered than the erratic and random music of Constantin Constantius's post-horn.

With these reflections from the religious discourses in mind, we turn back to *The Concept of Anxiety* and to what is one of the most condensed discussions of time in Kierkegaard's authorship. In *The Concept of Anxiety*, Chapter 3 ("Anxiety as the Consequence of that Sin which is Absence of the Consciousness of Sin"), Kierkegaard sets out to examine two key ideas. The first, which he tells us in the opening paragraph is simply another way of saying that the human being is a synthesis constituted by spirit, is to see "anxiety as the moment" (6 170/CA 81). The second is the now-familiar category of transition, which, as Kierkegaard says, has become a much-used category of contemporary logic. However, he adds in a footnote, Aristotle already understood that the transition from possibility to actuality, *kinesis*, "is not to be understood logically but in terms of historical freedom" (6 171/ CA 82).[20] These ideas converge in the assertion that, if there is to be a transition from one state to another, then there must be a moment in which that transition occurs. But how can such a moment be conceptualized? What can set a system in movement if it is not itself already in movement? How can radical novelty actually arise?

Kierkegaard's questions are at this point formulated logically and, in his sense of the word, dialectically, as the problem of *thinking* the category of transition. But, as he would be the first to recognize, the problem is not itself purely logical. It is the existential problem of the anxious human being, the being caught up in the passage from nature to freedom, the being asking the concerned question about its own being, the being that has become a question to itself. Anxiety, we have already heard Kierkegaard say, is ambiguous through and through, but the question is now whether such an ambiguously self-relating being, a being that is more properly described as a "becoming", a being in transition (a transition, moreover, that can be completed only in and as a leap), is thinkable.

Previous philosophical attempts to think "the moment" have, Kierkegaard says, offered only abstractions. A long footnote dedicated to Plato's treatment credits the Greek philosopher with having addressed the question. However, the concept of the moment that Plato himself came up with in the dialogue *Parmenides* is, Kierkegaard asserts, "a silent atomistic abstraction" (6 172/CA 84), lying "between motion and rest without being in time, and it is into this and out of this that what moves changes into rest, and what is at rest changes into movement" (6 172/ CA 83). The "moment" in Plato is thus a category of transition, but it is peculiarly atemporal. This is because it is formulated in response to the problem of alteration in metaphysical concepts rather than as a reflection on the actual human experience of time. This is what Kierkegaard now attempts.

He begins by recalling the definition of the human being as a synthesis of soul and body, a synthesis that is accomplished as and when the human being realizes itself as spirit. If, however, we also think of the human being as a synthesis of the temporal and the eternal we will be unable, Kierkegaard says, to find a third synthesizing factor within the human subject. But this would mean that, in fact, the elements of the synthesis would simply fall apart. From the human point of view, this would suggest that we fell back once more into the sheer temporality of unqualified and all-devouring flux.

It is customary, Kierkegaard notes, to speak of time as an infinite succession comprising past, present and future. However, this way of looking at time would not be possible if all we had to go on was the experience of time and nothing more. For to measure time in this way would require what Kierkegaard calls "a foothold", that is, a point of reference that would anchor any subsequent division. This foothold could only be provided by supposing a present, a moment in time that was presented to consciousness in unambiguous form. However, in line with a tradition of thinking about time already found in Augustine, Kierkegaard denies that any such moment is offered by the experience of time itself. Each moment passes away before we can think it. What happens when we imagine a moment of actual presence is that, instead of thinking it in its temporality, we spatialize it, and "let time be as represented instead of being thought" (6 174/CA 85).[21] But this representation is essentially empty. What it contains is, in reality, no more than an "infinite vanishing" (6 174/CA 86). Although we say of the person living a purely sensuous life that they live in and for the moment, this is, strictly speaking, inaccurate, since the sensuous person, in fact, has no "moment"; they are never present to themselves but, like time itself, are "infinitely vanishing" into oblivion.

The only possible basis for the experience of time as structured into past, present and future would, Kierkegaard claims, be if something were able to be or to give presence that is not itself subject to the temporal fate of "infinitely vanishing". This something, he states, is the eternal. Only the eternal can be present and give fullness to the present; only the eternal can ground the moment of awakening in which the self becomes "older than the moment", in which we are given the possibility of becoming selves who have transtemporal coherence, history, existence. Such a "moment" of awakening is something very different from the moment that is infinite vanishing. It is the moment in which time and eternity intersect. But can such a moment, such presence, be thought? If it is in time, as the moment, that the eternal intersects with human life, and if, as Kierkegaard has elsewhere warned us, it is not granted to us to know ourselves as we are *sub specie aeternitatis*, are we actually any further forwards? Can such an eternal presence be known by beings permeated as we are by time?

Kierkegaard acknowledges the problem in an oblique way by drawing attention to the word "moment" itself. Noting that the Danish term *Øjeblik*, like the German *Augenblick*, literally means "the glance of the eye", he comments that "'The moment' is a figurative expression, and in that respect is not so good to have to deal with" (6 175/CA 87). However, rather than trying to find a more literal expression he characteristically offers a brief meditation on what the metaphorical term itself says. He does so by reference to a popular contemporary reworking of an ancient saga, *Frithiof's Saga*.[22] Frithiof, the hero of the saga, is being sent away from Norway to the Orkneys in order to prevent his marriage to Ingeborg, with whom he is in love. She loves him in return, but her family deem the match unsuitable and, while Frithiof is away, they plan to marry her to another. Frithiof himself does not know this, but Ingeborg does. The moment in this story on which

73

Kierkegaard now focuses is that in which Ingeborg looks across the sea to the point on the horizon over which Frithiof's boat has disappeared, separating them for ever. This, Kierkegaard says, is paradigmatic for the concept of "the moment", "the glance of the eye". He comments:

> As something sounded, an outburst of feeling on her part, a sigh, a word, would already have more of the attributes of time in itself, and is present more in the manner of something vanishing and less in that of the eternal's way of being present – which, indeed, also means that a sigh, a word, etc. have power to relieve the soul of what weighs upon it, precisely because what weighs upon it, simply by being expressed, already begins to become something of the past. A glance therefore indicates time, but it should be noted that it is time in the fateful conflict when it is touched by eternity.
>
> (6 175–6/CA 87)

What Kierkegaard seems to be saying here is that in relation to the pure experience of the eternal intersecting time, "the moment" in a pre-eminent sense, *any* form of representation will already be a falsification, even the inarticulate "representation" of a sigh. The only true relation to it is silently to mirror it in the glance. Even as presence, even in its presence, the eternal eludes cognition.

Kierkegaard's analysis echoes the analysis of religious intuition in F. D. E. Schleiermacher's *Speeches on Religion to its Cultured Despisers*, one of the key works of modern theology and widely influential beyond the world of academic theology in Kierkegaard's time. There, Schleiermacher insisted that religion was something *sui generis,* reducible neither to a form of knowledge nor to a morality. As such, he argued, it articulated a unique moment in the genesis and life of the self, a moment that he described as preceding the fateful separation of feeling and intuition and that, therefore, necessarily eluded any attempt at definition. Already to say of it (as Schleiermacher himself could say) that it was an intuition of the infinite or a sense of oneness with the universe was to impose intuition, that is, representation, onto what, in itself, transcended (or preceded) all possible intuition.[23] For Schleiermacher, as for Kierkegaard, the appeal to such a moment marked an outflanking of the Fichtean–Romantic conception of the self-creative, self-intuiting "I" and opened up an approach to the self as grounded less in autonomous self-assertion and more in dependence on a transcendent Other. In these terms, Kierkegaard could not have been unsympathetic to Schleiermacher's aim. However, his concept of the moment radicalizes Schleiermacher's account, precisely by virtue of the role it gives to time. The self portrayed by Kierkegaard is a temporalized self in a way that the almost Spinozistic self of

Schleiermacher is not. This means that the Kierkegaardian paradigm of the moment in which the eternal intersects the plane of the temporal and gives time to the self that is ready to apprehend it is more fragile, more ambiguous, and, indeed, more anxious than the ecstatic self of Schleiermacher's speeches. As it is experienced in time, the eternal is always already being lost in the infinite vanishing of time that it nevertheless supports and to which it gives meaning, or, more precisely, for which it opens up the possibility of meaning that individuals must lay hold of and take to themselves in anxious concern.

As in the religious discourses, the way in which this process realizes itself is in terms of the individual's relation to the future: "the future is in a certain sense the whole of which the past is a part, and the future can in a certain sense signify the whole," writes Kierkegaard, adding that, in this way, "the future is the incognito in which the eternal, as incommensurable with time, nevertheless wills to preserve its association with time" (6 177/ CA 89). It is only through the expectant relation to the future, that, as we have seen, is also a form of the self's relation to itself, that the eternal can become "present". And, Kierkegaard adds, it is only on the basis of this double relation that the past acquires significance, since as long as the future remains open, the meaning of the past is itself also open: "If I am made anxious about a past misfortune, then this is not because it is in the past, but because it may be repeated, i.e., become future" (6 179/ CA 91).[24]

The fullness of time that is bestowed by the presence of the eternal is therefore no simple given or datum of consciousness. It is something that can only be "had", with and under the temporal conditions of existence, in the anxious concern for the future. But that also means that it is not something that can be "had" once and for all. It can be possessed or acquired only if it is also, constantly, "repeated". As the opening lines of the novella *Repetition* make clear, this is precisely what distinguishes the philosophy of modernity from that of the past, and from any philosophy that, whether in a Platonic or in a Hegelian way, makes the recollection of the past methodologically central. Such recollective thinking necessarily abstracts from and places at a distance what can only properly be thought in the dynamic movement between present and future, as given-possibility-in-process-of-actualization.

> *Repetition* is a decisive expression for what *"recollection"* was to the Greeks.
>
> As they taught that all cognition was recollected, so modern philosophy will teach that the whole of life is a repetition ... Repetition and recollection are the same movement, only in opposite directions. For what is recollected has been and is repeated backwards, whereas genuine repetition is recollected forwards.
>
> (5 115/FTR 131)

Perhaps strangely, Kierkegaard himself makes relatively little further use of the term "repetition" once he has finished writing the book of the same name. Nevertheless, there are a number of terms that he uses throughout his authorship that do similar work. Such terms are "patience" in the religious discourses or "contemporaneity" in the *Philosophical Fragments*. And what is this work? It is to secure the possibility of a transtemporal coherence in the self that goes beyond the "identity" given by innate attributes or social roles. As inseparable from the leap into freedom, it qualifies this leap by showing that it cannot be a one-off leap but, instead, can exist only as a sustained and constant process of self-choosing – something that, despite its character of "leap" and "moment" is as settled as the almost monotonous wind that has learned to be at home in the mountains. Putting it like this can scarcely be said to demonstrate the coherence of Kierkegaard's own analysis, but it does perhaps help us see the question that he is attempting to clarify.

Anxiety and language

Questions of language are of constant importance in Kierkegaard's authorship and this is as true of anxiety as of other areas, for language is given a central if rarely noticed role in Kierkegaard's account of the Fall that complements a number of the points we have already examined from other angles. These especially concern the self-relation that is at the centre of the whole scenario of anxiety. In the discussion of the Fall in *The Concept of Anxiety*, Kierkegaard brushes aside a common objection to the biblical narrative, focused in the question "Who told Adam not to eat from the tree of the knowledge of good and evil?" Such a question, says Kierkegaard, is a difficulty "we need merely smile at". For, as he continues,

> Innocence can certainly talk and, to that extent, possesses in language a means of expression for everything that belongs to Spirit. To that extent, one need only assume that Adam talked with himself. The imperfection in the narrative, that another spoke to Adam about something he didn't understand thus falls away. Of course, because Adam was able to talk, it does not follow that he was able to understand what was said in a deeper sense. Above all, this is true of the difference between good and evil, which is indeed [expressible] in language, but only is [i.e. is only actual, only present] for freedom. Innocence can indeed speak this difference but the difference is not for it … (6 138/CA 44)

A page later, speaking once more of the prohibition and the penalty attached to it, Kierkegaard effectively repeats the same point. "The imperfection in the narrative, whereby someone should come to say to Adam something he is essentially incapable of understanding, falls away, if we consider that the speaker is language, and thus it is Adam himself who speaks" (6 139/CA 45).

But does this make sense? Can "*language*" be the speaker? And how, more specifically, could "*language*" have uttered the commandment and prohibition? Does Kierkegaard mean that God or an angel manipulated Adam's capacity for language so as to get him to formulate the commandment to himself without being aware of the hidden agent pulling the levers? It is certainly possible to imagine a kind of theological explanation that might run something like this, but it would seem to be alien to Kierkegaard's own procedure and would, indeed, be precisely to call on the dogmatic presuppositions that the introduction had declared to be outside the boundaries of a purely psychological investigation. So what might Kierkegaard mean? Let us attempt a possible reconstruction of the conceptual hinterground of this strange remark. Since *The Concept of Anxiety* itself, teasingly, says nothing more about it, we shall have to go elsewhere, to *Works of Love*.

The first discourse of the second part of *Works of Love* contains one of Kierkegaard's more extended comments on the nature of language. Here he claims that "All human discourse, even the divinely spiritual discourse of Holy Scripture is essentially metaphorical [literally, 'trans-ferred', cf. the Danish *overført*] discourse" (12 203/WL 209). Why so? From the moment of birth, Kierkegaard states, every human being is, as such, characterized as spirit. However, as *The Concept of Anxiety* also argues, the individual does not become conscious of their spiritual destiny at once. In infancy and childhood (although, once again, Kierkegaard is not specific about the precise terminus of this period) a person's consciousness is developed in exclusively sensuous–soulish forms. It is, however, in this period of life that we first acquire language, largely by imitation. It follows that we learn our basic grammar and vocabulary long before we really know what it means. Even a three-year-old can speak of love, death and God, but will do so without understanding, even though she may have a certain sensuous, imaginative picture illustrating such words: cuddles with mummy, the dead bird in the garden, an old man with a beard and so on. The advent of spirit does not, of course, destroy either grammar or vocabulary, but, to use a term that has become familiar in discussions of the brain–mind relationship, spirit *supervenes* upon language and fills the sensuous–soulish forms with meaning. The person who has or who exists as spirit understands what it means to speak of love, death and God. But, spirit has only the same language that has been prepared by the preceding development. "Because Spirit is invisible, so then its language is a secret one, and the secret consists precisely in this: that it uses the same words as the child or simple person, but uses them in a transferred sense ..." (12 203/WL 209–10). For human beings who are conscious of themselves as spirit, then, language is necessarily twofold, in the sense that it simultaneously operates at the sensuous–soulish level, and is also the bearer of a spiritual meaning. The relationship between these levels is that of transference or metaphor. It follows that language is always potentially equivocal or, at least, indirect: that the meaning of language cannot simply be read off from what it directly appears to say. As Kierkegaard puts it in *Works of Love*, there is no word that cannot become a word of love, just as there is no word that is necessarily and unambiguously a word of love, and, similarly, there is no word that cannot be upbuilding, just as there is no word that is, of itself, necessarily upbuilding. Everything depends on context, speaker and intention, that is, the spiritual investment made in the word: that I, the speaker, mean it as a word of love, of comfort, or encouragement.

It is entirely unsurprising that this relationship within the co-posited twofoldness of language closely parallels the structure of the human subject itself, as delineated in *The Concept of Anxiety*. Here too spirit is what synthesizes the psycho–physical duality of life into a meaningful human existence. Significantly, it is precisely in the moment when "Adam" hears the word of prohibition and penalty (that is also, as we have been told, a word that he himself speaks) that this duality is said to be "concentrated" into a moment pregnant with spiritual meaning.

Having excluded any external speaker – and, as I have argued, this means also excluding God as the occult agent of Adam's speech – Kierkegaard has thrown the full weight of his argument on to Adam's capacity for language. But is it possible for us to conceive of language alone performing what Kierkegaard ascribes to it? If Kierkegaard's position is to make sense at all we have to ask whether and how it is possible to conceive of prohibition and penalty arising from within language itself, without invoking the presence of a further, external actor in Adam's drama: someone who actually forbids Adam to eat the fruit and threatens him with punishment if he does so.

One way of approaching this might be to think in terms of the relationship between language and the world represented in it. The clearest statement of how Kierkegaard understands this relationship is in the unfinished *Johannes Climacus, or De Omnibus Dubitandum Est*. Here, in a paragraph entitled "How must existence be constituted for doubt to be possible?", Climacus writes:

What is immediacy? It is reality. What is mediacy? It is the word [but, perhaps, we could also translate here: "verbality", "speaking", "having the capacity of speech"]. How does this [verbality] cancel that [immediacy]? By being spoken [given voice, spoken *out*]; for that which is spoken, is always presupposed. Immediacy is reality, language is ideality, consciousness is contradiction. In the moment I give verbal expression to reality, the contradiction is there, for what I say belongs to ideality. The possibility of doubt thus lies in the consciousness whose essence is a contradiction, which is brought forth by and which itself brings forth a duplicity.

(Pap IV B 1: 146/PF 167f.)

Kierkegaard–Climacus is, of course, saying not that this contradictory structure *necessarily* gives rise to doubt, but that it contains the *possibility* of doubt, that is, the possibility of sundering the bonds that unite the subject to its world in an immediate, spontaneous and naive fashion. For language abstracts the subject from its concrete being (Pap X 2 A 235/JP 2324). If language opens up the possibility of consciousness, of a reflected, self-aware relation to the world, it also distances us from that world and sets in place the possibility of confusion between the world and the linguistic representation of the world. A linguistic being can all too easily come to confuse saying that something is so with its actually being so.

Is this, then, how Adam's being able to talk occasions his Fall? What would it mean if it were so? In the first instance, it would suggest that what was at issue in the Fall was a matter of representation: that Adam's error was to confuse image and reality, fact and reflection. But the mere fact of language can scarcely be seen as causing the Fall in this way. Adam could have remained in the truth. His linguistic representation of the world could have been a faithful reflection of the kind of which Kierkegaard speaks in several upbuilding discourses, when he invokes the image of the sea that in its depth and stillness is perfectly transparent and capable of reflecting the heavens above without distortion or obscurity. Moreover, seeing the Fall as an error in representation would seem to bring us back once more into the orbit of Kierkegaard's critique of Hegel in the *Postscript*, a critique that builds on the material originally planned for *Johannes Climacus*. For, as we saw in Chapter 1, the error of speculation is precisely to have confused thinking with what thought should be thinking *about*: to have confused representation with reality. Is this, then, a repetition of Adam's original Fall? And is it the fault of language, in the sense that it is language that opens the space of possibility into which Adam, losing his foothold in reality, vertiginously falls?

This may seem appealing. But it is not quite adequate as an explanation of what is going on in *The Concept of Anxiety*. For on this account Adam himself would be a proto-Hegelian, whose fault, to be repeated many centuries later by German philosophy, was by means of language and the deceptive possibilities contained in language to reflect himself out of reality and into a free-floating world of possibility, melting the solidity of Being-in-itself into the thin air of abstraction. But if this were so, then the Fall would first and foremost be a matter of representation, of cognition, a change in our cognitive relation to the world, as if we somehow slid out of control on the ice of language. But it is hard to see how such a merely cognitive fall could, of itself, make its subject, the human being, culpable, or be the occasion for *sin*. It would, simply, be a mistake, a mere accident. As such it would also be entirely commensurable with psychology and there would be nothing to be said about it that psychology could not say. Nothing, in other words, would be left over for dogmatics.

However, as we have already seen, the doubling that occurs in language functioning as the reflection in ideality of a given reality is, for Kierkegaard, twinned by another doubling, the internal doubling of language by which the sensuous–soulish dimension of figurative representation is made a vehicle of spirit. The surface of language, then, the plane on which its sensuous–soulish figures take shape, is doubly reflective, doubly slippery. It is the reflection of sensuous externality *and also* the reflection of spirit. In this way it is the intertwining, the mutual folding-in of spirit and its world. Thus language is not only about the world, but also about its speaker, the one who is spirit. Spirit itself is the breath – *ruach*, *pneuma*, *spiritus*, *Ånd* – that animates the reflective plane and renders it meaningful.

The relation of language to spirit, however, means that the question as to the adequacy of language in relation to that which is to be represented in it is not just a question about the relationship between language and the external world; it is a question in which spirit itself – our human subjectivity and freedom – is also stirring. This gives a different tenor, indeed a different direction to the discussion, for language is no longer being seen simply as the occasion for Adam (= us) to confuse the real world with the merely represented world. It is also the occasion for Adam wilfully to corrupt representation itself. For we not only make *mistakes* in language, we also use language *ironically, deceitfully, maliciously*. Speech may come to be used to conceal as well as to reveal the mind. In a late journal entry headed "Would that Human Beings Could not Talk!" Kierkegaard laments the damage that the gift of language has wrought upon humanity:

> The reason that everything is so easy to understand in the animal world is simple – it is because the animals have the advantage over human beings that they cannot talk. The only thing which talks in their existence is their life itself, their action.
>
> When, for example, I see a hind in heat, then I see what this signifies, it is in the grip of a powerful instinct and there is nothing

more to be said. If it could talk, then one might well hear nonsense about it being governed by a sense of duty, that it was seeking to propagate the species out of a sense of duty to society and its kind, and that it was because this would be to perform the greatest possible act of charity, etc.

… [T]hat which confuses everything is this advantage that human beings have over animals, that they can talk. So it can happen that while a person's life expresses what is lowest, their mouth babbles on about the highest, and assures us that this is what is motivating them.

Language, the gift of speech, spreads such a fog of drivel and trickery over the human race that it is <and> will be its ruin. Only God knows how many there are in any generation whom speech has not ruined, turning people into babblers or hypocrites. Only the most significant personalities amongst the human race can know how to carry the advantage of being able to talk.

(Pap XI 2 A 222/JP 2337)[25]

But language *qua* psychological structure cannot be to blame for this outcome in any causal or moral sense. Since language is what it is as the expression of spirit, the threat that language poses to spirit's self-identity, to spirit's truthfulness, is the work of spirit itself. The question as to the limits of language's capacities for the transferring of meaning from what is said to what is intended, limits that stretch to the point of equivocity, is not simply a question about language and the world, but a question about spirit, and thus a question of responsibility. If it is in the interests of spirit to communicate its meaning clearly and directly, to communicate understandably, then spirit itself must seek to limit and control language's polysemic capacities. And this is therefore a requirement that spirit, *qua* spirit (and therefore freely), places upon itself. If spirit is to communicate with spirit in language, then limits must be set to what words are able to mean.

Is this, then, the logic whereby Kierkegaard is able to say that it is no external speaker but language itself – Adam's own linguistic capacity – that engenders the prohibition? For if language is born as the opening up of an infinite field of communicative possibilities, it must simultaneously subject itself to the discipline of determinate discourse, resisting the temptation of intentional equivocation – ironic or malicious – if it is really to communicate "in truth". Such an acceptance of determinate boundaries of meaning bespeaks a self-imposed obligation of concreteness that is the condition of any actual communication, just as freedom, if it is to be truly free, cannot endlessly indulge the anarchic whimsy of Romantic idealism. In each case the claim of actuality is a claim requiring self-limitation, a self-imposed "prohibition". Such a self-limitation would not be a "grasping at finitude" since it would be itself a work of freedom, a spiritual act. "Grasping at finitude" is, rather, when, having become anxious in the face of its own possibilities and not daring to submit them to the obligation of concrete, responsible communication, spirit flees responsibility for its limitation and projects the responsibility on to another: a forbidding voice, a tempting serpent. But, if Kierkegaard's comments about language and the Fall are any guide, then there is really nothing external to us that can either provoke or lure us to such a flight from freedom, only our own vertiginous anxiety at the immensity of the responsibility to speak the concrete or actual word of truth that, as free, spiritual beings, is ours to speak.

Kierkegaard, existentialism and phenomenology

We have covered a lot of ground in this exposition of the concept of anxiety, although we are far from having done justice to the variety and depth of Kierkegaard's illustrative materials, to the nuances of his argument, and to the wealth of references he makes to the history of ideas. Even so, the materials presented here already raise considerable and far-reaching questions. One such question is whether or how far the whole structure of Kierkegaard's anthropology actually presupposes the religious and more specifically Christian framework that becomes explicit at many points of his work and that he himself said was decisive for understanding it. Can the attempt to offer a Kierkegaardian anthropology without reference to these Christian presuppositions even get off the ground? This, as I have previously indicated, will be dealt with in Chapter 4.

What perhaps needs to be addressed more immediately is the relationship between Kierkegaardian psychology and the twentieth-century philosophies of *Existenz* and existentialism. Without venturing into the textual questions as to how far either Heidegger or Sartre deliberately adopted and adapted Kierkegaard's portrayal of the human condition into their own philosophical work, the Kierkegaardian resonances of many of their themes, metaphors and concepts is hard to avoid. Anxiety, fallenness, guilt, despair, freedom, temporality, the moment and repetition are merely a sample of Kierkegaardian terms and concepts that reappear at crucial moments of existential philosophy. Thus, in the section "The Origin of Nothingness" in *Being and Nothingness* – a section, we might add, that is foundational for the whole subsequent discussion – Sartre acknowledges the relevance of Kierkegaard's contribution to the understanding of anxiety ("anguish" in Hazel Barnes's English translation). However, his subsequent discussion is even more Kierkegaardian than he himself appears to acknowledge (or to be aware of). He writes:

> Kierkegaard describing anguish in the face of what one lacks char-
> acterizes it as anguish in the face of freedom. But Heidegger, whom
> we know to have been greatly influenced by Kierkegaard, consid-
> ers anguish instead as the apprehension of nothingness. These two
> descriptions of anguish do not appear to us contradictory; on the
> contrary the one implies the other.[26]

Sartre is right. They do indeed imply each other – but Kierkegaard, in his account of anxiety as dreaming innocence, has already said just that. "Anxi-ety and nothing always correspond to each other", he wrote in *The Concept of Anxiety* (6 183/CA 96). Sartre correctly interprets Kierkegaard as empha-sizing that the point, the "object", of anxiety is never anything external to the self but simply the self itself and its own possibilities and, like Kierkegaard (although it is not clear whether this is a deliberate allusion), Sartre illustrates the point by using the example of vertigo, where, as he says, it is not the fear of falling off the precipice that is the dominant factor, but the anxiety concerning one's own ability to let oneself fall.

Examples of Kierkegaard's intertextual presence in twentieth-century existentialism (and the problem of evaluating these examples) could be multiplied. But whatever the more exact relationship between the details of Kierkegaardian and existentialist anthropology, there are other and larger questions. Not the least of these is the question raised by the fact that both the Heidegger of *Being and Time* (where, it is generally thought, the Kierkegaardian influence was most prominent) and Sartre insisted on the atheological and atheistic nature of the philosophical task. This raises from another angle the question as to whether or how far it is possible simply to have the big picture of the self drawn by Kierkegaard without what he regarded as its religious fulfilment. That existentialism itself was readily portrayed by religious apologists as well as by secular opponents as a thinly secularized Christian anthropology is one aspect of this question.

But there is a further question that is also larger than the matter of this or that Kierkegaardian borrowing by Heidegger or Sartre, and this is a question that concerns how we actually read Kierkegaard himself. It is a question as to the kind of intellectual exercises we take Kierkegaard's anthropological descriptions to have been. Both Heidegger and Sartre, in their different ways, claim to have been pursuing a form of phenomenological research in their two big works *Being and Time* and *Being and Nothingness*. Moreover, in each case this was directed towards a fundamental ontological explication of the meaning of human existence that was to precede any of the more particular findings about human beings that are the subject of the special sciences, from physiology to historiography. For Heidegger, the link between phenomenological method and ontological ambition was fundamental. As he defined his task in the Introduction to *Being and Time:*

> With regard to its subject-matter, phenomenology is the science of the Being of entities – ontology ... Ontology and phenomenology are not two distinct philosophical disciplines among others. These terms characterize philosophy itself with regard to its object and its way of treating that object. Philosophy is universal phenomenological ontology, and takes its departure from the hermeneutic of Dasein, which as an analytic of *existence,* has made fast the guiding-line for all philosophical inquiry at the point where it *arises* and to which it *returns.*[27]

What Heidegger is aiming at, then, is a "universal phenomenological ontology", that is, an interpretation of Being as such, that is valid for every form and manifestation of Being. Phenomenology is of value in so far as it serves to direct us towards these universal and fundamental features of Being. It can (he hopes) do this because although phenomenology starts with actual human experience, it offers a method by which to skim off the accidental and fortuitous elements in that experience and to discern what is truly basic in it. As far as Heidegger himself is concerned, he is clear about the value and the limitations of Kierkegaard for this project. Despite all the extensive traces of Kierkegaard throughout *Being and Time,* Kierkegaard is mentioned only in three brief footnotes.[28] Although these are at least as teasing as they are illuminating, they do set out the basic parameters of Heidegger's attitude to Kierkegaard and, indeed, to other theological sources. The footnotes cover the topics of anxiety, existence and temporality, with special emphasis in this last being placed on "the moment" (or "the moment of vision", as Macquarrie and Robinson felicitously render the German *Augenblick*). From these footnotes we learn that, on the one hand, Kierkegaard is "The man who has gone furthest in analysing the phenomenon of anxiety" (SZ 190 iv), who "explicitly seized upon the problem of existence as an *existentiell* problem, and thought it through in a penetrating fashion" (SZ 235 vi), and that he "is probably the one who has seen the *existentiell* phenomenon of the moment of vision with the most penetration" (SZ 338 iii). All of this sounds very positive. But there is another side to Heidegger's take on Kierkegaard, for Christianity in general is said to have dealt with the phenomenon of anxiety "ontically and even (though within very narrow limits) ontologically" and Kierkegaard is judged to have remained within these limitations (even if he also went furthest) by analysing anxiety only "in the theological context of a 'psychological' exposition of the problem of original sin" (SZ 190 iv). Similarly, Kierkegaard's sense for the *existentiell* problem of existence is countered by the fact that "the existential problematic was so alien to him that, as regards his ontology, he remained completely dominated by Hegel and by ancient philosophy as Hegel saw it" (SZ 235 iv). And, finally, his "penetration" in seeing "the *existentiell* phenomenon of the moment of vision" "does not signify that he has been correspondingly successful in interpreting it existentially" (SZ 338 iii).

What Heidegger is saying, then, is that Kierkegaard's thought remains on the level of the ontic, the *existentiell*, or the psychological and that, as a result, although he is to be acknowledged for having brought certain key phenomena such as anxiety, existence and temporality to the attention of philosophy, his own manner of dealing with them is not philosophical. Seen from Heidegger's own perspective on philosophy, this means that, whatever else he may be doing, Kierkegaard is not doing phenomenology and is not aiming at uncovering the universal ontological structures, the "existentialia" as Heidegger calls them, of human existence. At best, we might say, what he offers is prephilosophical, prephenomenological, pre-ontological; he is a purveyor of materials to philosophers, but far from being any kind of philosopher himself.

Is this a fair or even adequate characterization? Undoubtedly there are many Kierkegaard scholars who think not. Whether with specific regard to Heidegger's views or not, there is a strong body of Kierkegaard interpretation that insists on claiming him as a kind of phenomenologist. This can mean various things, and may sometimes be simply a way of drawing attention to Kierkegaard's emphasis on "the narrative quality of experience" (Mark C. Taylor[29]), to the way in which he links "the metaphysical and the eternal" with "the accidental or fortuitous" (Arnold B. Come[30]) or the self-consciousness of freedom (Jörg Disse[31]).[32]

A particularly forceful case for seeing Kierkegaard as a kind of phenomenologist has been made in recent years by the Danish philosopher of religion Arne Grøn. Grøn, like Sartre, correctly emphasizes the self-reflective nature of Kierkegaard's account of anxiety and despair, underlining that this is not a matter of learning something abut a neutral object "out there" but is both self-analysis on the part of the writer and a demand for self-analysis on the part of the reader, who, as Grøn says, "must be able to imitate in himself the movements that are described."[33] Grøn lays special weight on Kierkegaard's own account in *The Concept of Anxiety* of what he there calls his experimental method.

> He who has used a regular measure in the field of psychology and psychological observation, has acquired for himself an ability to

insinuate himself into everything human, an ability that makes him able to summon the example he needs in an instant, which, even if it does not have the authority of a fact, has another kind of authority ... [The psychological observer] ought to have a poetic originality in his soul that enables him in an instant to make a whole, a regular whole, out of what is only ever present in the individual in a partial and irregular manner. When he has perfected himself in [this capability] then he will not need to fetch examples from the literary repertoire or poetize half-dead reminiscences, but brings his observations out fresh from the water, still jumping and playing in all their colourful brightness. Nor does he need to run himself to death in order to find something to notice. On the contrary, he sits quietly in his room like a police agent who nevertheless knows everything that is going on. What he needs, he can give shape to instantly ... If he should grow dubious, he is nevertheless so oriented in human life and his gaze is so sharp, sharp as an inquisitor's, that he knows just where to look and easily discovers the kind of individual [example] he needs for his experiment. (6 147–8/CA 54–5)

But is this really a portrait of a phenomenologist? Although the "experimenter" is credited with an extensive experience of life, he also seems to be given permission to "invent" his examples in a manner far more reminiscent of a creative writer than a disciplined "scientific" phenomenologist.[34] There is certainly nothing in this passage that would seriously count against Heidegger's designation of Kierkegaard as a Christian psychologist, more interested in the *existentiell* problems of concrete life than in developing – through phenomenological investigation – a universal ontology. Indeed, different as Hegelian and Heideggerian forms of phenomenology are, we might ask whether the project of a universal ontology must not ultimately fall under the same charge of abstracting from the concrete and immediate situation of individual existence that Kierkegaard made in relation to speculation. What interest could someone persuaded by Johannes Climacus's characterization of the subjective, interested, passionate approach to existence have in developing a universal ontology? Nor is it clear that the question is made less sharp by the fact that such an ontology sets out from the kind of characterization of existence given by Climacus himself, for the moment that it moves beyond or away from the kind of passionate interest in existence – that is, *my own* existence, and not *Dasein's* – that Climacus advocates, such an ontological quest would seem inevitably to become prey to possibilities of self-forgetfulness that closely parallel those of the speculative philosopher. And if one of the complaints levelled against the system by Climacus was that it had and could have no place for ethics, it is striking that the broad (if not total) consensus of Heidegger commentators is that Heideggerian ontology is similarly lacking in ethical interest in the very precise sense that the philosopher's interest in his own personal ethical choices has no place within the project of fundamental ontology. *Qua* philosopher, the philosopher is duty-bound to look away from himself – which is just what the Kierkegaardian individual should never do. Which of the two, the fundamental ontologist or the existential thinker, has chosen the better part is, of course, a whole other matter.

We shall return to these questions when, in Chapter 3, we have looked more closely at Kierkegaard as a moral philosopher and, in the light of that, are also able to take further the question as to the kind of philosopher he is (if, indeed, he is a philosopher at all). However, there is a further point that needs to be borne in mind when considering whether or to what extent Kierkegaard might count as a phenomenologist, for it is clear that if Kierkegaard is to be regarded as having sought to open up aspects of the basic ontological structure of human existence phenomenologically, and if we take seriously his own religious claims, then it would have to be possible for the basic religious relation on which his view of the human condition turns to enter into the field of phenomenal events and to do so in such a way as to be available for phenomenological investigation. Again, this is a question that can only finally be answered when we have examined more closely what Kierkegaard's view of the human being's God-relationship is. Even in terms of what we have seen so far, however, and especially with regard to the way in which Kierkegaard described the eternal's manner of becoming present in the moment, it would seem impossible for the pivot of this relationship, the moment itself, to be an object of phenomenological investigation. If even a sigh on the part of Ingeborg would already dissipate the actual fullness of the moment, if her relation to the moment can find expression solely in her "glance", then it is hard to see how the presence of the eternal in the temporal flow of existence could become articulated in any way that would be at all commensurable with the kind of cognitive relation required by phenomenological investigation. Even at the moment of its intersection with time, the eternal remains withdrawn from any possible mode of cognition.

There is one more point we should briefly discuss before leaving the question of Kierkegaard and phenomenology, and that is the question raised by the third of Heidegger's Kierkegaardian footnotes, where he writes:

> He clings to the ordinary conception of time, and defines the "moment of vision" with the help of "now" and "eternity". When Kierkegaard speaks of "temporality", what he has in mind is man's "Being-in-time". Time as within-time-ness knows only the "now"; it never knows a moment of vision. (SZ 338 iii)

Given that, at the start of the footnote, Heidegger has praised Kierkegaard for the penetration with which he has grasped "the *existentiell* phenomenon of the moment of vision" he is clearly not denying that some form of the moment of vision is known to Kierkegaard. The problem seems to be that Kierkegaard's ability to think through what it means is hampered by his inability to move beyond "the ordinary conception of time", clinging to the thought of time as a kind of container within which the events of human life happen, rather than, as Heidegger proposes, seeing human being itself as time. On the Kierkegaardian view of time-as-container the moment of vision can only be a moment of access to something outside time, to an "eternal" that, in itself, is essentially foreign to time. The argument, it should be said, is not clear-cut. Nevertheless, on the basis of what we have read of Kierkegaard's account of time, and of the relationship between the moment and the eternal, it would seem that Heidegger is oversimplifying Kierkegaard's position. Clearly, Kierkegaard does see the eternal as transcending time in some important sense. Nevertheless, even if we concede to Heidegger that Kierkegaard's "eternal" is "outside" time, it is far less obvious that Kierkegaard's human subject has anywhere to go or any way of being other than that of temporality. For even in the encounter with the eternal the subject is not taken out of time but is given time in a new way. The eternal is what makes possible the experience of time as "fulfilled", but this is something quite different from being taken out of time into a timeless eternity. The eternal is not the negation of time but, in the incognito of the future, it is what makes possible the wholeness of time or the experience of life in time as a whole. But this is precisely what Heidegger wants to claim for his own account of the resolution that is made possible by the moment of vision, that is, that it opens up the possibility of experiencing temporal existence as a whole. In this connection, we might add, Heidegger's wish to base the authentic experience of time on an act of resolute self-affirmation could, from a Kierkegaardian perspective, be subject to an analogous critique to that brought against Romantic self-creation. The impossibility of the subject itself generating a position from which time could be grasped as a whole entails the infinite deferral of any conclusion within time, and makes it necessary for genuine selfhood to be given rather than asserted. Although we are not obliged to interpret all talk of "givenness" as necessarily theological, it is plausible that if, just at this point, Heidegger demonstrates an "anxiety of influence" by downplaying the relevance of Kierkegaard's thought to his own question, then, this, once again, may turn on Heidegger's problematic relation to religion and to the question of God, a question that, at this point, he wishes to keep as far away from philosophy as possible. But, the Kierkegaardian interlocutor might reply, can a "moment of vision" that does not find its ground in the eternal, in God, really expect to raise itself above the level of temporal relativity? Can it really open the way to the "Being" that Heidegger is seeking? Perhaps Heidegger himself came to doubt it. Certainly he never claimed to have "found" Being or to be able to define it. Later he would have to write it under erasure.

We are moving on here from the problematic of *Being and Time* with its search for a universal fundamental ontology and we are approaching the problematic of the later Heidegger, where there does begin to be talk of time as "given". We shall return to the relationship between Kierkegaard and the later Heidegger in Chapter 4, and here merely note John D. Caputo's comments on what he sees as the "severity" of Heidegger's strictures on Kierkegaard, arguing, against Heidegger, that what Kierkegaard in fact accomplished was "a destruction of the history of ontology as the metaphysics of presence" that Heidegger himself did not get round to until the second half of his philosophical career. "It would take more than a footnote on Heidegger's part to fix his relationship to Kierkegaard", Caputo comments wryly. "It took the full force of his turning in his later writings to get as far as *Repetition*."[35]

CHAPTER THREE

The good

Choosing the self (*Either/Or 2*)

We have now had the opportunity to consider what Kierkegaard called the aesthetic life from several angles. In Chapter 1 the Romantic ironist appeared as an individual version of the Fichtean absolute "I", inventing himself in what Kierkegaard judged to be an arbitrary and capricious manner. Unfortunately for the ironist, this meant that he deprived himself of a genuinely vivifying contact with reality and is likely to end up, like the Seducer of *Either/Or 1*, living at one remove from real life, behind the gauze. Despite the ironist's self-image being capability of playing infinite variations upon any given mood or situation, Kierkegaard's analysis portrayed him as inevitably succumbing to the ebb and flow of moods that are, ultimately, beyond his control. In Chapter 2 this characterization was extended by the depiction of the aesthetic life as a kind of atrophy of the self, a perpetuation of the state of childhood that bore the hallmark of chronic anxiety. For all the glitz and glamour of his self-presentation, the aesthete is, finally, someone who lacks the courage for responsible adult life. It is a life that remains under the spell of its own endless possibilities, but that never really succeeds in actualizing any of them. And there are hints of something darker; the violence of the aesthete's invocation of an annihilating vortex and the cruelty of a Nero suggest that this is more than a matter of whimsical poets and ageing hippies incapable of connecting with the demands of practical affairs.

But while recognizing that Kierkegaard's portrayal of the aesthetic life has proved one of the most effective parts of his authorship – and leaving aside the question as to how far it was also a self-portrayal of his own life prior to his re-conversion to Christianity – it is clear that, as far as the "official line" of the authorship is concerned (as represented in, for example, *The Point of View*), the aesthetic is presented as a stage that is always already overcome. If *Either/Or 1* gives the aesthete leave to speak in his own voice and to set out the aspirations of the aesthetic life from within, then *Either/Or 2* sets up an alternative that, if it is not Kierkegaard's last word, marks a line behind which he is not willing to retreat in the further exploration of what it means to become the selves we potentially are.

This alternative is set out by a character called "Assessor" Wilhelm, sometimes appearing in English-language Kierkegaard literature as "Judge William", "assessor" being a particular legal title that is similar although not identical to "judge" in British or American usage. As indicated in the Introduction, the Assessor is not, strictly speaking, a pseudonym but more of a regular fictional character. Therefore he is far from being simply a mouthpiece for Kierkegaard's own views. At the same time, he presents ideas that anticipate or parallel those of other pseudonyms (such as the analysis of the concept of anxiety) or Kierkegaard himself (as in his criticism of the impatience of the aesthetic attitude, which recurs in Kierkegaard's religious writings). If Wilhelm insists on the priority of what he calls the ethical – the "or", which he opposes to the aesthetic "either" – he also insists that the ethical has its source in a freedom that is not simply the capacity for choosing between alternative goods, but that defines the self's way of being, its responsibility for the manner of its existence. This insistence is focused in the second of the Assessor's two letters to A on the concept of choice.

The slogan "either/or" is one that appears in the early pages of *Either/Or 1,* where A mockingly writes what he calls "An ecstatic lecture" on the principle of either/or that begins: "Marry, you will regret it; don't marry, you will also regret that; marry or don't marry, you will regret both …. Laugh at the follies of the world, you will regret it; weep over them, you will regret it, laugh at the world's follies or weep over them, you will regret both" (2 40/EE1 38). On this view, there is no real significance to any of the choices we make in life nor to any of the attitudes we take to it; all are equally meaningless. The Assessor shows himself to be aware of this way of looking at either/or, but counters with his own alternative: that there is really only one either/or and that is decisive for a person's whole life. "Choice is itself decisive for the content of the personality", he writes. "By means of the choice [the personality] immerses itself in what has been chosen and, if it does not choose, it goes into a consumptive decline" (3 154/EE2 163). In this spirit, and in direct contradistinction to A's philosophy of non-choice, even not choosing becomes a kind of choice. As the Assessor goes on to say, the fact that we live in time means that life itself moves forwards even as we hesitate on the brink of choosing, and so our situation, and our self with it, becomes something different from what it was. We have already heard from Constantin Constantius that the important thing is that everything happens at the right time, and while a strategy of not choosing may be innocent enough in the time of childhood, it becomes something else again when we are or should be ready for the responsibility involved in choice. "The personality has an interest in the choice even before it is made, and if one postpones the choice, then this is in fact an unconscious choice on the part of the personality or a choice on the part of obscure powers at work within it" (3 156/EE2 164).[1] The Assessor follows this assertion with a detailed description of how A makes a habit of playing around with the idea of either/or, spending a year and a half on thinking about whether he should become a parson or an actor, only to let the whole thing fizzle out and re-emerge in a new idea, such as that he might become a lawyer, or perhaps a hairdresser or a bank clerk. But this, as the Assessor insists, is not merely not choosing: it is, after all, to allow one's life to be defined in a certain way and is, therefore, a choice. A cannot escape responsibility for who he is simply by not choosing in that way. In the terminology of twentieth-century existentialism, it is a free flight from freedom. In this perspective, the Assessor adds, it doesn't even matter so much if a person chooses the wrong thing, since that shows a readiness to accept responsibility and, he adds:

> Therefore, even if a person chose the wrong course, he will nevertheless discover by virtue of the energy with which he chose, that he chose the wrong. For insofar as the choice is undertaken with all the inwardness of the personality, his being is cleansed and he himself is brought into an immediate relation to the eternal power that is all-pervasive throughout existence. (3 158/EE2 167)

But, as the Assessor goes on to explain, the choice he is talking about is not really the choice between good and evil in the conventional sense. It is not simply that we find ourselves in situations where we can choose to do a good turn or to do harm.

> What is it then that I distinguish with my either/or? Is it good and evil? No: I wish only to bring you to the point where this choice can acquire meaning for you. This is what everything hinges on. Only when one can get a person to stand in such a way at the crossroads that there is no way out for him except by choosing, then he will choose rightly. (3 158/EE2 168)

Following this declamation, the Assessor goes off into a lengthy polemic against modern philosophy, that is, speculation and the doctrine of mediation, which, he thinks, serves to undermine the seriousness of choice. Certainly, he says, choices can always be explained retrospectively, always be mediated, and it is philosophy's privilege to treat the past in this way. But, for now, we live in time, and "As truly therefore as there is a time to come, so truly is there an either/or" (3 163/EE2 173). It is not at this point that Kierkegaard uses the expression frequently associated with him that "life is lived forwards, but understood backwards", but that is very much of a piece with what Wilhelm is saying. Seen from the first-person perspective of the one who chooses, the outcome of the choice and, consequently, its meaning for the chooser's life, cannot be completely determined in the moment of choice. In marrying or accepting a new job, there is always the possibility that I *might* be making a terrible mistake, no matter how many good reasons I have for choosing the way I do. That I choose, then, cannot depend solely on the motivating power of these reasons. There must be a "more", and this "more" is freedom itself. Wilhelm is thus able to sum up his philosophical polemic as being in the cause of freedom, the future and either/or, which, for him, are three intimately interconnected and mutually reinforcing concepts.

What is really at issue in the act of choice, then, is not simply whether this particular relationship is strong enough to undergo the transformation of getting married or whether this job really is the right one for me: what matters is rather the activation of the freedom to choose and, with that, the readiness to accept responsibility for the choice once made. What is chosen is, essentially, the self, *my* self.

> But what is it, then, that I choose; is it this or that? No, for I choose absolutely, and the absolute element in my choice is precisely that I am not choosing this or that. I am choosing the absolute, and what is the absolute? It is myself in my eternal validity. I can never choose anything external to my self absolutely, for then I am choosing something external, then I am choosing something finite, and therefore do not choose it absolutely. (3 199/EE2 214)

Now this might seem as if the Assessor too, like the Romantics whom Kierkegaard criticized in *The Concept of Irony*, is subscribing to some sort of Fichtean programme of absolute self-assertion, envisaging the self as the sole, absolute creative power in existence. However, as he goes on to explain, there is, in his view, a significant difference between self-creation and self-choice. In choosing myself absolutely, I unconditionally accept that there is no "alibi for being".[2] I am who I am and as I am and there is no parallel universe into which I can escape. I am infinitely responsible for the self that I am, and there is no one else who is or can be responsible for it in the same way. But this choice is not *ex nihilo* or contextless. Precisely as an act of self-choice, and not an act of self-creation, the self we become through this choice is also a received self. This can be fleshed out in various ways.

For example, it is plausible to see the Assessor's argument as pointing to and illuminated by the crisis of anxiety and freedom experienced in adolescence. For the adolescent is not a *tabula rasa*. The adolescent is someone who already has a history, who has a network of family and other relationships that, depressing as they may be for the adolescent, constitute the reality that must be faced and dealt with (even if the chosen ways of facing it and dealing with it turn out to be walking away and dropping out). The adolescent is also someone with a certain range of interests, aptitudes and skills that have been acquired in childhood, through a combination of nature and nurture. But now these must be taken over and, in the language of contemporary psychotherapy, be "owned" (or, it may be, actively *disowned*, as when a young person chooses *not* to pursue the successful singing career planned by his or her parents but to become a financial consultant instead). Self-choice is thus always *situated* and, once more to anticipate the language of twentieth-century existentialism, it occurs as a "thrown project", that is, the taking over of life-possibilities that are given on the basis of a "thrownness" (Heidegger) or "facticity" (Sartre) and that precede my choosing them.

In the Assessor's vocabulary, choice is characterized by the fact that the one who chooses it thereby acquires a history, that is, he accepts himself as the person he has become through the experiences that have brought him to this point. Perhaps puzzlingly, the Assessor adds that the act of choice can therefore also be called "repentance". Why? There seem to be several levels to this idea. The first is constituted by the fact that the awareness of self that accompanies the need for choice is always an awareness marked by a sense of lack or inadequacy: I have to choose precisely because I am not yet all that I could or should be. But, then, at the second level, there is also the thought that, as a matter of common experience, few if any actual human beings reach the point at which they decisively choose themselves without having fallen short of the best standards of morality. To choose or to accept myself absolutely is to accept myself as someone who has lied a little, stolen a little, coveted a little, who has been a little idle, a little careless of others and so on – and no matter how "little" the "little" is, it still, morally, needs recognizing as what it is: repenting of. But the Assessor seems to suggest something more. For, as he explains, a person who repents does so "back into the self, into the family, the race, until he finds himself in God" (3 201/EE2 216). At this third level, it is not only my own prehistory of moral failure that I repent of in choosing myself, it is also the prehistory of both the immediate ("the family") and the general ("the race") human experience in which I participate as a non-negotiable condition of my being what and as I am. Repentance in this perspective carries with it a recognition of what theologians once called "solidarity in sin", with the implication that I cannot be a morally perfect being solely on the ground of my own good will if

I am also, through circumstance, the inheritor of a manifold history of failure and wrongdoing. I, as this individual that I am, did not choose that there should have been a slave trade, colonialism and anti-Semitism, but all of these historical realities have shaped the world that I now inherit as my world, and, if I am a white European Christian, these realities require my "repentance" if I am to be the self that I really, historically am. If, therefore, the "absoluteness" of self-choice might seem to echo Romantic idealism, the insistence on repentance emphasizes that this is so far from being envisaged as absolute self-creation that it requires a total acceptance of the individual and collective history by which I have become the self that, on the threshold of choice, I am, even when this history contradicts the values by which I now want to shape my life.

But choice is not only about accepting the past. It is also inseparable from my freedom and my concern for the future. If, as the Assessor insists, the self chooses itself in its concretion, this also applies to its relation to the present and the future. Although I alluded to Heidegger's idea of thrownness to bring out one aspect of what the Assessor is saying here, there is a difference from Heidegger. In ethical self-acceptance the individual is not simply coming to terms with a past that is merely a collection of more or less arbitrary happenings. He is also committing himself to realize an ideal that the Assessor does not hesitate to call universal. "The task that the ethical individual takes on is the transformation of the self into a universal individuality" (3 241/EE2 256). The past is accepted, but in the act of self-choice it is accepted as a task: as something that needs to be reshaped and to be ordered in the light and under the influence of the archetype of universal selfhood that we have within ourselves.

The universality of the ethical choice reveals itself in the individual's attitude towards society. In contrast to one whom he describes as a mystic, the person who chooses rightly, will, the Assessor says, be ready to commit himself to the obligations that come his way as a member of a quite concrete social body. This means a readiness to work, to marry and to cultivate friendships, and it allows for a legitimate enjoyment of the aesthetic pleasures of a common cultural life (as opposed to the cultivation of rare aesthetic experiences that can only be enjoyed by self-selected superior artistic personalities).

That the Assessor seems to move unproblematically from talking of self-transformation in the direction of the ideal archetype of humanity to the internalizing of the life of a concretely given social order, from "morality" to "ethics" (*Sittlichkeit*), has set him up for denunciation by many commentators as a kind of Hegelian or, simply, a social conformist of the most banal kind. It can almost sound as if his advice to A boils down to something along these lines: "Pull yourself together. Give yourself a break from all this airy-fairy, self-indulgent arty stuff, and get your feet back on the ground. Get yourself a good job, find a nice girl, bring up a family and generally be a good chap, one of us." It is hard to deny that there is a tone of complacency in much of what the Assessor says (and we must remember that he is only a fictional personality and not even a pseudonym), but we should not over-state the myopia induced by his bourgeois conformism. Three points in particular need to be made. First, as will by now be clear, self-choice can only happen as the first-person free act of the person concerned. It cannot be produced by the intervention of any external moral or social power. If it leads to the realization of universal values, it does so only in and through the individual's free action. Secondly (as the Assessor has underlined in a previous letter to A), although the person who marries thereby acquires a home, a position in society and so on, these things do not constitute adequate reasons for getting married. The Assessor is Romantic enough to insist that one marries chiefly because one has fallen in love with the person one marries, and that marriage accords with the spontaneous wish of the lovers to be together for ever. *Qua* social institution, marriage does not restrict the individual's freedom but provides a support and context for it. And, thirdly, in the later work "Observations on Marriage", included in *Stages on Life's Way,* the Assessor gives serious attention to the question concerning the justified exception. Although his default position is that the realization of true selfhood will generally take the form of active engage-ment with the given forms of social life, he here concedes that there may, after all, be justifiable exceptions, such as a person who refrains from marriage. Such exceptions, however, will only be "justified" if they also accept the legitimacy of the social practices from which they except them-selves. Their action (or their renunciation) is not therefore to be construed as an attack on society or on the universal values expressed in social life (see 7 152ff./SLW 169ff.).

Yet if the Assessor's view of life culminates in the principle of either/or, it could also be described in terms of both/and. Indeed, he himself repeat-edly argues that by choosing to live ethically, the aesthete will not lose the capacity for enjoying beauty or love, but will keep them in a higher or, as he puts it, concentric unity with the central act of self-choosing freedom. And, crucially, becoming ethical does not mean losing the freedom that A values but – in return for surrendering the freedom merely to abstain from choosing, acting or involving oneself with the life of society – self-choice offers the freedom to make freedom itself the defining feature of one's existence. This both/and character exposes the Assessor's thought to opposing criticisms. We have already heard the criticism that he represents a local version of the kind of social conformism that some also find in Hegel. But he might also be criticized for the same reasons that many moral philosophers criticize existentialism: that he makes everything depend on what is, finally, a purely arbitrary act of wilful self-assertion.

This is a criticism with which Alasdair MacIntyre is especially associated. In *After Virtue* MacIntyre writes that "the doctrine of *Enten-Eller* [*Either/Or*] is plainly to the effect that the principles which depict the ethical way of life are to be adopted *for no reason,* but for a choice that lies beyond reasons, just because it is the choice of what is to count for us as a reason."[3] MacIntyre's criticism is embedded in a larger debate with Kierkegaard that is in turn part of a yet larger attack on the ethical inheritance of the Enlightenment. We cannot, then, briefly rebut the entirety of MacIntyre's charge, involving as it does both narrowly textual and larger history-of-ideas issues nor is it relevant to probe the incoherence of MacIntyre's broad account of Kierkegaard at this point. However, it seems odd to say that the Assessor offers *no reason* for making the act of self-choice that he recommends. In fact, he offers a range of reasons of various kinds. First, he demonstrates that what, at least in this particular case, is the main alternative to an ethical life is internally incoherent, despairing and, as such, cannot be maintained with any degree of self-respect by a person indulging in it.[4]

Secondly, he claims that although the choice is intrinsically a *free* one, *what* is chosen in it is the archetype of ideal humanity. And although he does not himself spell it out, this would seem at the very least (i) to count as *a reason* for choosing it and (ii) to allow for a discussion as to whether what he proposes does, in fact, count as such a universal ideal. If, with regard to this last point, many commentators have found that what the Assessor calls the universal is, in the end, only a privileging of the values of the Biedermeier period of bourgeois society, this does not mean that what he has offered is not a reason, but simply that he has confused what we might call a local vision of being a good human being with a genuinely universal ideal. But that, we might allow, is the sort of mistake that moral philosophers from just about any known tradition are likely to make. And, of course, the fact of being able to make this kind of objection does suggest that it is, still, a reason.

Thirdly, where MacIntyre seems to hold that the problem with Wilhelm's position is that, confronted with the claim of ideal humanity, it appears to be entirely arbitrary whether I accept this claim or not, Kierkegaard could argue that there is no blinding ourselves to the inevitable gap between a purely theoretical approach to moral problems and actually *doing* something. I can perfectly well accept that there are good reasons for undertaking a particular ethical task – I know I *ought* to do it – but, still, I *don't* do it. A criminal, for example, can theoretically accept the principle that robbery or murder is wrong, but does what he does anyway. Equally, there will always be the possibility of some reason or other, some excuse or other, for not acting. It is precisely this indefinable *something* that Kierkegaard is especially interested in: the *something* that makes us capable of taking the step from believing something to be right to acting upon that belief. In a strange way, indeed, the kind of history of Western society promoted by MacIntyre and other cultural pessimists itself invites a similar question: for if what "classical" Catholic Christianity offered was so compellingly reasonable, why was it so easy for the West simply to shrug and walk away from it? How could someone whose moral education had been in the hands of a good and wise Thomist priest grow up to find the habits of virtue in which he had been brought up so lacking in moral persuasiveness in the face of the life-problems that crowded in on him in adult life? This is not just a complaint against Thomism, since it is questionable whether there has ever been a moral system that was not only able to demonstrate its claims with irresistible rational force at the theoretical level but also able to move us to live by them. If even the smallest chink in the claims of reason is once allowed then it would seem that the Kierkegaardian principle of choice has found a foothold.

Moreover, and fourthly, the Assessor also insists that ethical choice does not operate in a vacuum, but calls upon interests and motivations that are larger than those provided by reason alone, narrowly understood. As we have seen, the self that chooses itself also chooses at the same time its embeddedness in a preceding individual, familial and collective history. But that moral life is embedded in larger psychological and social practices is something that MacIntyre and other practitioners of virtue ethics might seem to endorse. Indeed, if the Assessor has been charged with being a Hegelian, it might seem no less pertinent to charge him with being an Aristotelian, one for whom "morality" is not a sphere separated off from the rest of life, but concerns the good life for the whole person. MacIntyre says of Kierkegaard's ethical stage that it "is presented as that realm in which principles have authority over us independently of our attitudes, preferences and feelings",[5] but this is only partially correct. It is true that "preferences and feelings" are relativized by the Assessor (and MacIntyre does not seem to have a problem with this), but "attitude" seems to be pivotal to his whole account of the ethical. For being ethical is not simply subscribing to a set of principles, nor even being in the way of putting them into effect; it is also, crucially, a matter of the attitude we take to our lives: of whether we regard ourselves as beings on whom the matter of ethics has any claim or not. In other words, it is a matter of what we take to be worthwhile human aspirations; it is a concern for the whole of life, and not just for morality.

In response to criticism of his Kierkegaard interpretation MacIntyre has conceded some ground, acknowledging that the ethicist does offer reasons why it is better to live an ethical than an aesthetic life. However, he argues, this does not solve the problem, since these reasons would be unintelligible to someone still pursuing an aesthetic existence: "what can retrospectively be understood as rationally justifiable cannot be thus understood prospectively," he writes.[6] From the point of view of the aesthete, the choice to become ethical will still seem criterionless. Yet this seems a singularly weak point. Someone in the grip of Nazi ideology, for example, would probably be incapable of seeing any point in arguments against a racially based approach to human identity, but that inability does not in any way invalidate those arguments. It merely shows how, in the world we actually live in, philosophy and argument will generally require the supplement of an appropriate rhetorical presentation, and that alongside ensuring that we have good arguments we also take care that they can be heard by those who need to hear them. And here, of course, is where Kierkegaard is in his element. At this point the philosopher (MacIntyre) seems, simply, to require too much of an engaged ethical thinker. In life as it is lived we rarely wait upon all available facts and arguments being laid out before making our decisions. And although it is true that the insufficiency of our rational preparedness may often lead us into moral error, it is at least arguable that postponing important life-decisions until we are fully rationally prepared would lead to even greater disasters.

The unity of the self (*Purity of Heart*)

MacIntyre goes on to link Kierkegaard with Kant. One element in this linkage is Kierkegaard's acceptance that a moral action is defined as such by its universalizability: that it is an action such as I could wish all other agents to take in similar circumstances. In the next section of this chapter we shall return to Kierkegaard's wrestling with the problems posed by such a principle. However, there is another "Kantian" aspect to Kierkegaard's view of the ethical and that deserves comment. It also opens another angle of illumination on the dubiousness of MacIntyre's strictures on Kierkegaard. This Kantian element is Kierkegaard's insistence on the principle of unity in the moral life.

It may not at first seem particularly interesting to assert that the ethical agent is and must be characterizable as strongly unified, but it is clear that this is something of great importance for Kierkegaard. We have already noted the Assessor's use of the image of "concentricity", with which he means to suggest how the act of ethical self-choice unifies the self around this act, synthesizing (another important Kierkegaardian term) the manifold of the self's aesthetic and social involvements into a coherent personality. The strongest statement of this principle in Kierkegaard's work, however, is in the collection of religious discourses, published under his own name, entitled *Upbuilding Discourses in Various Spirits*, the first part of which, "On the Occasion of a Confession" has been published separately in English under the title *Purity of Heart*.[7] This title nicely focuses the theme of the discourse itself, which Kierkegaard offers as a meditation on the Letter of St James, 4:8: "Draw near to God and he will draw near to you; cleanse your hands, you sinners, and purify your hearts, you double-minded." From this Kierkegaard infers that if those who need to purify their hearts can be described as "double-minded", then having a pure heart could be appropriately described as being single-minded or willing one thing. He comments that "the one who in truth only wills one thing *can only will the good,* and the one who only wills one thing, when he wills the good, *can only will the good in truth*" (11 30/UDVS 24, original emphasis). Kierkegaard thus sets up what will be the pivot around which the discourse turns: that there is a threefold interconnection between the unity of the will, truth, and the good. Opposed to this is what he calls double-mindedness. This is variously characterized as willing the good but doing so for the sake of something else (e.g. a reward) or as willing what, since it is not the good, is inherently manifold (such as the person who, like the aesthete, wills to live for pleasure but, in doing so, delivers himself over to an infinite range of possible fulfilments).

The Kantian ambience of Kierkegaard's argument can be indicated by reference to Kant's comment on the categorical imperative that, as opposed to the hypothetical imperative (in which "the practical necessity of a possible action" is represented "as a means to achieving something else that one wills"[8]): "there is one imperative that, without being based upon and having as its condition any other purpose to be attained by certain conduct, commands this conduct immediately."[9] Kant also calls this the imperative of morality and he conceives it – to use another key Kantian term – as inherently autonomous: as not subject to any external force or condition. Only when the will determines itself in line with such a categorical imperative can we talk of the good or moral will. For this reason Kant opens *The Critique of Practical Reason* by distinguishing the practical reason, which, in the strictest sense of the term he identifies with the moral will, from the various deliverances of the faculty of desire, that is, the forces that impel us to act for attaining one or other animal or social goal but that, in themselves, are only good in a derived sense: good for survival, good for career development, good for sexual satisfaction and so on. As opposed to such promptings of desire, the good will wills what is good simply and solely because it is good.

Kierkegaard would seem to agree. A striking feature of *Purity of Heart* is the way in which he takes case after case of double-mindedness and shows how the person who wills in that way is not and cannot be willing the good. More fundamentally, however, his aim is not just to show up the *immorality* or *amorality* of the double-minded person but positively to recommend the strategy of willing the good. In the overall context of Kierkegaard's work this appears to have important, if controversial, interpretative implications. On the one hand, and leaving aside his use of the biblical text, his starting-point seems to be a conception of the ethical that is not only Kantian but, specifically, autonomous: a conception of the ethical that does not invoke supra-ethical religious or theological factors. What he offers is a description of what it is to be a moral agent that any humanist can understand, although, naturally, not all will subscribe to just this particular model of ethical life, preferring utilitarian, Aristotelian or other options. Jeremy Walker is one commentator who, acknowledging the Kantian aspect of Kierkegaard's argument, sees the strategy of *Purity of Heart* as being to start with an autonomous model of ethics but to develop it in such a way that it ends by showing the necessity for ethics to find its ultimate term in an objective concept of the good that is, in turn, identical with God. As Walker puts it, Kierkegaard begins with philosophy but ends with theology.[10] If one sees the argument of *The Critique of Practical Reason* as a genuine attempt to establish the requirement of belief in God via the concept of the supreme good as the sole proper object of practical reason (i.e. moral willing), then the Kantian analogy is strengthened still further. If, on the other hand, one sees the true outcome of Kantian ethics as existential voluntarism, where whatever the subject arbitrarily wills becomes its supreme value, then Kierkegaard's text would seem to be offering an important counter-argument, which, at the same time, gives subjectivity its proper due.[11]

What *Purity of Heart* seems to be offering is an argument that hinges on identifying the power that gives unity to the self with the good, understanding this last as an object (indeed, the one true object) of moral striving for all possible moral agents, and that can therefore serve as a principle of moral community that is also supra-individual and supra-subjective. This power may, psychologically, be regarded as the "spirit" to which we heard Kierkegaard appealing at many points in Chapter 2, but it may also be identified with the act of self-choice recommended by the Assessor. Like that act – and like the action of the practical reason in relation to the psychological manifold of individual life in Kant – it both synthesizes the diverse elements of the self *and* puts the one who wills into a moral relation to others. For, if, *qua* "the good", the formal structure of *what* the individual who is seeking to actualize his potential as a unified self wills is what all other individuals must similarly be seeking, then the self's concern for its own integration and unity is no longer a purely psychological preoccupation. The self becomes what it is by willing what all other (potential) selves must also have as their *telos*. Self-realization is thus also the realization of the good, or, to repeat an expression of the Assessor's, the realization by the individual of the archetype of ideal humanity, a concept that is similarly explicable in Kantian terms.

If there is "theology" here, then, it would seem to be a theology that takes its departure from moral reflections that are not inherently determined by any particular theology or faith tradition. But, even if we allow that, in this work at least, Kierkegaard is offering us a purely autonomous path from the ethical to the religious, a way that supplements the psychological scenarios sketched in *The Concept of Anxiety* and *The Sickness unto Death* and deployed *ad hominem* against the aesthete A by Assessor Wilhelm, there would seem to be an almost insurmountable obstacle in the way of any over-all reading of Kierkegaard along these lines. That obstacle can be indicated by naming what is perhaps Kierkegaard's best-known (and certainly most-discussed) work, *Fear and Trembling,* and the problem around which *Fear and Trembling* is conventionally viewed as revolving, namely, the so-called "teleological suspension of the ethical". Seen from the point of view of this work, and whatever we might find elsewhere in his writings, aren't we pressed to concede that, for Kierkegaard, religion (and, therewith, the real truth of the human situation) always and necessarily presupposes the shipwreck of even the best moral and ethical strivings?

The exception (*Fear and Trembling*)

Although generally expecting that the ethical individual will be a person who acts in conformity with the social morality – the *Sittlichkeit* – of his or her time and place, Assessor Wilhelm, is not blind to the fact that unless such conformity springs from internal motivation, from the will to become ethical, it will be merely empty. At the same time he is aware that there may be occasions when even a person who has such a will may not be able to find expression for it within the prevailing social morality. He will not allow the mere desire to rebel or to be different to fall into this category, since a justified exception will be a person of fundamental good will or benevolence towards society, someone who affirms the legitimacy of the common good, yet is unable to tread the common way. Perhaps he will abstain from marriage, for example. But this is to state the problem rather weakly, and it is not hard to ratchet up the stakes. For it is one thing not to conform to the ethical life of society by simply dropping out, as in not marrying. But it would be something else again actively to transgress that ethical life, as, for example, in adultery. And the question may be posed as more than one of simple social morality. While acknowledging the value of an ethical point of view that centres on the relationship of benevolence between the individual and society, there may be more to morality than what a given society happens to hold to be right. If morality is more than local *Sittlichkeit* and might claim some kind of universality, then it becomes infinitely harder to justify any purported exceptions.

The idea of universal moral law is, in many areas of contemporary discourse, somewhat discredited. For example, as far as sexual morality goes, the general opinion in Western societies has moved away from the idea that sex within monogamous heterosexual marriage is the only morally legitimate form of sexual activity. We are more likely to think that the way in which sexual relationships are evaluated and regulated is almost entirely culturally relative. The language-game of morality cannot be separated from the concrete form of life in which it is embedded. Yet the idea that there should be certain universals is hard to shake off. The person who has learned not to bother too much about the sacredness of marriage and social prejudice against gays and lesbians is also likely to insist that it is simply and universally wrong to be prejudiced against someone on the grounds of their sexual orientation and practice. When, in a much-contested philosophical myth, Wittgenstein shook a red-hot poker at Karl Popper and challenged Popper to give an example of a universal moral rule, Popper is said to have countered with the words "Not to threaten visiting lecturers with pokers".[12] It is hard not to take Popper's point and hard to miss the more serious cases to which it might be applied. Although the problems of defining and securing consensus around universal laws are well recognized, there are still areas where the aspiration towards such universality remains vigorous, the field of human rights being only one salient example.

We have already indicated the Kantian resonance of some aspects of Kierkegaard's moral thinking and universalizability was, of course, one of the key tests that Kant required of any proposed action that laid claim to be moral. A moral action is an action that I could desire every individual to perform in similar and appropriate circumstances. The example most associated with this test is that of lying. Just as we would never wish to be lied to by others, argues Kant, so there can be no circumstances in which we ought to lie. Commentators have reacted against the whiff of rigorism in such a demand, drawing attention to situations where things might not appear so black and white, as when a resistance fighter is asked under torture to betray the names or whereabouts of his comrades. And, in fact, Kant himself was well aware that moral situations come in much more complex and nuanced forms in reality than they do in philosophy textbooks.

Kierkegaard's example, however, seems to raise none of the complexities or nuances of, say, lying in order to protect others. It is what many would regard as the most basic of all moral laws: you shall not kill. Leaving aside the question as to whether the state (whether through the judicial process or in time of war) has the right to override this law, Kierkegaard confronts us with a case where an individual citizen not only sets out to commit murder but believes himself to be justified in so doing. Even worse, the murder he intends is that of his own son to whom, over and above the general prohibition on killing, he owes the active duties of care and protection. Finally, to crown the whole story, the religious tradition has enshrined the story of this individual and his murderous intention in its holy scripture and the man concerned is hailed in every Church throughout Christendom as the prototype of faith! The man is, of course, Abraham, and the story is that related in Genesis 22, in which Abraham believes himself to have been called by God to take his son Isaac (his only son, through whom, as he also believes, God will secure his posterity in many generations) and sacrifice him, although, at the very last moment, when the knife is already drawn, an angel calls upon him to stop and points to a ram that has been caught in a nearby thicket that he is to offer instead.

This story provides the occasion and focus of what Kierkegaard himself predicted would become his most-discussed book, *Fear and Trembling*. But how are we to go about reading this remarkable, even unique, book? One commentator, Mackey, opens an essay on the work by stating that *"Fear and Trembling* ... is an attempt to understand the story of Abraham and Isaac recounted in Genesis 22."[13] That the book in some sense belongs to the genre of biblical commentary is true, although, for reasons that go beyond the pseudonymous author's repeated declaration that he cannot understand Abraham, one might question whether "understanding" the story of Abraham and Isaac is exactly what the book is about. Mackey himself and other, more recent commentators have drawn attention to the possibility that, as biblical interpretation, Kierkegaard is also taking up a long-held Christian theological practice of reading the Old Testament typologically, that is, reading it in such a way that a situation or action in the Old Testament is seen as foreshadowing an event in the life of Christ that is its "real" meaning. On this reading, *Fear and Trembling* is not so much about a limit-problem of ethics, but about the possibility of redemption through Christ.[14]

But, whatever else it may be or do, *Fear and Trembling* does highlight in an extraordinarily vivid and anguished way a problem that properly belongs to moral reflection, not least to moral reflection that sets out from Kantian premises. As Lippitt has pointed out in his recent introduction to the book, each of the three "Problemata" begins with the assertion that "the ethical is, as such, the universal" (with only the omission of the "as such" in one case). This would seem to underline the importance to Johannes/Kierkegaard of the question as to whether moral laws can indeed by understood as universal and, if so, whether there could ever be such a thing as a "justified exception" or, as the first "Problem" section of the book asks, "Is there a teleological suspension of the ethical?" That is, can moral universals be "suspended" in certain circumstances?

Until now I have avoided being drawn into the issue of Kierkegaard's textual strategies, but it seems almost unavoidable in the case of *Fear and Trembling*. For although, as I have just suggested, the book is concerned with a question that might, quite rightly, be posed as a question for moral reflection, it does so in a unique way. Nor is this simply because it takes its bearings from a biblical text. *The Concept of Anxiety* also did that, while broadly maintaining a linear, treatise-like structure. And although other Kierkegaardian works also break away from textual linearity, they do so in recognizable ways (in the case of Kierkegaard's "novels" – *Either/Or*, *Repetition* and *Stages on Life's Way* – by playing upon models found in contemporary "novels of education"). *Fear and Trembling*, however, is different again. It is subtitled "A Dialectical Lyric", which already confronts the reader with something of a paradox. "Dialectical", in Kierkegaard's vocabulary, usually has to do with conceptual analysis (as in the subtitle of the *Postscript* – "*A Mimical-Pathetical-Dialectical Compilation, An Existential Contribution*"), whereas "Lyric" suggests anything but that, implying a spontaneous, impassioned, distinctly non-analytical outpouring. *Fear and Trembling* will, indeed, contain both. Then, after the customary Kierkegaardian Motto and Foreword (each of which raise issues I shall not pursue here), comes a section entitled "Attunement", aimed at getting the reader in the right mood for what is to come.[15] This includes four alternative versions of the Abraham story, written as pastiches of the biblical narrative but with very different tonalities and outcomes from what we find in Genesis 22.[16] These are then followed by a "Eulogy of Abraham". Only then do we come to the three "Problemata", which seem to offer something like a sequence of recognizable philosophical questions and arguments: "Is there a teleological suspension of the ethical?", "Is there an absolute duty to God?" and "Was Abraham ethically responsible in keeping silent about his plan to Sara, Eliezer and Isaac?" However, before we get started on the first problem, Kierkegaard inserts a "Preliminary Expectoration" (which A. Hannay translates as "Preamble from the Heart"). Finally, comes an epilogue. Matters could become further complicated if we noted that the closing section discusses the very same philosophical problem of motion that is taken up on the first page of *Repetition*, published (under another pseudonym) on the same day, and that the final section of *Repetition* takes up the question of the exception that, as we have seen, is pivotal to *Fear and Trembling*. Nor should we overlook the riddle of the pseudonym itself: Johannes *de silentio*, which, as some commentators have noted[17] might be taken as indicating that the book is also "about" silence, a suggestion strengthened by the fact that, as the title of the third problem indicates, the silence of Abraham, Abraham's secret, is explicitly thematized in the text.

All of this makes it clear that, whatever we find in the book, it is something other than the simple statement of a problem and the attempt to solve it, which would be a merely "dialectical" exercise. The question of mood, "attunement", and the possibilities provided by multiple perspectives and multiple genres of writing within a single work (as well as the overt allusion to the complementary *Repetition*) suggest that Kierkegaard is not likely to be simply giving us his "answer" to the question posed. Rather, we might guess, he is trying to get us to see something of the scope and depth of the question itself. Nevertheless, even if we manage to abstain from looking for answers in *Fear and Trembling,* there seems to be no reason why we should not attempt to understand the question it is asking and to get some take on the kind of question it is.

At one level it is a question of a quite straightforward problem: whether moral laws are universal and, if so, whether there can ever be exceptions to them and, if that is so, how one might justify such an exception. As such it can be seen not only as probing a fairly obvious issue arising out of Kantian ethics, but also as articulating a problem that was to haunt the nineteenth century and, with a prototype in Napoleon, to find powerful expression in Stendhal, Dostoevsky, Nietzsche and many others. Although not all of these give the question the religious charge it has in Kierkegaard, they all reveal a fascination with figures who remove themselves from the moral accountability of their contemporaries and act as if they are "beyond good and evil". Although such "supermen" would seem to be clearly anti-Kantian, they also, in another way, give expression to another Kantian theme, the pursuit of maximum autonomy, although, typically, their version of self-direction has shed the aspiration to model their autonomy rationally and, instead, placed the main emphasis on willing and feeling.

Although the kind of heroic "superman" we see in Nietzsche (or the typically *failed* supermen of Dostoevsky's novels) have gone out of fashion in our own times, the basic pattern remains influential. It is, I would argue, implicit in many of the basic assumptions about the self made in the modern counselling movement. Carl Rogers, one of the seminal figures in this development (who claims to have back-up from Kierkegaard), describes the changes taken by "clients" in the following terms: "Away from Façades", "Away from 'Oughts'", "Away from Meeting Expectations", "Away from Pleasing Others", "Towards Self-Direction", "Towards Being Process", "Towards Being Complexity", "Towards Openness to Experience" and "Towards Trust of Self". Acknowledging that some people will see in this a recipe for evil, for "releasing the beast in [the] self", he answers, in remarkably Nietzschean terms, that, yes, it does assume that such a person "is, in some basic sense, a constructive and trustworthy member of the *species leo* … To be sure, he kills when he is hungry, but he does not go on a wild rampage of killing, nor does he overfeed himself."[18]

Kierkegaard's own fascination with Abraham, and Johannes's speaking of Abraham as the "hero" whose poet he himself is, might seem to set him in this line of thought and it might even be tempting to see his Abraham not merely as a "father of faith" but as a prototype of Nietzsche's Zarathustra.[19] Although, if so, we might need to apply the analogy proposed by Georg Brandes, that, in relation to Nietzsche, Kierkegaard was like a Columbus who, having discovered America, believed that he had merely discovered the Indies by another route. In other words, although he intuited the new humanity whose prophet Nietzsche was to become, Kierkegaard persisted in interpreting this in the light of traditional Christianity and was, therefore, unable fully to embrace his own discovery. A similar criticism is made by L. Shestov, who accuses Kierkegaard of failing to grasp the infinite freedom, the life beyond good and evil, that he comes so close to describing in Abraham. The clearest sign of this, Shestov thinks, is Kierkegaard's obsession with "justifying" Abraham's exceptional life ethically, since this quest for justification imposes an alien requirement on freedom that, in and for itself, has no need to answer the complaints of ethics.[20]

One obvious answer that Kierkegaard might seem to be giving to his own question is that the case of an Abraham is very different from that of the atheistic Raskolnikovs and Zarathustras of the world. He had, of course, read neither Dostoevsky nor Nietzsche, but his criticism of early Romanticism had been aimed at the hubris of self-creation and self-assertion, absolute egoism, that he saw in their reworking of Fichtean idealism. Such would-be supermen cannot, in fact, make good their own claim to be "justified" exceptions, since all they have to support them is, precisely, their own self-assertion, their own claims on their own behalf. And it is doubtful if Kierkegaard would lend a sympathetic ear to any arguments invoking moral luck on behalf of would-be exceptions, since, in his terms, that would be precisely to make the meaning of a free act dependent on external circumstances and, therefore, another example of double-mindedness. Abraham, however, is no absolute egoist, but a man of faith, a man committed to obedience rather than self-creation.

To tease out some of the issues here, let us leave the literary and hypothetical supermen of nineteenth-century literature and turn to a real-life example that reflects some of the most anguishing dilemmas in twentieth-century history, dilemmas that, in varying ways, were experienced by millions of European men and women. When Lukács joined the Communist Party in 1918, he explained his action in terms that appealed at least as much to *Fear and Trembling* as to the correctness of Marx's analysis of the contradictions of capitalism. He wrote:

> To believe is different from knowing, to believe means just a conscious irrational mentality that one follows when facing his life ... Lenin and Trotsky excellently recognised the revolutionary situation, but they could have been just sitting in a library. But, where faith begins, to live means to die for something – and to die for something means [not only] to live but [also] to kill someone else ...[21]

Or, as he further explained his idea in a letter, "the soul has to be sacrificed in order to save the soul; on the basis of a mystical morality one must become a cruel political realist and thus violate the absolute commandment: 'Thou shalt not kill!'"[22] This is not far from the choice of Raskolnikov in Dostoevsky's *Crime and Punishment*, but only Lukács is not even allowing himself Raskolnikov's utilitarian justification of murdering one person for the benefit of the many. For Lukács there seems, at this point, to be only "a mystical morality", a voice of God without God, as it were. But what is to distinguish this from mere arbitrariness? Not much, it would seem. Moreover, as Andras Nagy points out:

> one major difference became obvious when quoting the sacrifice of Abraham for political reasons, which seemed to seek a secularized redemption in front of an empty sky: that the object of sacrifice was lost forever, that there was no longer anyone to save "Isaac". What was lost by this act, became lost forever. And not only for the one who sacrificed but also for all the innocent victims of such an act.[23]

Abraham is rather differently placed since his action is not something he has himself dreamed up. How could he have, since it is a presupposition both of the biblical story and of Kierkegaard's retellings of it that Abraham deeply and truly loves his son? It is a divine command. It is a matter not of self-assertion, but of obedience.

There are Christian views that would endorse a divine command theory of ethics, that is, that what makes an action right or wrong is neither some innate quality of the action itself nor the disposition of the agent, but simply whether it accords with what God commands. This might seem problematic in the case of Abraham, however, since, although it is true that at this point in the biblical narrative God has not yet issued the table of laws that includes the prohibition of murder, He plainly condemns Cain's murder of his brother, Abel; moreover, God has himself promised Abraham that through Isaac he will become the ancestor of many nations. Yet one could say that, within the horizons of the Jewish or Christian belief systems, there is an analogy with the case of miracles: just as God has created certain natural processes (the orbit of the sun, for example) and is therefore uniquely able to suspend those same processes if he so chooses (by, for example, making the sun stand still – see Joshua 10:12–14), so too he can suspend the laws of ethics if, for whatever reason, he so chooses.

Such an argument might be enough for a believer, although, of course, even believers are likely to question whether, in any given case, such-and-such an outrageous action could ever truly be commanded by God. As Kierkegaard points out, the parish priest who has preached so eloquently about Abraham on Sunday will in all likelihood be scandalized if one of his parishioners subsequently declares that he was so taken with the sermon that he intends literally to emulate the example of Abraham. Part of Kierkegaard's point here is to have a go at what he regards as the rather thoughtless complacency with which the Church treats its biblical heritage. That is to say, he wants to show that Christianity is something far more demanding than what is on offer in the rather cosy, self-satisfied environment of established religion. But, in a sense, the priest is right. It is not enough simply to be able to say "But God told me to do it!" There are, after all, modern terrorists (and for that matter the criminally insane) who, unlike Lukács's communist terrorists, appeal to divine authority for their actions. From the point of view of Kantian ethics, however, there is nothing really to choose between the person who justifies such an act simply in terms of some inexplicable claim to be the exception and the person who claims to be called by God. Kant explicitly takes Abraham to task and, like Kierkegaard's parish priest, says roundly that such a thing should not be done, no matter who tells you to do it or why. It is simply an offence against a universal and exceptionless prohibition of murder. And here again we might repeat MacIntyre's objection that Kierkegaard's whole view of ethics culminates in the privileging of actions that are, ultimately, unmotivated and unreasonable, sheer, blind, arbitrary acts of will. That these involve invoking God does not make one iota of difference.

One way of moderating the severity of a simple appeal to divine commands is to point out that this was not the first time that God had intervened in Abraham's life. On the contrary, the whole story only makes sense against the background of a series of divine interventions, which include the promise of Isaac's birth and other assurances of God's favour towards him. Abraham therefore has grounds to trust God and to believe that whatever God tells him to do will work out for the best. Theologians could add that Abraham not only had his own private experience to go on, but the assurance of a divine covenant.

Abraham, Kierkegaard insists, had faith: he "believed and he believed for this life" (5 21/FTR 20). The character of this faith is further illuminated by a distinction that is forcefully made in the "Preamble from the Heart", namely the distinction between resignation and faith. To practice resignation (or, as Kierkegaard puts it, to be "a knight of resignation") is to be willing to surrender what one loved most without hope of return (one might think back to *The Concept of Anxiety* and to Ingeborg, who lets her lover go knowing that they will never be together again). A knight of faith, however, is one who makes what Kierkegaard calls "the double movement of faith". He is ready to give everything up, perhaps he does indeed give everything up but, at the same time and "by the power of the absurd" equally expects to get everything back. Something like this, Kierkegaard says, is true of Abraham: he both resigns Isaac *and* expects to get him back. How does he expect to get him back? Does he secretly expect there to be a last-minute substitute, that God won't really ask him to go all the way? Or does he expect Isaac to die and yet, somehow (since with God all things are possible) be restored to him? Or will God send him a second Isaac? Does it make a difference?[24] Kierkegaard doesn't go into these questions and, of course, for him to do so would be to begin to explain what he says is inexplicable, a point reinforced by Johannes's repeated exclamation that he cannot understand Abraham.

Abraham, then, "believed and he believed for this life". But is his preceding God-relationship really enough to make sense of this belief? Kierkegaard himself alludes to this prehistory at various points. However, as he implies in his eulogy of Abraham, precisely these previous experiences of God's favour could have made what he was being asked to do now all the more bitter, as if all that he had been through, all that he had been promised, had led only to this, as if God's good favour had been "only a whimsy, a passing fancy" (5 20/FTR 19), and, indeed, in these early chapters of the biblical narrative, God doesn't seem averse to changing his plans according to circumstances or inexplicable fancy. Somehow, appealing back to Abraham's long-term God-relationship or even to the covenant, doesn't quite seem to make sense of the story in any of the versions that Kierkegaard offers. Certainly it would scarcely be enough to satisfy a hostile critic who wished to maintain the universal validity of the prohibition of murder or who suspected Kierkegaard of eulogizing irrational and unmotivated or inadequately motivated wilfulness.

Sacrifice and selfhood (*Fear and Trembling*, continued)

But what if the story of the *Akedah* (the "binding" of Isaac, as it is referred to in the Jewish tradition) as retold by Kierkegaard is not really about

Abraham? What if we are to read it not as a real-life moral problem, as, say, in Lukács's decision to join a terrorist organization, but as a parable, a story about what it is to become a self and the kinds of things that will de demanded of us if we are really to grow as moral persons? Reading the book in this way might even provide a way of countering the sort of criticism we have heard from MacIntyre, and making Kierkegaard a serviceable text in the cause of virtue ethics. For what now moves centre-stage is not Abraham's act, but *how* he is in his act: *the kind of person* he is.

On this reading the key to the relationship between resignation and faith is not so much to do with the difficulty in believing that those we kill might nevertheless be restored to us, but with growing out of the desire to be the managers of our own lives. As Ed Mooney puts it:

> Relinquishing Isaac as absolute center of value means that Abraham must relinquish any claim to possess, master, or control the mean-ing Isaac will have as the aged patriarch advances towards his death. Isaac was to be the promise of his immortality, the consolation of his mortality, the continuance of his seed.[25]

Abraham has to learn that, however well laid his plans, life does not go according to plan and one has to become open to life in another way. In this other way, Isaac will be returned, but no longer as the centre, no longer as the guarantee that Abraham's name will live for ever. "Johannes de silentio shakes us from the idea that the key to moral or religious earnestness is in the public sphere where we discover and can then conform to a lucid list of rules. Johannes puts our eyes on underlying motive and transcendent orienting vision."[26] In these terms, what is crucial is the "how", the man-ner of Abraham's acting. On this basis, Mooney argues in a previous book that "A great deal of what Kierkegaard deems important to faith is compat-ible with Abraham *refusing* God's demand."[27] For what we see in the story of the *Akedah* is a dilemma of a kind that simply defies what Mooney calls "systematic ethics or Reason". Given the premises of the story, "It's *plain wrong* to refuse God and it's *plain wrong* to kill Isaac."[28] The point cannot then be to praise what Abraham does, for what he does is wrong, either way. The issue is rather how he does it. What Johannes holds up to us then is not a paradigm of how exceptional individuals are entitled to act but how all individuals should act: that is, with the seriousness, earnestness, anguish and hope of an Abraham.

This brings Abraham much closer to the world of tragedy than Kierkegaard himself seems to allow. Kierkegaard does, in fact, incorporate into *Fear and Trembling* a reference to one ancient tragedy that he takes to be sufficiently close to the story of Abraham to provide a useful contrast to it.

This is the tragedy of Iphigenia, whom Agamemnon, her father, is called upon to sacrifice in order to placate the goddess Artemis, who has been withholding the winds that would enable the Greek fleet to sail against Troy. The difference from the case of Abraham is clear enough. Agamemnon acts entirely within the public sphere of an accepted system of belief and cultic practice, and his sacrifice of Iphigenia, although cruel, is also justified on utilitarian grounds relating to the great affair of the Greek confederacy's war against Troy. Agamemnon, in other words, has reasons for his action that are public and comprehensible. Abraham does not. Yet, if we are as interpretatively generous towards the assumptions of the biblical text as we customarily are with regard to Greek tragedies (where our lack of belief in Zeus, Artemis and so on does not seem to prevent us from sympathizing with the actions and passions of those who do), then something similar to Agamemnon's situation does start to emerge. Abraham is, after all, the head man of the tribe whose God is the final arbiter of the laws of the tribe and the success or failure of its undertakings. There is no structure of statehood or other public sphere quite like that represented in the tragedy of Iphigenia, but there is something analogous to it.

However, if we are to reconceive Abraham's dilemma in tragic terms, we need to be careful. A text worth noting here is the essay from *Either/Or 1* on "The Tragic in Ancient Drama Reflected in the Tragic in Modern Drama". In this essay, Kierkegaard draws a contrast between the ancient and modern worldviews that hinges on a difference in degree and even kind concerning the relationship between individual and society. In the ancient world, Kierkegaard argues, people experienced their lives as integrated into the social body, whereas, in the modern world, we are what and as we are on the basis of reflection and choice: I do not explain who I am by telling the story of my tribe but by recounting my own life-experiences and choices. This, Kierkegaard suggests, is crucial to understanding ancient tragedy. The example he uses is Antigone, whose conflict with King Creon over the burial of her brother, an enemy of the state, is not so much a conflict between incompatible personalities, as a conflict between the great substantial powers of family and state. Antigone is not acting merely as Antigone, but as the guardian of the substantial values of the family, and likewise Creon is acting on behalf of the values of the state. The individualization of modern life, however, tends in the direction of dissolving the tragic, since a thoroughly reflective, autonomous agent will be without that dimension of fateful participation in a larger sphere of value that makes tragedy really tragic. The modern individual gets into unpleasant situations, experiences suffering and dies, but that is not tragic if the individual or the ensemble of individual agents involved acts on the basis of free decisions. Modern drama, Kierkegaard suggests, may have more pain, in so far as I recognize that the bad thing that is happening is *my fault,* but less sorrow, for in sorrow the individual pain is diffused throughout the larger, supra-personal life of the community and is thereby eased. As an example of how ancient tragedy would have to change in order to become modern he again takes Antigone, only this time it is Antigone's role as the daughter of Oedipus. Let us imagine, he says, that Oedipus's crimes, killing his father and marrying his mother, have not been discovered and that Antigone alone knows the secret. As she loves her father she cannot betray his guilt to the world. This alone is not tragic. But now she falls in love. If she is to marry, can she be appropriately honest towards her husband by telling him all? Or would that be to betray her father? She resolves to remain single, to resign her love (to use the language of *Fear and Trembling*) and remain single. But now, Kierkegaard adds, her beloved reciprocates her love and will not leave her alone. Knowing her great love for her father, he even persists in surprising her at Oedipus's grave and imploring her by the love she has for her father, not knowing that it is precisely this that makes it impossible for her to give herself over to her love.

Leaving aside how successful Kierkegaard's modern drama might be in its own terms, what would happen if we were to apply the same principles of modernization to the story of Abraham and to do so in terms of a tragic reading of his story? Where we might come out, I suggest, is not very far from the reading offered by Derrida in *The Gift of Death*. Here, where Johannes emphasizes the exceptional nature of Abraham's predicament, Derrida suggests that it is in effect the most common, universal experience of ethical life. "Duty or responsibility", he writes, "binds me to the other, to the other as other, and ties me in my absolute singularity to the other as other." But whereas this other is named in the religious tradition as "The Other", that is, as God, Derrida's (modern) experience reveals to him that *"Every other is every wholly other [tout autre est tout autre]"*, in other words, the incomprehensible, secret otherness of God meets me in every single other person to whom I am obligated in duty and responsibility.[29] And every one of these others similarly demands of me, in obligation, the sacrifice of all the others who might claim me. As Derrida goes on to illustrate, in feeding my cat I am neglecting all the cats who may be dying even now of malnutrition, in devoting myself to my professional life, I am ignoring the crying need of all those who, even now, are dying of starvation or sickness:

> As soon as I enter into a relation with the other, with the gaze, look, request, love, command, or call of the other, I know that I can respond only by sacrificing ethics, that is, by sacrificing whatever obliges me also to respond, in the same way, in the same instant, to all the others.[30]

Lippitt, critically but not unsympathetically, asks "why we need the story of Abraham and Isaac to make this point".[31] Part of the answer to that could lie in the previously mentioned tactic of suggesting that an important element in the message of *Fear and Trembling* is to draw out the kind of passion, the kind of seriousness and anguish that is appropriate in ethical existence. Lippitt suggests that, on Derrida's reading, there cannot be any of the aloneness that the Abraham of *Fear and Trembling* appears to endure, since we all daily experience that very same thing. But is that right? For although we might – Derrida appears to – recognize that solitude, that silence, as something that each (and therefore *all*) must suffer, to recognize it is not the same as to be relieved of it. After all, I know that you will die, but does that really help me confront the ineluctably individual reality of my own death? Moreover, if we read Derrida's account against the background of Kierkegaard's strategy of modernizing ancient dramas, Kierkegaard himself would seem to say that the difference between the ancient and the modern tragedy is precisely that the modern quasi-tragic individual is bound to a kind of secrecy and a kind of silence that is inseparable from the knowledge of their own responsibility. The heroes and heroines of ancient tragedy can speak because they are not merely articulating their own pain but are giving voice to a matter of common experience, and what they endure is commensurable with the inherent publicness of language. This is not so in the case of the modern tragic personality, for to the extent that the source of her pain is in her, she cannot share it with any other. She alone must stand trial for it. There is no alibi in being. In this regard, Abraham – despite (or maybe because of) his biblical provenance – is already more "modern" than either Agamemnon or Antigone.

Returning to Derrida, it might seem that these last comments undermine his way of linking Abraham's predicament with that of the person who neglects all the other cats in the world in feeding their own. What is to stop me looking over the fence and sharing my grief over neglecting all these millions of cats for the sake of one? If this was the only example of such a predicament, then we should seem to be presumptuous in claiming the example of Abraham as a prototype of our own everyday dramas. But isn't the point perhaps that the hyper-complexity of contemporary life and the overwhelming mass of information about need, pain, murder, war and general mayhem make for an accumulation of moral shortcoming such that we can, in reality, *never* talk about *all* the others we are sacrificing in pursuing our own local tasks and interests? It's all too much and we can never give voice to the distress of having to let so many die without stirring ourselves to save them. The point – Derrida's point – is, I suggest, at least debatable and not to be dismissed as negligible.

We are far from having solved the riddle of *Fear and Trembling*, and it would be foolish to imagine that such a limited treatment could do more than open up some of the complexities and challenges of this singularly problematic text. In any case, we have (not, perhaps, entirely successfully, since it is a rather artificial exercise) been attempting to look at it in only one aspect, namely, as a text dealing with a particular problem in ethics. But the discussion of ancient and modern tragedy and of Derrida's rewriting of the Abraham scenario in terms of our daily experience of sacrifice as a condition of exercising moral obligation points up two issues that take us further into the interpretation of Kierkegaard as a modern moralist. These are (i) whether Kierkegaard's ethics (which, as we saw in the first section of this chapter, is strongly concerned with the unification of the self in the inwardness of its own willing) in any way allows for the encounter with the human other that is so central to Derrida's interpretation, and (ii) just what kind of writing is appropriate to the task of writing about ethics for a modern audience. It is to these two questions that the remaining sections of this chapter will be devoted.

The Other (*Works of Love*)

In considering Kierkegaard's view of the ethical, we have largely had in view what might be regarded as the inner crises of the individual self, as it seeks to realize the archetype of ideal humanity in itself and so to unify itself around a single-minded purpose, or as it discovers that in some way or other its assumptions concerning the universality of its aims and values are radically insecure and, even if correct, cannot help it in the moment of action. But when we talk about morality or ethical life, we do not normally mean a kind of drama that the self conducts with itself but the action or behaviour that takes place when two or three are gathered together. Morality, in other words, must mean more than the self's relation to its own actions. It must also have to do with the relations between selves. But does Kierkegaard have anything to say about morality in this sense? Many commentators have thought not. We have already considered the charge of acosmism with regard to Kierkegaard's epistemology and ontology of the self, but something similar now recurs in the sphere of ethics, namely, the charge that the Kierkegaardian self – and that includes the ethical no less than the aesthetic self – is all alone in the world.

It is undeniable that at many points in his authorship and in many different ways Kierkegaard promoted a kind of individualism. Summing up the "movement" of his authorship as a whole, he wrote that it is "*from* the public, to 'the individual'. *Religiously*, indeed, there is no public but only the individual, for the religious is earnestness and earnestness is the individual"

(18 68/PV 10). The term translated "individual" here has also been variously translated as "the single individual" or "the single one" to indicate that Kierkegaard gives it special emphasis and uses it as a kind of technical term in his work. Noting, but putting to one side for now, the point that the specific contrast he draws is between the public (elsewhere "the crowd") and the individual, his constant heavy stress on "the single individual" cannot but raise the question as to whether what he has to offer is, in the last resort, some kind of moral solipsism.

The question is one that has troubled many commentators, including those who have acknowledged important debts to Kierkegaard. Martin Buber, one of whose central themes was precisely that of the self as essentially relational, essentially interdependent with other selves (as, most famously, in the I–Thou relationship that Buber popularized), offered an interesting and nuanced partial defence of Kierkegaard on this point. Contrasting Kierkegaard with Max Stirner, Buber argues that the Kierkegaardian "single one" is, in fact, capable of relationship. Yet his essay starts by emphasizing the "radical nature of [Kierkegaard's] solitariness" and contrasting Kierkegaard with both Augustine and Pascal with regard to the fact that where "beside Augustine stood a mother and beside Pascal a sister … the central event of Kierkegaard's life and the core of the crystallization of his thought was the renunciation of Regine Olsen as representing woman and the world."[32] However, Buber goes on to argue, only one who is a "single one" in a Kierkegaardian sense is capable of coming into relation to God: "Not before a man can say *I* in perfect reality – that is, finding himself – can he in perfect reality say *Thou,* that is to God. And even if he does it in a community he can only do it 'alone'."[33] Nevertheless, Buber disagrees with what he sees as Kierkegaard's understanding of this God-relationship on the part of the single one. For Buber does not wish to see the God-relationship and the relationship to the world as exclusive. On the contrary, it is one of the most pervasive themes of his whole philosophy that these two relationships are mutually supportive. You cannot, finally, have one without the other. For Kierkegaard, however, the exclusivity of the God-relationship demands the sacrifice of the relationship to the world, including relationships with other human beings.

For Buber, this criticism of Kierkegaard is not so much a reason simply to reject him, but rather a way of identifying what is important and valuable in his thought and of reinterpreting it in a broader context. Others have taken a far more hostile line, seeing Kierkegaardian individualism not merely as inadequate but as actively thwarting the creation of a genuinely ethical discourse about the self. Two especially influential critics have been T. W. Adorno and K. E. Løgstrup, and we shall therefore briefly examine their objections to Kierkegaard.

Adorno's position is succinctly stated in his article "Kierkegaard's Teaching on Love", in which he focuses on Kierkegaard's book *Works of Love*, an important point since it is just this work that other commentators appeal to as providing a counterbalance to some of the other more individualistic works. Where Buber sees Kierkegaard's single one as manifesting "concrete singularity",[34] Adorno sees the Kierkegaardian individual solely as an individual manifestation of a universal concept of humanity, with regard to which he comments that:

> According to Kierkegaard, the Christian love commandment is directed towards the human being as such, without regard to its specific constitution and also without regard to any natural feeling for a particular person. For the purposes of love the other person is merely what the whole external world is in Kierkegaard's philosophy, a mere "occasion" for subjective inwardness. This essentially knows no objects: the substantiality of love is objectless.[35]

In the light of this he adds that "The *credo quia absurdum* ['I believe because it is absurd'[36]] is translated into *amo quia absurdum* ['I love because it is absurd']."[37] And what is this absurdity? It is, Adorno argues, that *precisely because* love, *qua* subjective intention, cannot be commanded – cannot be an "ought" in the same way as a commandment of the law (as in "Thou shalt not kill") – it is, with conscious reference to this very impossibility, made by Kierkegaard into an "ought". There is even, Adorno suggests, a hint of the demonic in the way in which the Kierkegaardian individual uses the mere occasion provided by the existence of others to demonstrate its "sovereign" capacity to carry out this impossible commandment and its virtuosity in self-sacrifice. The complete irrelevance of the actual neighbour is further demonstrated by Kierkegaard's utter indifference to the outcome of our acts of love and his exclusive focus on motives. Kierkegaard retells the stories of the Good Samaritan and the widow whose small offering in the temple box was worth more to God than the great gifts of the rich (the so-called "widow's mite") in such a way as to argue that even if nothing at all results from an individual's works of love, this simply does not matter. His "love" is therefore love without others, love without a world. In this regard it is quite different from the love of neighbour recommended in the gospels, where love is portrayed in a world peopled by the "fishermen and farmers, shepherds and tax-collectors", who were concrete individualities and not just representatives of an abstract idea of "the neighbour". In this abstractness Kierkegaard simply reinforces – albeit against his own intentions – the reification and objectification of human beings in the conditions of bourgeois society. Kierkegaard's "misanthropy" (as Adorno does not hesitate to call it) has, however, one positive result, in that it helps him to expose the pseudo-love and pseudo-virtue of this society for the sham it is, and he is also prophetic of the dumbing-down consequent upon modern mass communications in a society that serves the interests of the capitalist world-order.

Løgstrup's critical emphasis is on what he sees as Kierkegaard's way of defining love exclusively in terms of helping the neighbour to love God, rather than helping ameliorate any concrete worldly problems the neighbour might be facing. Crucially, Løgstrup also gives special prominence to Kierkegaard's argument that true Christian love will always meet with opposition in the world as it is. For this reason he believes that although *Works of Love* insists on the acid test of my loving intention being my willingness to love those I find unlovely and strongly disbars preferential relationships from counting as love in the strong, Christian sense,[38] Kierkegaard's reflections are nevertheless determined by issues arising from my relation to those I do find attractive or sympathetic. For it is precisely in such relationships that it becomes so extremely difficult to be sure that I am really behaving morally towards that person. When, for example, I put aside my original plan of spending the weekend watching sport on television and volunteer to help them dig over their garden, am I "doing good" or simply indulging the pleasure I find in their company? The result of this preoccupation, Løgstrup claims, is that Kierkegaard's "loving" individual (strangely enough) ends up worrying far more about others' reactions than his own intentions, since their negative response becomes the proof of the genuineness of his love. His "works of love" will, in fact, be experienced by others as hateful and anti-social. But this is also to underline the impossibility of any positive relation between self and others. *Works of Love* as a whole, Løgstrup thinks, is a "brilliantly conceived system" for resisting any claim the other might make on me, especially when that claim threatens to become intimate.[39] For Løgstrup himself, it should be added, it is precisely the empirically given and phenomenologically interpretable encounter between people that is the foundation of the ethical demand.

Both Adorno and Løgstrup, then, take the view that the "other" doesn't really come into the picture at all in *Works of Love,* supposedly Kierkegaard's most "ethical" work. Others, of course, disagree and disagree strongly.[40] Nevertheless (and given that both Adorno and Løgstrup are able to make use of some fairly damning quotes from Kierkegaard himself), there would seem to be a serious case to answer. In particular, the following interconnected points need to be considered: whether Kierkegaard's view of love is centred on God in such a way as to diminish or entirely to obscure the human other as the proper object of moral conduct; whether the practice of love that he recommends amounts to more than the individual realizing a universal human value without regard to the concrete situation of the one to whom love is to be shown; whether the content of the act of love, as conceived by Kierkegaard, is indeed "absurd" or misanthropic; and whether there is, finally, something almost demonic about Kierkegardian "love".

It must, of course, be conceded that Kierkegaard's view does have a theological background. *Works of Love* itself opens with a prayer in which Kierkegaard declares that it would be impossible to speak rightly about love if God were forgotten, since God is the source of all love, "on heaven and on earth" (12 10/WL 3–4). In her closely argued study of *Works of Love* Jamie Ferreira indicates that the resources used by Kierkegaard for giving content to the love command are theological: God as the model of love, Scripture as a criterion of reflection on the requirement of love and the concrete imitation of Christ.[41] Kierkegaard further uses the divine command to love the neighbour as the main focus of the first part of *Works of Love*, especially emphasizing the fact that loving for the sake of obedience to this command is different from (and, he claims, superior to) loving on the basis of simple preference, that is, the fact that I like such and such a person and feel benevolently inclined to help them. But does this mean that Kierkegaard forces us towards being concerned with whether or not we are keeping the divine command at the expense of really attending to the need of the neighbour? Is this a real choice?[42]

Before *Works of Love*, Kierkegaard had already insisted that the God-relationship required us to be involved with other human beings, and not only in the sense of the Assessor's promotion of social life as a part of being ethical, with its possible connotations of simply conforming to social expectations. In one of the *Eighteen Upbuilding Discourses*, he wrote that "the one who loved human beings and only learned to love God through this love would be only imperfectly educated, but the one who loved God and in this love learned to love human beings, such a one was strengthened in the inner being" (4 93/EUD 97). The love of God is, then, crucial (and is not merely a cipher for the love of human beings), but the love of God requires us and perhaps even enables us also to love human beings. Similarly, in the discourse known as *Purity of Heart* (where, as we have seen, Kierkegaard is especially preoccupied with the self's inner unification), he concludes by asking: "And what is your attitude towards others? Does willing one thing bring you into concord with others? ... Do you wish for all what you wish for yourself, or do you wish to keep the highest for yourself, for you and yours, or to make you and yours the highest?" (11 131/UDVS 144). This, of course, leaves many of the questions we are considering unresolved, but it does underline the point that Kierkegaard regards the God-relationship not as excluding human relationships but, on the contrary, as affirming what he goes on to call the "blood relation" of all human beings. In *Works of Love*, among many possible examples, he reflects on what the everyday saying "God be with you" might mean if we took it seriously, if, for example, a person of aristocratic demeanour who did not care to engage with the life of the lower orders, really "went with God" out into the streets. "[T]hen", ponders Kierkegaard:

> he would perhaps try to hide from himself and therefore also from God what he saw, what God saw he hid. For when one walks with God, one does indeed walk safe from danger, but one is also forced to see in a quite unique way. When you walk in God's company, you need only see one single case of human wretchedness, and you will find yourself unable to flee from what Christianity wants you to understand, human equality. (12 80/WL 77)

That one understands the duty of love as a duty laid upon one by God, then, is so far from blinding one to the need of the neighbour that it should open one's eyes to this need in an especially forceful way. In one of the most quoted expressions of *Works of Love*, "God" becomes a "middle-term" in human relationships. As Kierkegaard puts it in words he himself emphasized, "*Worldly wisdom thinks that love is relationship between one person and another; Christianity teaches that love is a relationship between: a person – God – a person: that is, God is a middle-term*" (12 107/WL 106–7, original emphasis). However, as Kierkegaard understands it, this so little excludes the urgency of the claim made by the neighbour that it in fact grounds and underlines this claim. It does so by transforming my obligation to the other from being a matter of inclination to being a matter of duty. Only then, Kierkegaard says, can we really speak of "neighbour-love", that is, a love that is owed equally to all. In this respect "God" and "neighbour" become interdependent terms, so that Kierkegaard can also say that "love is only definable as a matter of conscience when either God or the neighbour is a middle-term, and so not in the case of romantic love or friendship" (12 140/WL 143). Kierkegaard, however, wants to say not that one cannot be in love or have friends, but that the love-commandment and the transformation of love into a matter of conscience will also introduce a further dimension into these kinds of preferential or inclination-based associations. Even one's spouse must become a "neighbour" in this sense if one is to speak of moral duties towards him or her.

The problem, although posed with reference to God, is not simply theological, however. There are many kinds of theological ethics that emphasize attention to the concrete needs of the neighbour. The problem seems rather to be the intense focus maintained by Kierkegaard on the intention involved in any particular loving act, a focus that ultimately leads, or seems to lead, to the actuality of the other disappearing from view. In other words, what critics object to is as much the Kantianism of his approach as its theological nature. The practice of love, on Kierkegaard's model, will thus end up being more a matter of self-scrutiny – making sure one's got one's motivation right – than of really being interested in what the other needs.

Kierkegaard does undeniably emphasize intention to an extraordinary extent, and seems perfectly comfortable with abandoning utilitarian calculations as a part of morality. In order to stress just this point he rewrites the stories of the Good Samaritan and the widow's mite in a discourse in *Works of Love* significantly entitled "Mercy, A Work of Love, Even if it can Give Nothing and Achieve Nothing". In 1986, addressing the general Assembly of the Church of Scotland, Margaret Thatcher famously remarked that "No one would remember the Good Samaritan if he'd only had good intentions – he had money as well." Kierkegaard, however, offers a pre-emptive counter-example to just this sort of view. He asks: what if the Good Samaritan had not had anything with which to bind up the wounds of the man attacked by robbers? What if he had not had an ass on which to place him but had carried him as best he could on his shoulders? What if he had no money and the innkeeper would not take him in? What if the man had died in his hands? "Would he not then have been as merciful, just as merciful as that [other] good Samaritan?" (12 304/WL 317). Or else, what if there had been two men together who had been attacked and robbed, and while one of them could do nothing but lie there and groan, "the other forgot or overcame his own suffering in order to speak a mild or friendly word, or … struggled to where he could get a refreshing drink for the other, or, if both of them had been rendered speechless, one of them nevertheless sighed silently in prayer for the other" (12 310/WL 324). Wouldn't this be an act of mercy? As for the widow, what if a thief had stolen her two small coins (which Kierkegaard imagines as having been wrapped in a little cloth) and substituted another cloth in their place? Wouldn't the intention of her gift have been just as good, just as praiseworthy, as in fact it was? To these reworkings of familiar biblical stories, Kierkegaard adds his own parable. Imagine, he says, that there was a poor widow with one daughter. This daughter loves her mother, but has no abilities or skills with which to give any practical help, although this is what she would most like to do in the world. Whatever she can do, she does, although it is never enough really to change the situation. This, Kierkegaard says, is true mercy.[43] But now, imagine further that there was a rich benefactor who, from time to time, visited them and gave generously to them. "the poor girl would stand there ashamed", Kierkegaard suggests, "because 'he' can do so much and his mercy completely covers over the girl's" (12 312/WL 325). That kind of benefaction, because it involves something external – money – could be the subject of a painting, Kierkegaard says, but the girl's mercy never could be, because it has no outward manifestation.

Adorno, supported by Baroness Thatcher, would seem to agree that such fruitless mercy is scarcely worth praising. At one level, of course, this would seem simply to be a clash of two very different and long-standing approaches to ethics that have taken a variety of historical forms. Kierkegaard is only one of many representatives of a deontological approach, even if it is also true that he places an extreme and unusual emphasis on intention alone. But it is clear that good intentions do not exclude practical applications. Indeed, even in terms of the stories that Kierkegaard tells, the good intentions of the Samaritan, the widow and the daughter are a commitment to action to the extent that action is possible. The Samaritan, indeed, probably has to labour rather more than the Samaritan of the biblical parable, especially the "wounded Samaritan"! The widow believes she is giving, while the daughter, Kierkegaard expressly says, does do whatever she is able to, even though it is pitifully inadequate.

True, Kierkegaard denounces as expressive of worldly wisdom the view that "*the chief thing is … that need must in any way possible be relieved, and that, if possible, everything should be done to relieve need*" (12 312/WL 326, original emphasis), but it by no means follows that he thinks need should *not* be relieved, simply that the relief of need does not exhaust the ethical task. Even if all material wants were to be relieved, he argues, there would still remain the question as to whether it had been mercy that had done this (as opposed, say, to the enlightened self-interest of global capitalism). The question is one of priorities. But if the prioritization of intention does not exclude addressing the concrete needs of the other, is it not likely to encourage a kind of moral navel-gazing, such that we become self-obsessed about the purification of intention in a way that, if from a slightly different angle, also contributes to diminishing the urgency with which we actually engage with the alleviation of others' suffering?

That such a situation could be the outcome in some cases is very possible, but it is clear that Kierkegaard himself offers a perspective that helps us see why this might be regarded as pathological. A key to this perspective is his idea of conscience. If Kierkegaard's emphasis on the principle of the unity of the self as interdependent with the striving to actualize ethical freedom is, as I have suggested, Kantian, his idea of conscience strikes a very different note from that of both Kant and Kant's idealist successors. For if, in Kant, conscience seems to be more or less identical with the principle of intentionality itself, and if, for the post-Kantian idealists (although importantly not for Kant himself), this principle could become transparently self-conscious in a kind of moral intuition, Kierkegaard's idea of conscience is entirely lacking this kind of self-reflection. Where the idealist could, in principle at least, make sense of the project of scrutinizing his own actions and motives to see if they were in accordance with his foundational moral intuition of the good, Kierkegaard envisages conscience in such a way as to make this quite impossible. Like much else in Kierkegaard's philosophy his idea of conscience has a religious flavour, although whether it is indissolubly tied to its religious origins is arguable. "In conscience", he writes, "it is God who beholds a person, in order that the person may behold God in all things" (12 359/WL 377). To live conscientiously is to live as if one's life were being lived constantly "before God", or, as the rabbi in Woody Allen's *Crimes and Misdemeanours* puts it, "the eyes of God are always watching you". How does this change things? It means, first, that, since (as is axiomatic for Kierkegaard), we can never see ourselves as God sees us, we have no final way of knowing whether or not our motives are in fact as they should be. Only God, who sees in secret, knows. Therefore, secondly, it means that we can never exhaust the ethical demand: there is no point at which we can, so to speak, wipe our hands and say "There's a job well done", since we are not ourselves in a position to determine the scope of the ethical task before us. The task itself is open-ended, infinite. As the title of another of the discourses of *Works of Love* puts it, as long as we live, we have to remain *in the debt of love*. We can never pay off the claim that love has upon us. And this, once more, directs the agent away from the scrutiny of his or her own motives and towards action. The question must always be, not "Have I acted rightly?", but "What more is there for me to do?" Thirdly, it follows that we must always be hesitant in regarding ourselves as virtuous and in claiming in any given case to have had right on our side. Conscience of this kind is an invitation to self-scrutiny and to make a realistic acknowledgement that self-deception is as likely to afflict me as much as it is (plainly!) a fault of the other person. Conscience, in other words, teaches love to be humble.[44]

But can such a theologically determined idea of conscience contribute to the secular debate about ethics? I have argued elsewhere that there is a strong case for interpreting Kierkegaard's use of expressions such as "before God" in a regulative sense, that is, as hypothetical exercises that help us to see ourselves and to direct our conduct in new and liberating ways.[45] Although the feeling of always being watched by the eyes of God seems clearly heteronomous (and in this respect also a clear shift away from Kantian models), it can serve to free up the self from attachment to short-term goals or local pressures towards one or other kind of conformity or complacency. In *After God*, Don Cupitt has argued that what he calls "the eye of God" motif is one of the residual elements of the theistic legacy that

will survive its metaphysical destruction by Hume and Kant. Cupitt summarizes this motif in the following terms:

> To believe in God is to live as if under the eye of God, and to assess
> oneself and one's world as from the standpoint of eternity. The
> person who truly and seriously believes in God is a person who has
> a special mediated (or, as I shall call it "bounced off") kind of
> consciousness ...[46]

But this, Cupitt says, can be understood in an entirely non-realist sense. The
very silence of God in the modern world supports this image since, Cupitt
says, it corresponds perfectly well to the silence with which a therapist listens to a client: yet, although the therapist says nothing and only listens, the
fact of having the therapist to talk to can of itself help transform the client's
self-understanding.[47] Perhaps that is not the latest or best therapeutic practice, but we see the point. Working out how I am to be or what I am to do
is best construed *not* as something I work out by myself in the inwardness
of consciousness, but as answerability, as responding to claims, however
implicit (as in the case of the silent therapist), that do not originate in me
but reach me, as it were, from outside. Understood regulatively – non-real-
istically, Cupitt would say – the idea of conscience as "the eye of God" thus
becomes a shorthand for the way in which my moral self is what it is and as
it is only as answerable to an infinite ethical claim that comes from outside
the orbit of the self's self-concern, from the other. Yet, because I freely
choose to see myself – or to let myself be seen – in this way, this need not
be a matter of reverting to a form of heteronomy. Whether such a "regulative" reading of Kierkegaard's idea of conscience requires us to go along
with Cupitt's non-realism, that is, whether it excludes the belief that we
actually *are* being watched by the eyes of God, is a question to which we
shall return in Chapter 4.

But, if we can allow that, however it is to be more precisely understood,
the God-dimension of Kierkegaard's concept of love does not exclude but
requires human "works of love", it might still be objected that the other
human beings who are the objects of these works are not regarded by the
one who loves as of interest in themselves, but are merely the occasion to
satisfy the demands of God or conscience. There can be no final answer to
this objection, since much depends on how we understand Kierkegaard's
various examples, which, in many cases, are as open to differing interpretations as any New Testament parable (a point to which we shall shortly
return). Is the wounded traveller who crawls away to get water for his friend
to be construed simply as doing what he does in order to satisfy his conscience? Can he be moved by his friend's need without that falling under the

ban of acting on mere inclination or preference? Do we most naturally imagine him, in his weakened state, as thinking "Must get water … Jim needs water …"?[48] In such inarticulate mutterings we see that the motivational force of the concrete act is derived from the friend's actual need, even if the readiness to allow oneself to be thus motivated might well be the result of a long training in conscientiousness.

In another discourse, Kierkegaard insists that the concept of "neighbour" (a concept that, as we have seen, is closely correlated with the idea of a commanded love) must apply, in principle, to just anyone whose need is presented to us, and not just the family and friends we choose to be with. When you get up from your prayers, he says, the very first person you meet when you go out is your neighbour in this sense. Adorno castigates Kierkegaard for this since, he claims, it reduces the ethical relationship to pure heteronomy in that there is no intrinsic reason why I should concern myself with just this person rather than someone I was, perhaps, better equipped to assist. Why should I pause to help the alcoholic if I know by experience that (i) I'm not very good at dealing with alcoholics and (ii) I'm on my way to give counselling to a troubled teenager, which is where my expertise really lies? Why should I sacrifice a human service for which I have prepared and trained myself for such an arbitrary encounter? This should not, of course, trouble a critic such as Løgstrup, since his own account of the ethical demand hinges precisely on the other becoming dependent on me in such a way that, in principle, I have their life in my hand. The demand is made before I have a say in the matter and it persists whether or not I am able to respond adequately to it. Here, of course, we might well recall Derrida's thoughts concerning the inescapability of sacrificing possible good acts for actual good acts in any moral action. Kierkegaard's view does not, of course, mean that I simply cancel my obligation (in this case) to the troubled teenager I'm on my way to help. It simply confronts me with a further claim to which, somehow or other, I must respond. Life's like that, he might say, and in terms of the individual's experience of individual morally charged encounters he'd be right. Adorno, one suspects, is partly looking in another direction, since he would wish (as Kierkegaard does not) to offer a defence of strategic social practice as a means of addressing human needs. Whether Kierkegaard's position necessarily excludes such collective action is debatable, although he would certainly resist conceding to it a status superior to that of the obligation of love towards the individual neighbour that lies at the centre of his argument.

But doesn't the whole idea of conscience as deriving from a vision of oneself as seen from the outside, by the eyes of God, return us to what critics such as Adorno and Løgstrup do not hesitate to call the inhumanity or misanthropy of Kierkegaard's moral position? Precisely the fact that, on such a view, the moral demand is infinitely unsatisfiable, suggests that we are falling into a potentially demonic situation, condemned to an unending servitude to a God who just goes on and on making demands, a Chronos-like father figure who will sooner or later consume us utterly. In considering the motif of the "eye of God", I argued that it might be possible to use such an idea regulatively, without necessarily buying in to a realist or objectivist view of God. But even on such a non-realist reading we might say that the whole idea is stultifying rather than helpful, placing the ethical subject in a kind of self-imposed cage, stifling the freedom that should be the hallmark of moral action. Having postponed the question as to the legitimacy of a non-realist account of Kierkegaard's God (and, therewith, of his account of conscience) to Chapter 4, I must now do the same again, since the full answer to this question depends on a closer examination of the idea of God that Kierkegaard is invoking. What can, briefly, be said here is that, unsurprisingly, much depends on how one envisages God. If one does think of God as the angry, infinitely demanding father, then to submit one's conduct to the unblinking gaze of such a God might well be adjudged to be a gesture of moral suicide. But if there are hints of such a God in Kierkegaard, there are also clear statements of an alternative view, such that to know oneself watched by the eye of God is not to find oneself annihilated but, rather, recreated, strengthened and, to use a characteristically Kierkegaardian term, built up or edified. Once again, it seems as if the final resolution of a Kierkegaardian problematic requires a step beyond ethics and, indeed, a step beyond philosophy, and that it is in his religious thought, in his theology, that the threads of Kierkegaard's thinking come together.

How to teach ethics

Nevertheless, there is one further matter to consider before moving on to engage directly with Kierkegaardian religion, for, even in their own terms, questions of ethics are seen by Kierkegaard as questions of a very distinctive kind. In order properly to understand such questions, it is vital that I relate to them in the right way. And that, clearly, is not in the way that speculative philosophy relates to them (if it relates to them at all: it is Kierkegaard's – arguable – view that Hegel's system, many would say like Heidegger's, had no ethics [9 103/CUP1 121]). They are not questions capable of a simple theoretical answer but questions to be asked existentially, anxiously, passionately: as questions that concern my own existential fate in the world and, it may be, my eternal destiny. It would, then, seem to be just as inappropriate in Kierkegaardian terms for a philosopher to write a system of ethics as it would be to construct a would-be metaphysical system. Writing about ethics that does not stimulate the reader's aptitude for ethical action, in however small a measure, is, simply, unethical. How should one go about it?

Here, then, we begin to engage with the questions of communication that lie at the heart of Kierkegaard's own account of himself as an author. Famously, Kierkegaard declared the strategy of his authorship to be one of indirect communication. This strategy was, at one level, connected with what he saw as the particular problem of Christendom and the failure of the established Church really to communicate the things of God. However, there is another strand in his writings on communication that more specifically concerns ethical communication in general.

The most accessible single source for Kierkegaard's views on the problems of ethical communication is a set of unpublished lecture drafts that he wrote when considering putting himself forwards for a teaching post in Denmark's pastoral seminary. The notes are entitled "The Dialectics of Ethical and Ethical-Religious Communication" (JP 648–57). These lectures begin by making a fundamental distinction between art and science. The problem with the modern world, Kierkegaard says, is that it has forgotten this distinction and treats all subjects as if they were branches of science, even when they are, in fact, arts. By art, it should be said, he does not in this instance mean fine art, such as painting, poetry or literature, but art in an older, Aristotelian sense: art as a practical skill (as, perhaps, in the art of archery or flower-arranging or even the art of government). This confusion, he says, is especially fatal when it comes to ethics, for ethics is not about having a correct theoretical view of the world. Ethics is about right action. But surely, one might ask, one has to know what is right before one can do it? However, for Kierkegaard (as we have been seeing), readiness to act, intention, is itself a condition of moral action, and readiness to act is a function of the subject. If this were not so, then one could imagine that there might be experts in ethics, just as there are experts in history or biology: people equipped with a knowledge that places them in a position to instruct others. But this is not so in ethics. Here there can be no experts. Ethical teaching has therefore to be teaching that in some way engages and stimulates the learner's readiness to act. In doing so it crucially presumes that the learner is someone capable of such action. The learner must already, at least potentially, be a moral agent, a member, with the teacher, of a moral community. One example Kierkegaard uses to illustrate this point is the relationship between a drill sergeant and a raw recruit. No matter how rough the sergeant's treatment of the recruit, the whole process of training depends on the assumption that the recruit has it within him to become a soldier. The training aims to realize this potential. Perhaps the example is not well chosen in relation to a modern, technological army, but Kierkegaard has other examples, such as learning to swim, that do not involve anything other than the learner's own mind–body unity. Of course, the person who learns to swim learns something they did not know how to do before, but what they learn is not the theory of swimming; indeed, they might be altogether ignorant of why it is that human bodies can float in water. What they learn is, simply, to swim. And to do that, they themselves must do it. Teaching ethics is teaching what Kierkegaard calls a "should–can", that is, helping the learner to become aware of standing under a certain obligation and of their capacities for responding to that obligation. It is learning how to engage myself with my life and my world in a certain way. And everybody has this potential.

This has a number of important implications. First, the one who "teaches" does so in only a qualified sense. He is, as Kierkegaard's chief model for a genuine ethical teacher, Socrates, said of himself, a midwife, someone whose work consists in bringing to birth what is already stirring in the learner. In these terms, the teacher does not have any kind of authority in relation to the learner. He cannot tell him what he should do, since that would be precisely to overrule the learner's freedom, which it is the whole object of the exercise to arouse. He is not "above" the learner, but on a level with him. No matter how skilled in his maieutic (midwife's) art, the teacher serves rather than manages the learner. Indeed, in the moment that one person wants to be another's teacher he must beware of forgetting that *qua* ethical subject the same demand is placed upon him as it is upon the learner:

> With regard to the ethical, the one human being cannot have authority in relation to the other because, ethically speaking, God is the master and every human being a pupil. If someone were to say to people: You should do what is ethical, it would be as if in the same moment one heard God saying to this important man: Nonsense, my friend, it is you who should do it.
> (Pap VIII 2 B 81 8,16/JP 649: 272)

The teacher too is a member of the moral community, and it would be a glaring contradiction if in seeking to arouse the moral concern and engagement of others he neglected his own duty to live morally. Once again, this puts ethics on a very different footing from any kind of "science". In the case of an abstract science such as geometry, the personality of the teacher is neither here nor there. In the case of a humanistic discipline such as history, a teacher does not have to be a great politician or military leader in order to be able to teach about the rise of women's suffrage or Napoleon's campaigns. Even in the case of the arts, it is possible to teach art or literary appreciation without being a great painter or writer. But to teach that one should always do the good, while neither doing it nor even attempting to do it, is (Kierkegaard thinks) to confuse matters utterly.

A further important feature of ethical teaching to which Kierkegaard draws attention is that it always occurs in a quite concrete situation and that the concrete situation in which the teaching is given fundamentally affects the meaning of the whole teaching–learning event. To revisit the example of swimming, it is one thing to teach swimming on dry land, by lying the learner over a chair and teaching him or her the correct strokes, but it is something else for the learner to do this in the water, and something else again to do it in a turbulent sea over 70,000 fathoms of water, as opposed to a 1.5-metre-deep swimming pool. Kierkegaard's point here is not the relativistic point that different things are right in different contexts, but simply the pedagogical point that if the situation is not taken into account, then whatever is learned will not really engage the learner's whole personality; it will remain abstract, superficial or irrelevant. One cannot just talk about morality or the good in abstraction; they must be related to the learner's actual circumstances.

But how, more precisely, might this be done? In *Works of Love* Kierkegaard emphasizes that such a teacher must not only be able to attract learners, but he must also learn to repel them and to practise self-renunciation by not allowing himself the indulgence of having disciples. Instead, and even – *especially* – when they *don't want* to face up to it, those he is "instructing" must be put into or returned to the situation that (since ethical teaching, as we have just seen, is always *in situ*) requires a decision that only he or she can make. This, I suggest, provides a context in which to understand the sense of Kierkegaard's insistence on the ethical communicator making himself repulsive to the learner as something quite different from the misanthropic obsession to which Løgstrup acribes it. The point is precisely that it is not the teacher who is at issue, but the learner, and, especially, the possibility of the learner becoming free from "the teacher" and claiming, through action, his or her own moral identity. In this connection (and in addition to the defining role model he found in Socrates), Kierkegaard seems both to recall Kant's promotion of moral autonomy and to anticipate Zarathustra's polemic against having disciples.[49]

Also relevant in this connection is what might be called the aprioristic character of much of Kierkegaard's writing about ethics. Although, as we read in Chapter 2, the Kierkegaardian psychologist prides himself on his rich and diverse experience of life, his examples (or "experiments", as he calls them) are invented to suit the point he is trying to make. Even where he takes his material from some other source (the Bible, literature, the newspapers), it is unashamedly reworked in terms of the problem under consideration. Yet Kierkegaard is not so much trying to write from life (which, in terms of his basic categorical structures, would be to work from the actuality of existence to the possibility of thought), as working out how thinking (possibility) might be related or applied to life (actuality). Once we recognize the priority of this movement from possibility to actuality in Kierkegaard's ethics, then we see again why it is problematic to construe Kierkegaard as a phenomenologist, since, in ethics, this would reverse the order of moral reflection. A significantly different approach is offered by Walker's suggestion regarding what he calls moral "depositions". With both Kierkegaard and Socrates in view, Walker writes that self-knowledge is not necessarily to be thought of as the kind of knowledge we might come to via the kind of psychotherapy that helped us to retell the story of how, through childhood trauma and adolescent crisis, we became the adults we are; that is, it is not primarily narrative-driven. Rather, it is a matter of deciding the principles that are determinative for our moral existence. To have self-knowledge in this sense is to be able

> to produce ... an account of the kind we call a "deposition" (*Forklaring*).
> And what is this? What is it that the individual cannot become confused about or forget, once he has become clearly aware of it? In a nutshell, his moral principles and aims ... the kind of account of his activity and existence that [Socrates] gives in the Assembly and in prison.[50]

On this view, there will therefore be a qualitative difference between the individual's psychological development, in which the potential for freedom is actualized via anxiety, and the moral life, in which this freedom acquires a specific and singular character by virtue of the principles (or axioms, as Kant would say) that we choose to be determinative for our conduct or by which, if we fail to live up to them, we are never the less willing to be judged. A certain psychological maturity is therefore a presupposition of being able to live ethically, but living ethically is more than having discovered the centre of the self or having brought the manifold materials of psychological life into the orbit of freedom's unifying energy. It is also to have principles and to have considered them with care. Putting it like this also helps us to see how, although close to Kant at many points, Kierkegaard finally takes a step beyond Kant or, perhaps more accurately, makes central to his ethical thinking what are only hints in Kant. There are two points to emphasize here.

First, Kant, famously, speaks of an inclination or propensity towards evil, of which the most serious form is "the depravity (*vitiositas, pravitas*) or ...

the *corruption* (*corruption*) of the human heart", defined as the power to choose "maxims that subordinate the principles of the moral law to others (not moral ones)".[51] This propensity, Kant adds, is "a subjective determining ground of the power of choice *that precedes every deed,* and hence is itself not yet a *deed.*"[52] This is, precisely, the domain within which the Assessor's talk of choosing to choose belongs. But whereas Kant appears to see such a possibility of a corruption in the choice of maxims as a more or less marginal phenomenon of ethical life, Kierkegaard judges it to be possibly the most prevalent feature of ethical life as we know it: instead of living as the free, moral beings we have it in us to be, we typically sink back into the morbid self-concern or self-loss of despair, postponing the urgent moral choices we should be making for the sake of one or other form of self-obsession. The challenge faced by the ethical teacher, then, is how to stimulate the learner's own innate capacity for acting morally in face of the same learner's no less innate capacity for allowing his or her own heart to become corrupted.

Secondly, choosing to live "as if before God" is not quite the same as living by a set of principles, no matter how carefully these may have been chosen, for the eyes of God are not – as we might imagine "principles" being – outside time. Rather, they follow us through time, tracking each twist and turn of our moral journey and entering into the close grain of every act of moral decision. In order to know what is required of us "before God", then, we need to produce nuanced schematizations of how it might be to live "before God" in such and such a situation. I suggest that Kierkegaard's category of "experiments" answers to just this requirement, giving flesh to a moral sensibility that would otherwise remain abstract and ineffective. This, it should be said, is the positive reason why these "experiments" should not be interpreted in terms of phenomenological observation, since to do so would be to subordinate the freedom of moral life to predetermined phenomenological data.

We have several times had occasion to refer to some of the retellings of biblical stories, domestic scenarios or other moral tales with which the pages of Kierkegaard's writings are crammed.[53] The multiple versions of the *Akedah* in *Fear and Trembling* are only the most famous of these. Many of them are strikingly pictorial mini-dramas, as it were, on the stage that Kierkegaard created for himself in his writing. This "theatrical" quality has often been noticed by commentators. Martin Thust, a German Kierkegaard scholar of the early twentieth century, spoke of "Søren Kierkegaard's puppet theatre", interpreting the pseudonyms and the various characters in them as representatives of spiritual types, rather than as fictional characters intended to represent "actual" people.[54] Edward Mooney has recently drawn attention to the inclusion in Kierkegaard's notes for a work satirizing contemporary urban culture the idea of "Some Sketches for the Spiritual Peep Show for Use on Sundays by the Faithful", and that at one point he had the idea of treating the story of Abraham in this way.[55] Noting Kierkegaard's own stress on the idea of "situation" as an essential ingredient in ethical reflection, we might adapt this slightly to suggest that it is not so much the "types" Kierkegaard is wanting us to be thinking about, as the *situations* that are represented. The point, then, is not to provide a kind of gallery of spiritual possibilities in which the reader might recognize his or her own image – as in the adolescent's fascination with the theatre – but to set up a sequence of dilemmas that are unresolved within the text and therefore require interpretative deliberation and reflection on the part of the reader. These, then, are Kierkegaard's enacted "experiments", not so much "thick descriptions" or phenomenological analyses of ethical situations as a means of stimulating the kind of deliberative processes that are appropriate to moral decision-making. In examining Constantin's eulogy of the theatre we noted that he drew a sharp contrast between the kind of innocent aesthetic fantasy enjoyed by all adolescents and the harsh world of real moral choices. What Kierkegaard's indirect moral pedagogy – his ethical "puppet theatre" – offers is, in this respect, a means of helping the learner to negotiate the middle ground between the aesthetic and the ethical: between the aesthetic absorption in mere possibility and the reality of the ethical life in the choices that here and now confront me with ineluctable urgency.

Certainly, Kierkegaard does seem to affirm a number of recognizable positions in moral theory: he privileges moral intentionality over utilitarian outcome; he regards the subject as capable of choosing the maxims that are determinative for his moral life and so on. But it is open to question how far, for example, he "teaches" that there *is* a justified exception to the laws of morality. When we have once noted the importance of the pedagogical dimension of Kierkegaard's ethical thought and recognized that, for Kierkegaard, morality, no less than religion, is the matter of indirect communication, then we will be chary of simply identifying Johannes *de silentio*'s praise of Abraham (for example) with Kierkegaard's having taught that Abraham was right to do what he did. Rather, Kierkegaard might be read as asking us simply to consider how, if we once concede that situations analogous to this do arise in the lives of individuals seeking to live the moral life, we ourselves might act in such a pass. That is to say, it is not a teaching but, simply, a question and a provocation.

CHAPTER FOUR

The infinite qualitative difference and the absolute paradox

The problem

The religious dimension of Kierkegaard's thought has now been touched on a number of times. Of course (and as I noted in the Introduction), the mere fact that a thinker is also religious or occupies himself at a number of points in his writings with religious questions does not immediately disqualify him from counting as a philosopher. But just as the communist poet V. V. Mayakovsky promulgated artistic principles concerning the subordination of art to the Communist Party that proved self-destructive for his own career as a poet in Soviet Russia, so too a thinker like Kierkegaard might seem to have espoused particular theologically motivated principles that must be intellectually suicidal for anyone wishing to be taken seriously as a philosophical thinker. Whatever Kierkegaard himself may have thought or wished concerning this, it must constitute a stumbling-block for those who want to take him seriously as someone with something important to say in our contemporary philosophical situation.

What, then, is the problem? It can be indicated in a preliminary way by reference to the two theological "slogans" to which the title of this chapter alludes: the infinite qualitative difference and the absolute paradox. These should not be conflated, since the former might be understood in a sense that would be acceptable to believers in such non-Christian theistic traditions as Judaism and Islam, concerning as it does the general relationship between God and the world. The latter, however, is a specifically Christian formulation, referring to Christian belief in the Incarnation of God in one man, Jesus Christ. It is this, Kierkegaard says, that is the absolute paradox: something that thought cannot think. Even worse, it is something that thought must find inherently offensive, a scandal or stumbling-block, to use the language of the New Testament (e.g. 1 Peter 2:8), or, as Kierkegaard also puts it in a somewhat bold translation of the Greek of Luke 2:34, "a sign of contradiction". But even the most general or weakest of these formulations, that there is an "infinite qualitative difference" between God and human beings, already carries serious implications for philosophy. When the theologian Karl Barth declared in the preface to the ground-breaking second edition of his commentary on St Paul's Letter to the Romans (entitled *The Epistle to the Romans*), that, in so far as he had a system, it was identical with Kierkegaard's promulgation of the "infinite qualitative difference" between God and human beings, he gave it to be understood that he was removing theology as a discipline exclusive to Christian faith from the scrutiny of philosophical reason.[1]

Now, it might be objected that not only are these terms all subtly distinct, but they are also characteristic of distinct pseudonyms or, at least, distinct works. The "absolute paradox" is an expression derived from Johannes Climacus and his *Philosophical Fragments,* the "infinite qualitative difference" from Climacus's *Postscript* and the "sign of contradiction" from Anti-Climacus's *Practice in Christianity*. However, the fact that we find such seemingly convergent ideas distributed across a number of pseudonyms might seem to suggest that what we are dealing with is a very distinctively *Kierkegaardian* theological attitude, an attitude that regards human reason in general and philosophy in particular as having no business in religion's holiest of holies. But – worse still – this is not just a matter of demarcating a restricted domain of knowledge in which philosophy has nothing in particular to say (as one might say that philosophy has nothing in particular to say about the military reasons for Napoleon losing the Battle of Waterloo or what makes the painting of Cézanne different from that of Monet). For God and the God-relationship is not just one question beside others in Kierkegaard's thought. As we have seen in a number of connections, human identity itself – our being the selves we are – is seen by Kierkegaard as inherently dependent upon the God-relationship, as are human ideas concerning the good, the meaning of existence and even, by implication, certain issues in logic. That Kierkegaard's idea of God is that God is necessarily incomprehensible or even actively offensive to reason might therefore seem to have retroactive significance for virtually every important aspect of his thought. In the measure that God is conceived of as being beyond the scope of reason or even opposed to it, so too does human existence come to seem beyond the scope of reason or even actively irrational. That certainly is what some Kierkegaardians and some anti-Kierkegaardians have concluded (with Shestov, perhaps, being the only commentator to declare that Kierkegaard was not irrational enough![2]). Perhaps it is the conclusion we too will be compelled to reach, but we should not, as philosophers, reach it unless every other line of interpretation has proved fruitless. It is mere intellectual laziness to declare that "Kierkegaard is a fideistic irrationalist" and thereby absolve ourselves from having to think seriously about what he is saying. If even the tears and torments of the saints can become the matter of a philosophical hermeneutic,[3] so too, we might guess, can Kierkegaard's boldest ventures in the language of faith. And, we should remember, Kierkegaard himself (as he would certainly have been the first to emphasize) was also a human being like us, and whatever he thought should also, in principle, be thinkable by us. How, then, should we proceed?

Kierkegaard himself offers one line of approach. In the *Postscript* itself he appears to open up a path to the religious that takes its cue from questions that the author (Johannes Climacus, in this case) assumes to be comprehensible to anyone who cares to stop and think about them, questions such as: "What would it mean for my life if I could expect an eternal happiness at the end of it?" Climacus argues that anyone who makes this question central to their lives will naturally think about it in a very distinctive way. Their thought will be characterized, he says, by the "interest" of existential pathos as opposed to the "disinterestedness" of speculative thought, and he shows how this "interest" is developed through what he calls its initial, essential and decisive expressions (namely, respect or worship, suffering and guilt). These bring Climacus to an account of what he calls "the religion of hidden inwardness". However, it is crucial to notice that up until this point he does not invoke any of the special features of Christian revelation and what he offers, as he himself stresses, is a form of religion – he calls it "Religiousness A" – that is compatible with human experience in general. In its own terms, it is said to be compatible with life "outside Christianity" or "in paganism", even if it goes so far that the individual annihilates himself in the consciousness of his nothingness before God. As the *Postscript* also suggests, the same can be said of Kierkegaard's upbuilding discourses, the religious meditations published under Kierkegaard's own name and that accompanied the pseudonymous production step-by-step.[4] These, Climacus asserts, lie within the immanent possibilities of human beings. They do not presuppose any input, as it were, from anything that radically transcends these possibilities. Only at the point at which belief makes itself dependent on the singular revelation of the God in time does something more than human come into play, in what is here called "Religiousness B" or "dialectical" faith, but which can be said to be faith in God on the basis of the revelation in Jesus Christ.

In this passage from a humanly comprehensible form of religion to what intrinsically transcends human capacities, Kierkegaard is, of course, following a well-worn pattern in theological thinking. In the system of Thomas Aquinas this is articulated in terms of the distinction between natural and revealed theology and, with different epistemological presuppositions, something analogous was practised by the Anglican natural theologians who flourished from the seventeenth century onwards. In these cases the emphasis is on knowledge or on the propositional content of faith. Thus, some propositions concerning God (such as the propositions that God is good, omnipotent, omniscient, etc.) are held to be accessible to universal human reason, while others (such as the proposition that we can only be saved by faith in the blood of Christ) are limited to the regenerate eyes of faith. Some philosophers of religion (again most notably in the Anglican tradition) had also spoken of a "natural religion" that differed from natural theology in that it concerned not knowledge about God but forms of practical living that could be regarded as implying a certain God-relationship.[5] Kierkegaard, as I have said, can be seen as sharing this general pattern, even if he did not concern himself with the pre-Christian knowledge of God and even if his model of "natural religion" is far darker, more fractured and angst-ridden than that of the virtuous pagans celebrated by Lord Herbert of Cherbury and his successors. Indeed, although we can probably not find anything in Kierkegaard that might parallel Thomas's dictum that grace does not destroy nature but perfects it, he does (at least in the journals) express his agreement with the view he finds in Leibniz that faith is above but not against reason.[6] This, however, seems relatively little to put in the balance against the far more numerous polemics directed against the intrusion into matters of faith by reason and philosophy, polemics that can be found in just about every stratum of Kierkegaard's authorship. Nevertheless, we shall now attempt to see what the path from everyday human experience to faith might look like, according to Kierkegaard, and to test just what kind of "leap" might be required of one who desires to make the radical transition from "Religiousness A" to "Religiousness B". In doing so we shall begin by following the version of this path found in the early upbuilding discourses, commenting also on the closely related (but not identical) account of "Religiousness A" in the *Postscript*. One advantage of doing this is that it enables us to pick up on several points from the discourses that have been discussed in previous chapters. But it should also be noted that, as the discussion of concern and anxiety showed, where the *Postscript* uses the device of a hypothetical proposition concerning the possibility of an eternal happiness, the discourses take as their starting-point the simple question as to what the world means to me and what my life means for the world.

From concern to self-annihilation

We have already seen how Kierkegaard uses the possibility of "concern" to set in motion a counter-movement to the evanescence of temporal experience. The concerned self is a self that is learning to become "older than the moment" and to acquire continuity in time, although this continuity – having a self – can only be sustained by the constant renewal of concern. This renewal is treated in the discourses in terms of patience, but it might also be seen as corresponding to what Kierkegaard calls "repetition". Such a self appears to have lifted itself out of the empty, hedonistic and animal-like life of those who exist only for the moment (using the word in a non-radical sense), as mere links in the chain of natural causation or as waves in the endless ocean of becoming. If this self then goes further and sets itself the project of realizing the Good it would seem to have provided itself with an agenda for a full, demanding and yet rewarding life. But what is the self really capable of? How far can it go in lifting itself out of the stream of becoming and constituting itself as a self in the strongest sense? Is the project of a single-minded ethical purity of heart humanly feasible?

There is evidence that Kierkegaard himself thought not. Early on in his authorship, he made Assessor Wilhelm insist on the need for the ethical self to ground itself in an act of repentance, "repentantly" choosing itself from the hand of God, as he put it. In Wilhelm's own letters such repentant self-choice is firmly distinguished from the Romantic ideal of self-creation. But *can* the self choose to choose itself? Even Wilhelm seems to allow for such a question when he sends A a sermon written by a friend of his who is a parson in Jutland. The message of the sermon – which constitutes the "Ultimatum" that is the final part of *Either/Or 2* – is that "over against God we are always in the wrong", implying that the kind of repentant self-choice advocated by the Assessor himself can never become an assured possession.

If the upbuilding discourses offer the possibility of awakening concern and acquiring a self, they also draw attention to many of the perils surrounding such a venture. These include mistaking a merely imagined resoluteness for a readiness to confront the actual life-problems that beset us. But if one is once set on the way of confronting these, how far can one go? Some of the discourses seem to suggest the answer: not very far. In "To Need God is a Human Being's Highest Perfection", Kierkegaard sketches the awakening of concern in terms that are now familiar to us. "What then is a human being?", he asks. "Is he just one more jewel in the successive unfolding of creation? Has he no power? Is he himself capable of nothing? And what might this power be? What is the highest he is capable of willing?" (4 274/ EUD 307). Regarded simply as a natural phenomenon, Kierkegaard goes on to say, a human being is doubtless a very wonderful thing, but a person may nevertheless feel that there must be more to life than being "a weapon in the service of obscure desires, that is, in service to the world" (4 274/EUD 308), "an instrument in the hand of obscure moods" (4 274/EUD 308) or "a mirror ... in which the world mirrors itself" (4 275/EUD 309). This, then, is the moment in which concern awakens, the moment in which we "acquire a soul" or, as he now puts it, in which we fight not with the world, but with our self.

> Behold him now. His powerful figure is held in the embrace of another figure. They hold each other so tightly all around, pressed together with such equal suppleness and equal strength that the bout cannot even begin, since, if it did, that other figure would overwhelm him in that very moment – yet that other figure is himself. Thus he is capable of nothing.   (4 275/EUD 309)

Such a conflict is not only terrible because there is no prospect (it seems) of winning, but also because if what I am fighting against is nothing external, not circumstances but, simply, myself, then there can be no "illusion", no "escape", no "self-deception". "This is how a person gets annihilated," Kierkegaard says, "and this annihilation is his truth" (4 275/EUD 309). This is the scenario in which a person discovers that he can do nothing by his own powers and, if he is to do anything at all, then it can only be with the help of God. It is in this sense that this "annihilation" is a human being's "highest perfection", since it both makes a person ready for the God-relationship and also provides a ruthlessly honest knowledge of the self that cuts through all the flattering illusions we entertain about ourselves in moments of aesthetic fantasy. This description, we might add, seems to correspond closely to the account of what, in the *Postscript*, Kierkegaard calls the "essential expression" of existential pathos, which he calls suffering and defines as the consciousness of being capable of nothing, without the help of God. (In the *Postscript* itself this state is explored by means of a 50-page meditation on a man who takes it into his head to take an outing to the Deer Park – a leisure area on the northern edge of Copenhagen – and who comes to realize that even such an innocent diversion is only possible with the help of God!)

But are we actually capable even of admitting the self-knowledge that involves such an avowal of our own incapacity? Kierkegaard now seems to step back and begin again, offering a more detailed description of the interaction between the two selves. "When a person turns towards himself in order to understand himself, then it is as if he stepped into the path of that first self, bringing to a halt the craving and longing for its environment of the self that was turned towards outwards, calling it back from the external world" (4 279/EUD 314).

As Kierkegaard goes on to explain, what this means is that, in the first instance, the inner or deeper self persuades the first self (the self that identifies itself in terms of one or other worldly project) of the uncertainty and ambiguity of worldly success or enjoyment. Even if external circumstances seem favourable to the fulfilment of the first self's desires, the inner self holds it back, convinced that even "success" would mean merely the absorption of the self into its environment and therefore reverting to the state of being an "instrument in the hand of obscure moods". Achieving my goal of reaching the top of the corporate ladder, I discover that my reputation and the sustaining of my personal wealth have become dependent on the whole ensemble of financial and institutional relationships in which my self has become embedded. I may have achieved my ambition, but I have not overcome it. On the contrary, I have allowed it to rule me. The first self might – it almost certainly will – complain of the discipline imposed upon it. Perhaps if it does not seize the opportunity now, while there is still time, it will be gone for ever! Just this once, it pleads. And perhaps there are others willing to encourage the first self in the pursuit of its desire, egging it on with words of praise for its talents and opportunities. But, says Kierkegaard, to see the self in terms of fulfilling talents and opportunities is to see it as essentially infantile: "One can be thirty years old or more, one can be forty and still only a child. Indeed, one can die as an aged child. But it is so delightful to be a child! So, one lies on the breast of temporality in the cradle of finitude, and sensuality sits by the cot and sings to the child" (4 281/EUD 316). The work of the deeper self, then, is that of weaning the child from its infantile fantasies, or from what a later psychology would call wish-fulfilment. Yet this is a very drastic form of weaning, since it ultimately means putting the first self to death: if it was sensuality that sat by the cradle, "the deeper self sat with him at his death-bed in the final hour of self-denial, when the self arose to eternity" (4 281/EUD 316).

We are following Kierkegaard's narrative here, and therefore only comment that he does not at this point pause to consider an alternative scenario in which the desires of the first self might be dealt with by being moderated rather than extirpated. As other writings clearly show, he would regard such a compromise solution as actually serving the interests of the first self, which, he would say, thereby remains firmly in the driving seat. Such a strategy of compromise would be an example of the double-mindedness that he analyses in *Purity of Heart*, especially in the treatment of the worldly mind's use of "probability" and "cleverness" as practical maxims.

If we return to the path described in the discourse "To Need God is a Human Being's Highest Perfection", we now come to a point at which the two selves are "reconciled", as Kierkegaard puts it, although in a very different way from that exemplified in worldly compromise. For the first self has recognized the inability of the external world to provide fulfilment for the needs of the deeper self and therefore accepts the need for its own death. But this is not the end of the process. Thus far we have only reached what Kierkegaard elsewhere calls "stoicism" or, perhaps, what *Fear and*

Trembling called the "movement of resignation". Will the person who has learned to subdue the vehemence of his attachment to the world take a further step and learn to see the ultimate incapacity of even the inner self to resolve the contradiction of his life? Will he learn to understand himself as dependent on God? This new challenge might seem to belittle the heroism of the ascetic, world-denying self, but, once more appealing to the principle that no one is stronger than themselves, Kierkegaard suggests that even the inner self must now learn to recognize *its* incapacity and humble itself under its need of God (4 284/EUD 319).

It cannot be said that the course of Kierkegaard's argument is entirely clear at this point, and he seems to rely too heavily on the suspiciously glib argument that no one is stronger than themselves. One might object that, since the whole dynamics of Kierkegaardian anthropology seem to hinge on the self being a multi-levelled form of existence, there should not be a problem in claiming that one form of self (the higher or deeper self) *can* overcome the lower. Isn't such "overcoming" of the very essence of existing *as spirit*? And if it turns out that we are, finally, incapable of existing as spirit, what happens to all those passages in which – as in *The Concept of Anxiety* – Kierkegaard spoke of our existing as self-transcending spirit in apparent continuity with the anthropology of German Idealism?

Leaving that question hanging, I suggest that there are, in fact, at least three reasons more or less explicitly offered in the upbuilding discourses as to why the inner self too must ultimately be regarded as powerless and in need of God. The first of these takes its cue from the content of the original concern in which the self asked about the meaning its existence had for the world and what the world meant to it. It is crucial to hold on to this starting-point, since it reminds us that Kierkegaard is not actually concerned here with the kind of ascetic programme of self-denial offered in many religious traditions. What he is concerned with is *how the self understands itself in its existence*. But although we could imagine an heroic form of asceticism in which the inner self really did seem to triumph over bodily desires (and the history of religion provides some remarkable examples of this), it is more difficult for the inner self to answer the question as to the "why" and "wherefore" of its existence. Thrown into a situation where it must struggle to disentangle itself from its environment it may do its best, but even as it does so it may find itself plagued by the question as to why it has to be like this. Mind may overcome body, but consciousness cannot get behind its own facticity. In terms of the last of the *Eighteen Upbuilding Discourses*, what the inner self is really after is an *explanation*.

In this last discourse the self's search for meaning is articulated as a question about prayer. The phenomenon of prayer begins, often enough, as the mere intensification of the worldly desire for some external good (as in prayers for rain, good health, etc.). The title of the discourse, however, suggests a rather different view of prayer: "One Who Prays Aright Struggles in Prayer and Is Victorious – in that God is Victorious". Once again the self must learn to be weaned from its desire for a merely external satisfaction, and to see prayer not as a means of achieving worldly goals but of entering into and deepening its God-relationship. And the key to this God-relationship is precisely the "explanation", that is, the self-understanding that enables the self to find self-acceptance. Yet the "victory" that God wins over the self is that what is finally offered is not an "explanation" of a cognitive kind but an existential reordering of the self that Kierkegaard calls a "transfiguration", a shift registered in a word-play on the Danish words for explanation and transfiguration, "Forklaring" and "Forklarelse" respectively.[7] This is how Kierkegaard describes what happens in the moment of transfiguration:

> The outer world, and every demand he ever made on life, was taken from him, now he struggles to find an explanation, but he cannot fight his way through. At last it seems to him that he has become an utter nothing. Now the moment has come. Who should the one who thus struggles wish to be like if not God? But if he himself is anything [in his own eyes] or wants to be anything, then this something is enough to prevent the likeness [from appearing]. Only when he himself becomes utterly nothing, only then can God shine through him, so that he becomes like God. Whatever he may otherwise amount to, he cannot express God's likeness but God can only impress his likeness in him when he has become nothing. When the sea exerts all its might, then it is precisely impossible for it to reflect the image of the heavens, and even the smallest movement means that the reflection is not quite pure; but when it becomes still and deep, then heaven's image sinks down into its nothingness. (4 380/EUD 399)

Such a resolution of the agonized striving of the self for true selfhood is, of course, problematic in its own way for philosophy, since it seems to place this resolution in a non-cognitive or precognitive "experience" that might almost merit being described as mystical. At the same time, there is a clear theological structure in what Kierkegaard is saying that possibly holds open the door to philosophy, or, at least, to the possibility of a dialogue between philosophical and theological ways of seeing the question.

I shall return to this possibility, but there are still two further points to take into account in considering why the ascetic self needs to become a, so to speak, theological self. The first of these is the point that finds its most powerful expression in the discourse entitled "At a Graveside", from the collection *Three Discourses on Imagined Occasions*. As the title suggests, this is a discourse resting on the conceit that it is being spoken to the mourners at a graveside and, naturally enough, its topic is death. One of the central strands of the discourse is that there are two ways in which we can think about death, ways that Kierkegaard calls "earnestness" and "mood" respectively. "Mood" turns out to be a very broad category, comprising all the forms in which we seek to sanitize the thought of death and to inure ourselves against the threat that death poses to our self-image and our ensemble of life-projects: to think about death without taking it seriously. Not only such everyday expressions as that death is a "rest" or a "sleep", but also such images as the skeletal grim reaper and even the ataraxy of a Socrates contemplating the imminent separation of soul and body fall short of earnestness, according to Kierkegaard.

As Theunissen has argued, whatever hints of a body–soul dualism there may be elsewhere in Kierkegaard's writings, he here gives decisive expression to the modern, post-Hegelian view that death affects the whole person, body and soul. Death is, simply, annihilation, *my* annihilation, the end of *me*. Death is a teacher of earnestness, because only death confronts me with the real finitude of my existence. Every other alteration can be seen as provisional, partial or temporary, but the alteration effected by death is decisive, total and absolute.[8] As Theunissen also shows, Kierkegaard here closely anticipates the role that death is given by Heidegger in *Being and Time,* that is, the role of uniquely challenging forth the self's will to authenticity.[9] Only, for Kierkegaard, even such a will-to-death as *Being and Time* might seem to be teaching could also be regarded as the product of "mood" and of self-flattering illusion. We cannot will ourselves into a decisive relation to death, since death is completely beyond our control. It is, as he says, "inexplicable" (6 317ff./TDIO 96ff.) and, he adds, this is the last thing that should be said about it. We cannot draw death into any understanding of life. Death defies understanding. It is an inexplicable fact. Yet if this inexplicability might seem to bar the ultimate aspiration of the ascetic self to take charge of its own life by being one thing that the ascetic self cannot command or control (the ascetic can choose when to die but cannot choose not to die), it might also be taken as an incentive for the self to look beyond its own possibilities, and to "know its need of God". Whether Kierkegaard can be accused at this point of falling into his own trap and substituting "mood" for "earnestness" is open to debate. Adorno remarked that the step "from grief to comfort" provided by the Kierkegaardian hope of an eternal resolution of life's unanswered questions was so far from being "the greatest" step that it was, in fact, "the smallest" and an example of the crudest form of religious self-delusion.[10] To defend Kierkegaard at this point would involve weighing the extent to which, in formulating the hope offered by a religious "answer" to the inexplicable question posed by death, he remains true to his own critical demolition of the false comforts offered by "mood". Has the religious hope, in other words, really been stripped of wish-fulfilment, or is it just a carefully concealed form of just such wish-fulfilment? Has the religious person placed themselves *entirely* in God's hands, or have they reserved the claim that God is only to be believed in in so far as God secures the immortality or survival of the soul? But the fact that such questions can be turned against Kierkegaard by no means invalidates his critique of "mood". Indeed, they might be taken as corroborating this critique, since it is just this that is now being turned against Kierkegaard himself.[11]

The final reason for judging the ascetic self to be, in the last resort, inadequate, is to be found in a theme that runs through many of the discourses, a theme provided by what Kierkegaard called his favourite scriptural text, the Letter of James 1:17–22. Here it is especially the motif that "every good and perfect gift comes from above" that repeatedly attracts his attention. If, in one perspective, the self finds itself thrown into existence and confronted by the grim prospect of its own ineluctable decease, there is another perspective in which that same thrownness can also be experienced as a gift, the gift of existence itself. As the Assessor also argued against the Romantic ideology of self-creation, we cannot, in fact, create ourselves, but whatever we are or become, we are or become on the basis of choosing a life given to us from the hand of God. Although we must become responsible for the realization of whatever possibilities our lives may have, we are not ourselves the source of those possibilities. They are, at the deepest level, given. Throughout Kierkegaard's discourses then, there is a fundamental tone of gratitude for existence, a tone that can be heard even in those passages where he speaks of the suffering we must endure in our passage through life, since even this suffering may be understood as a "good and perfect gift".

At one level, of course, this is one of the most conventional of all pious thoughts. Yet, in his own way, Kierkegaard here anticipates the debate that, taking its cue from Marcel Mauss, has run on through Georges Bataille to Derrida, Jean-Luc Marion and, through these last, has become a major topic of contemporary philosophy of religion in the continental tradition. The debate has focused on the ambiguity of gift-giving observed by Mauss and other anthropologists.[12] To give a gift is to place the recipient in one's debt: it is, implicitly, to require a reciprocal act ("one good turn deserves another"). Gift-giving, therefore, for all its appearance of sheer gratuity, is deeply implicated in the whole structuring of social power relations and, as such, can be seen as a means of establishing and reinforcing social hierarchies. And if God is regarded as gift-giver, then, in these terms, that is only another way of insisting on God's heteronomous rights over the human subject. According to Derrida, this dynamic renders gift-giving impossible, since to give a gift – for it to be known that what I give is given as a gift – is actually not to give a gift but to impose an obligation.[13] Kierkegaard's position, however, seems to be that to identify an exchange or an event as a gift is to be able to be grateful for it, and it is precisely the giving of this possibility of being grateful that is of the essence of a gift. A relationship established on the basis of gift, in other words, is pre-eminently a relationship in which love can fulfil its defining desire to assign all that the lover has and is to the beloved. To be able to be grateful to God is to be able to bring my life in its entirety into the compass of the God-relationship. This is especially important in relation to such negative experiences as suffering, loss and bereavement, with which Kierkegaard deals in the discourse on Job's saying that "The Lord gave, the Lord takes away, blessed be the name of the Lord".[14] In existentially incorporating such experiences into the category of "gift" I become able to affirm existence in its entirety as a "good and perfect gift", although Kierkegaard is, of course, under no illusions as to the existential (as opposed to the theoretical) difficulty of doing this.

However, although it is tempting to assimilate Kierkegaard's position to that of Marion, when the latter also argues against simply succumbing to the structuralist veto against "the gift" and re-asserts the priority of "givenness" over Being, something he sees as the ultimate possibility of any philosophical ontology, there are also differences.[15] Kierkegaard would certainly agree with the religiously fundamental nature of "gift" and "givenness". Yet it is dubious whether he would endorse Marion's procedure of trying to establish the priority of givenness by means of phenomenological analysis. As a decisive feature of the religious self's God-relation, openness to the gift in Kierkegaard belongs to existence, not to philosophy, and Marion's procedure would also, in very different circumstances and in a very different style from 1840s' Hegelianism, have to be seen as an attempt at something like an "existential system". In this regard, it is important that the crucial passages in which Kierkegaard gives his teaching on the divine giving are precisely to be found in his upbuilding (i.e. religious) works and are not offered as the outcome of a philosophical analysis. Marion could well counter that he does not claim to offer a direct explication of what we might call theological or religious givenness from the quality of givenness that he believes is phenomenologically prior to Being. And, he could point out, Kierkegaard's own call for thought to direct itself to what is other than or precedes thought, as well as the emphasis on the self having to choose itself, could be read as a kind of external, that is, non-religious ground for the givenness that comes to light in the religious relation. But although Kierkegaard sees the religious relation as hinging on the possibility of our experiencing and receiving existence as a gift, and this gift-experience is also rooted in the very structure of human psychology (and therefore, in principle, open to every human being), it is nevertheless not open to philosophical scrutiny. The gift does not reside in the *structure* of our experience, but in the way that structure is actualized in first-person experience. As such it can never be adequately motivated or deciphered from within a purely philosophical perspective. Existence becomes a gift only in the freedom of our desire to see it as such.

Made in the image of God

Behind the theme of experiencing existence as a gift stretches a vast network of theological ideas centred on the idea of God as Creator. The recurrence of certain key metaphors shows how, for Kierkegaard, the theology of creation can be dovetailed into the experience of prayer as leading from an "explanation" to a "transfiguration", in which the self reflects or becomes transparent to the divine glory as "heaven's image sinks down into [the self's] nothingness". The allusion to "image" at this point reflects the traditional biblical and Christian idea of humanity being made in the image of God, a doctrine addressed by Kierkegaard in the second of the three discourses on "The Lilies and the Birds" that make up the central part of *Upbuilding Discourses in Various Spirits*.

Here again the idea of human nothingness is in play, and a contrast is drawn between the lilies and the birds, taken as representative of the natural world and human beings. Whereas the lilies and the birds bear witness to God (in the manner, perhaps, of natural theology) they do not bear the likeness of God: they are not Godlike. Kierkegaard continues: "When a person sees his image in the mirror of the sea, then he indeed sees his image but the sea itself is not that person's image and when he goes away the image goes too: the sea is not the image and cannot retain the image" (11 176/ UDVS 192). In the external world no one thing can actually *be* the image of another. In the world of spirit, however, where we are dealing with what is invisible, it is different:

> But God is Spirit, [He] is invisible and the image of the invisible is also invisible: thus does the invisible Creator reflect himself in that invisibility that is an attribute of Spirit, and God's image is precisely the invisible glory. If God were visible, then there could be nothing that could be like Him or be His image; for there can be no image of anything that is visible and in the whole realm of visible things there is nothing, not a single blade of grass, that is the likeness of any other or is its image: if that were to happen then the image would be the object itself. (11 176–7/ UDVS 192)

In the realm of visible things, in the world of space and time, existence is possible only on the basis of concrete particularization. Even if two entities share a common essence (like two birds of the same species) they exist only as separate and inexchangeable instances: each is a unique "this". Nothing visible can therefore be like God in this strong sense of "like". But humanity can be "like" God in so far as it is defined as and by Spirit: "To be Spirit: this is humanity's invisible glory" (11 177/UDVS 193). Humanity's God-likeness is not therefore to be found in its external distinction from the rest of creation: its upright carriage, its commanding gaze, its dominion over other creatures.

> [I]t is glorious to stand erect and have dominion, but most glorious of all is to be nothing in the act of adoration. To adore is not to exercise dominion, and yet adoration is precisely that wherein humanity is like God, and, in truth, to be able to adore [God] is what gives the invisible glory preeminence over the rest of creation ... Humanity and God are not to be likened in any direct way, but inversely: it is only when God has infinitely become the eternally omnipresent object of adoration, and humanity remains forever the one who adores that they are "alike". If humanity would seek to be like God by exercising dominion, then it has forgotten God, God has departed and humanity is playing at being Lord in His absence.
>
> (11 177/UDVS 193)

The external appearance of human beings (the upright carriage, etc.) may witness to God in the same way as any other work of creation, by inviting reflection on the divine power and wisdom, but that is not where we are to look for the image of God in the strong sense. That is found only in the relationship of worship and adoration. In this relationship we return to our original created being as bearers of the image of God, and become capable of fulfilling our primary creaturely vocation: to worship and to adore God our maker. Such worship and adoration provide the ultimate context in which the themes of the annihilation of the self and existing as the recipients of "every good and perfect gift" are to be understood, while the "earnestness" of the thought of death prevents us from slipping into the sentimentality of an "all things bright and beautiful" way of construing the theology of creation.

This theological excursus has, I believe, provided us with a context in which to re-read some of the familiar formulations of *Philosophical Fragments* with fresh eyes and so to refine our view of Kierkegaard's understanding of the relationship between philosophy and theology. How? *Philosophical Fragments* (together with passages from the *Postscript* that closely echo *Philosophical Fragments*) arguably provides Kierkegaard's strongest formulations of the inability of philosophy to deal with issues of religion. In Chapters 1 and 2 of *Philosophical Fragments* Kierkegaard draws a strong contrast between the Socratic teacher who awakens the learner's innate potentiality (whether this is a potentiality for geometry or morality), and the religious teacher who, discovering the learner to be so deeply mired in sin that he must be recreated or reborn and given a new nature, has to become a "redeemer" who "saves" the learner and makes him capable of learning about "the God". In theological parlance, what is offered in *Philosophical Fragments* is a theology of redemption, that is, a theology centred on the predicament of the fallen human being who is reckoned as so completely to have lost the divine image as to be incapable of re-establishing the God-relationship without the intervention of a redeeming God. There is no reference here to anything like a theology of creation. Yet it is clear – as we have seen – that Kierkegaard himself did have such a theology, and was prepared to publish it under his own name. But how might this theology of creation relate to the theology of redemption offered by *Philosophical Fragments*?

We can fine tune the issue by looking at one more discourse. This is the second of the four discourses published in December 1843, six months before *Philosophical Fragments,* and it is one of the discourses reflecting on the "favourite" text from the Letter of James, that is, on the idea that "every good and perfect gift comes down from above" (which is also the title of the discourse). Like *Philosophical Fragments* it seems to take the situation of fallenness as the presupposition of a religious life-interpretation, a theme also flagged in the discourse by means of another text concerning gift-giving: "If you who are evil know how to give good gifts, how much more will your heavenly father give good gifts to those who ask him" (Matthew 7:11, Luke 11:13). This in turn leads to some thoughts on the analogies (and disanalogies) between our experience of human fathers and the meaning of divine Fatherhood. Our acquaintance with earthly fathers is not the basis of our faith in the Fatherhood of God, Kierkegaard says, and we should not project the foibles of human fathers on to divine Fatherhood. The key point is, at its simplest, the conviction that God *gives* good gifts, a conviction that cannot be demonstrated by signs or wonders or by "the testimony of flesh and blood", which are necessarily exposed to doubt. Doubt can only be brought to a halt by the word itself, when it points to "the condition that makes it possible for him [the human being] to receive the good and perfect gifts" (4 126/EUD 136). This condition is said to be the impulse to the good. But, Kierkegaard says, "before this impulse awakens in a person, there must first occur a great upheaval" whereby "the individual can be what the apostle calls the first-fruits of creation" (4 126–7/EUD 136).

Now there can be talk of "a new order of things" in which the human being finds "nothing lying in between God and the self" and is "born by the word of truth" that is also "to be born *to* the word of truth" (4 127/EUD 137). This rebirth must be made one's own in the right way, namely by becoming swift to listen, slow to anger "and with meekness receiving the word" and "keeping watch with thanksgiving" (4 129/EUD 139).

Now, all of this might seem to read like a first draft of *Philosophical Fragments*, Chapter 1, section B, where Climacus describes how the one who is in untruth or sin receives the condition for knowing truth from the teacher (God), in a transformation that is characterized as "conversion", "repentance" and "rebirth". As the one who is the ultimate agent of this process, God reveals himself as "Saviour", "Redeemer" and "Reconciler".

The next discourse continues with the same theme, and a further adumbration of *Philosophical Fragments* is found when Kierkegaard begins to develop the problematic of the gift in a manner that anticipates the parable of the King and the Poor Maiden in *Philosophical Fragments,* which is itself a parable of the Incarnation, thus exemplifying Climacus's own concluding acknowledgement that his project in its entirety merely reproduces what has been given freely to everybody in the scriptures.[16]

Yet for all the similarities between the arguments of the discourse and that of *Philosophical Fragments* there are also significant differences. Where *Philosophical Fragments* speaks of the human being's relation to the Incarnation, this discourse on the gift speaks of the relation to God the Father, that is, to God as Creator, which means God as having a relation to all creatures, and not merely to the cognitive minority of believers. And where *Philosophical Fragments* speaks of the gift as merely hypothetical, the discourse emphasizes its unconditionality and actuality. Kierkegaard writes "It does not say, thus your heavenly Father knows how to give good gifts but it says that he gives good gifts" (4 124/EUD 133). The whole premise of the discourse's argument is that God not only can give good gifts, but that he has given them, does give them and will continue to give them. We cannot exist as creatures without being the recipients of divine gifts. We might even say that God is God *because* he gives good gifts, and especially *because* he is the source and origin of the Good and of our love for the Good. Kierkegaard thus emphasizes that the Good is what comes "from above", that it is that in relation to which human beings are entirely dependent on God, but he can also say that "If you do not wish to continue in this [way of understanding things], it is because you do not wish to remain in God in whom you live and move and have your being" (4 125/EUD 134). Our "wish to remain in God" is, in other words, integral to our knowing our dependence on God. And this "wish", which must be materially identical with the "impulse towards the Good" of which Kierkegaard spoke previously, belongs to our original possibilities *qua*

God's human creatures. To be the recipient of God's good gifts is not something we shall only experience in "that promised land" to which God is leading us, but is the very condition of human existence. The condition that is given as the possibility of redemption is therefore nothing other than the condition by which creation is maintained in being.

What we have here, then, are the clear outlines of what is, in fact, a classically Christian theological structure, in which the theology of redemption is not promulgated in a vacuum but is contextualized by reference to a preceding and encompassing theology of creation. As such it indicates that all human beings, by virtue of their fundamental creatureliness, always already stand within a God-relationship that comprises aspects of creation and redemption. As relating to creation, this God-relationship is not something descending arbitrarily from above, but corresponds to elements in our basic human constitution. "Religiousness A", described in the *Postscript* as a purely immanent position, can now be seen as susceptible to reinterpretation in a theological framework that both respects this immanence yet opens it up towards other possibilities. For, if a person who seeks to be religious in a purely immanent way gains insight into the inner structure of the human condition, he or she will see that immanence is not the same as self-sufficiency and that the internal crises to which immanence is exposed yield a desire for God that also has the form of a desire for redemption. The human condition thus provides a pattern of life within which the Incarnation may be experienced as a meaningful event.

Nevertheless, the philosopher might well retort that this is all very well, but it is, after all, a *theology* of creation and, as such, depends on the acceptance of certain principles (such as: that God exists and is the Creator of all that is, that human beings are made in the image of God) that human reason is not obliged to accept. To this objection we must concede that Kierkegaard does not argue for these principles in what he would call a disinterested or speculative way. His argument is simply his account of the self's concern over what it means to be a self thrown into a world of flux, incapable by itself of finally mastering its absorption in the external world, and being finally handed over, in its entirety, to death, yet in all of this also finding the possibility of understanding it all as a good and perfect gift and, despite recurrent defeats, the possibility of holding on to and nurturing the aspiration towards the Good. Whether this account is persuasive or not, it is not nonsense and, on Kierkegaard's own premises, it is an account capable of making sense to any "well-intentioned reader". It is certainly based on the religious presupposition that God is our Creator, but this religious presupposition itself requires those who hold it to articulate their faith in such a way that it is comprehensible to all and not reserved to a cognitive minority who are the beneficiaries of a more or less restricted revelation. In this perspective

Kierkegaard proves to be closer to those twentieth-century theologians such as Rudolf Bultmann and Tillich who took the existential analysis of existence as offering a point of contact for Christian apologetics, rather than to some-one like Barth, who insisted that faith is separated from any possible form of human experience by "the crevasse, the polar zone, the desert barrier" that separate human corruption from divine incorruption.[17] Revelation, Barth declared, comes down "vertical from above" and requires "the dissolution of all concrete things, and apart from THE TRUTH which lies beyond birth and death."[18] As Barth sees it, human beings are so deeply fallen that they cannot even correctly formulate the question concerning God. It is undeniable that Barth was able to find passages in Kierkegaard that seemed to anticipate these assertions, but it is equally undeniable that this is only one side of Kierkegaard, for whom the human being certainly cannot find fulfilment without God but for whom the possibility of the God-relationship is some-thing that we can never lose, as long as we remain human.

But if Kierkegaard's theology of creation provides a context that helps us to make sense of his theology of redemption it certainly does not (and can-not) go all the way in explaining the latter, for the theology of redemption brings with it articles of faith that could never be derived from our general knowledge of human beings, such as the assertion that it is only by faith in the God-Man Jesus Christ that our seeking after God can be brought to its right conclusion. Having asked what might motivate us to go beyond the purely philosophical–ascetic quest for authentic selfhood and to seek a theo-logical self, we are now confronted by an analogous question as to what would motivate anyone to go beyond a God-relationship understood in terms of creaturely dependence to faith in the Redeemer and, indeed, to just this Redeemer?

I shall attempt to answer this question in several steps. The first concerns the need for an individual, personal and historical expression of divine love; the second the dialectic of sin and forgiveness; the third the exigency of love; and the fourth the reasons why this particular person, Jesus Christ, might be seen as suitably fulfilling the expectation of such an individual, personal and historical expression of divine love.

Incarnation and history

The title page of *Philosophical Fragments* boldly sets out three questions that the book will address. They are reformulations of questions posed by Lessing and run: "Can there be an historical point of departure for an eternal con-sciousness? How can such [a point of departure] be of more than historical interest? Can one construct an eternal happiness on an item of historical knowledge?" These questions do not in themselves require us to consider the particular historical claims of Christianity, but it is clear that this was the issue underlying both Lessing's and Kierkegaard's interest in them, for, unlike several other religions, Christianity seems to make its message dependent on faith in a particular historical individual. It does not merely teach us to live so as to maximize the possibilities for violence to be overcome by love (for example), but also requires us to affirm that our own salvation and our own ability to carry out its ethical demands are dependent on our believing certain things about this historical individual: that he was in a unique way the son of God, born of a virgin, that he died in such a way as to remove the burden of sin placed on human beings as a result of the Fall, and that he rose again from the dead, sits at the right hand of God in heaven and "will come again with glory to judge both the living and the dead", as the Nicene Creed puts it. Although the clauses relating to Christ's current status and future work are not in any simple sense "historical" affirmations, the preceding clauses are. This is a double challenge to anyone wanting to press the claims of Christianity.

First, it must be shown that such historical facts are relevant to the quest for eternal life or the desire to live a spiritual life. This question was already familiar in the ancient world. Christians living in an intellectual atmosphere moulded by a more or less diffuse Platonism could interest their pagan auditors in the quest for an eternal blessedness in terms that corresponded to the pagans' own conceptions of a higher, less physical sort of existence. But in claiming certain historical events as decisive for the success of this undertaking they faced a more difficult task. Reflections of this tension can be seen in works such as Augustine's "On the Usefulness of Belief", in which the concept of "belief" relates precisely to those historical particularities that could never count as "knowledge" in the sense propounded by Augustine's Platonic contemporaries (as could such "truths" as the divine nature of the soul, its immortality, etc.).[19]

A second, further problem arose when, in the time of the Enlightenment, the question was raised as to whether the texts that testified to these events were themselves historically reliable. Whereas centuries of Christian apologetics had hailed the trustworthiness of the apostolic witness, Hume's remark (in the *Essay on Miracles*) that "the wise lend a very academic faith to every report which favours the passion of the reporter" summed up the new caution regarding historical testimony. Both aspects of the question are relevant to Kierkegaard's own generation, which lived through a period of dramatic change in the historical study of the New Testament documents as well as the new philosophical developments associated with Hegel. These were, indeed, closely interlinked.

Yet the first and fundamental question that confronts a Christian apologist in this situation lies several steps back from such narrowly historical questions as "Was Jesus born at Bethlehem?" or "Did Jesus perform the miracle at Cana of Galilee as reported in St John's gospel?" Before these questions can be answered one must show the credibility of the idea that our salvation – our "eternal happiness" (to use Kierkegaard's phrase) – might require there to have been one individual in whom God was personally present. Kierkegaard offers forceful and polemically couched remarks to the effect that such an idea is inherently offensive to reason. If we speak of God purely as the Unknown or the Absolute Other, he says, then each and every concept and idea will become confused and we will be unable to attach any clear notion to it at all. The "absolute paradox", however, is not this but the claim that one individual human being "is also" God; that the Absolute Other is, in other words, also identical with one "like unto us". This is not merely paradoxical, it is "offensive" and "absurd", yet it is this that lies at the heart of Christian faith. The pseudonym Anti-Climacus might be assumed from his name to offer something very different from Climacus. However, in his *Practice in Christianity* he seems to make an essentially similar point when he speaks of Christ as the "sign of contradiction". "A 'sign of contradiction'", Anti-Climacus writes:

> is a sign that, in itself, contains a contradiction. There is no contradiction in it being this or that and also a sign, since there must be some immediate something in order for there to be a sign at all. What is literally nothing is certainly not a sign. A sign of contradiction, on the other hand, is a sign that, in its constituent parts contains a contradiction. (16 122/PC 124–5)

And, as he goes on to make clear, this is precisely the case with Christ who is both an individual, particular, suffering, lowly man and yet also (according to Christian faith) God. As did Climacus, Anti-Climacus judges this to be inherently likely to offend the claims of reason. But is Kierkegaard overplaying his own hand here? Certainly the stark terms in which he states the problem serve his case, but might there be ways of broaching the idea of the Incarnation that make it more reasonable?

Kierkegaard was, in fact, well aware of the debates raging around the theological legacy of Hegel. On the one side were the so-called Right Hegelians who interpreted Hegel as being fundamentally compatible with Christianity. On the other were the Left (or Young) Hegelians who took Hegel's ideas in a direction that led in fairly short order to the militant atheism of Feuerbach, Marx and Engels.

There was, clearly, much in Hegel that resonated with traditional Christian thinking and traditional Christian rhetoric. The term "Spirit" itself and the language of the "soul", of "eternity" and, not least, of "God" seemed to indicate some kind of affiliation to the Christian tradition. Looking further, many other decidedly theological ideas seemed to play a decisive role in shaping the system as a whole. Not the least important of these was the idea of Incarnation. The question is, whether what Hegel meant by Incarnation was the same as what classical Christian doctrine meant by it. This question was sharpened by the kind of controversy stirred by such a work as David Friedrich Strauss's *The Life of Jesus Critically Examined*. In this study Strauss developed what he called the "mythical" method of interpreting Scripture. To the average reader this seemed to strip away virtually every cherished detail of the gospel narrative as a "mythical" accretion to a now inaccessible historical kernel. But Strauss himself argued that there was no need to despair, and that what criticism took away with one hand, speculation restored with the other. In place of belief in an individual Christ who lived a long time ago in circumstances remote from our daily life and essentially uninteresting to us, speculation offered a universal Christ or, more precisely, the idea of the unity of the divine and the human, for which the individual life of Jesus of Nazareth merely provided the occasion for his followers to articulate. Humanity is itself divine, and such ideas as that of a Christ or a Son of God are merely mythical expressions for what is, properly understood, the truth of humanity. Although Strauss can write of the evangelical narrative that it is "a beautiful sacred poem of the human race – a poem in which are embodied all the wants of our religious instinct",[20] the materialist development of this position is already glimpsed in his rhetorical question: "And shall we interest ourselves more in the cure of some sick people in Galilee, than in the miracles of intellectual and moral life belonging to the history of the world – in the increasing, the almost incredible dominion of man over nature ...?"[21] It is, in other words, in humanity's collective scientific and technological transformation of its natural environment that the "divinity" of the human race is to be discerned, a message that was both echoed and radicalized in Feuerbach and subsequently taken up into Russian nihilism.

Was Strauss, as he himself believed, simply spelling out what was implicit in Hegel? The Right Hegelians thought not. Strauss knew that theologians such as Philipp Marheineke believed that if humanity was to realize its own destiny as Spirit, then it was indeed necessary for God to reveal himself in the form of an individual life. Only so could we learn that Spirit was, so to speak, for us. Hegel himself is nicely ambiguous. "The consciousness of the absolute that we have in philosophy in the form of thinking", he says in the lectures on the philosophy of religion, "is to be brought forth not for the standpoint of philosophical speculation or speculative thinking but in the form of *certainty*."[22] In other words, although speculative thinking is able to lay hold of and to conceptualize the truth revealed in Christianity, it can only do so on the basis of a prephilosophical certainty that is not itself derivable from philosophy. But the condition for acquiring such certainty must itself be something concretely existing. As Hegel says:

> For it is only what exists in an immediate way, in inner or outer intuition, that is certain. In order for it [this divine-human unity] to become a certainty for humanity, *God had to appear in the world in the flesh* ... At the same time there is this more precise specification to be added, namely, that the unity of divine and human nature must appear in *just one human being* ... it is not a question of the thought of humanity but of sensible certainty; thus it is just one human being in whom this unity is envisaged – humanity in the singular ... Moreover, it is not just a matter of singularity *in general*, for singularity in general is universal once more ... That is exactly why the unity in question must appear for others as a singular human being set apart ...[23]

For Strauss such singularity would appear superfluous and Hegel would at this point seem to be closer to Kierkegaard, yet it does not follow that they are saying the same, since it is not clear that, the singular Incarnation of the God having once happened, it continues, on Hegel's account, to have the same significance for subsequent generations as it did for those on whom this revelation first burst. Having once learned the principle of divine–human unity, Hegel might seem to allow that we can now satisfy ourselves with developing it further in a purely philosophical way.

Kierkegaard was familiar with these arguments. Apart from any knowledge he may have had of Hegel's own Christological writings, he actually attended lectures by Marheineke in Berlin in which these issues were discussed and would already be familiar with them from the "Right" Hegelianism of Martensen. Several years before his sojourn in Berlin Kierkegaard had also intensively studied a critical commentary on Strauss's book in which, once more, Strauss's tendency to substitute an impersonal divine–human principle for a concrete Incarnation in a singular individual is carefully considered. The author, Julius Schaller, comes down strongly in favour of the need for holding fast to the Christian idea of a concretely individual God-Man.[24]

Reason, then, would seem not necessarily to be offended at the thought of the Incarnation of God in an individual human being. Unless Kierkegaard was completely mistaken, we have to ask what there was in *his* idea that would have been unacceptable to the philosophers. There seem to be two key points. The first, which has already been hinted at, is that the Kierkegaardian God-Man retains the same relation to all subsequent generations as he had to his historical contemporaries. His life did not merely offer a lesson that, having once been learned, can now be put into effect in historically relative ways. For this life was not merely the immediate form of the divine-human idea, but *he* remains the one who, in eliciting faith, becomes the unique agent of our redemption as the individuals we are. This is, for example, the point of the discussion in *Philosophical Fragments* of what Kierkegaard calls "the disciple at second-hand", that is, the disciple living at one or more generations removed from Christ and not having any opportunity of a first-hand personal encounter with Christ in his incarnate, singular life on earth. The second point finds expression in a rather contemptuous comment that Kierkegaard makes in the course of taking extensive notes on Schaller's book. Whereas one might have expected him to be largely sympathetic to Schaller's critique of Strauss – and to some extent he is – he notes that:

> In thus developing the concept of reconciliation Schaller is developing only the possibility of God's relation to human beings, which one can certainly concede to him can only take place when the existence of a personal God is accepted; but the wrathful God is still not reconciled by this, and the satisfaction and repose one finds in such an answer is only illusory, since this question has no real meaning for the Christian consciousness, though it may well be very important for philosophical "Vorstudien" ["preliminary studies"].[25]

In other words, what philosophy and speculation and even certain theological critics of philosophy and speculation take to be the decisive issue is something that does not of itself concern a purely religious consciousness. What concerns the philosophers and their critics are questions of epistemology and ontology: how can we come to know God (or the divine–human idea) and what it is that we are given to know in such knowledge? The person who approaches the question in a religious perspective, however, will be asking something different, something, perhaps, like Luther's "How can I find a gracious God?" The question that frames the believer's approach to God, then, is a question about salvation, about sin and forgiveness. Yet Kierkegaard would seem to allow that the philosopher's questions have a legitimate if merely "preliminary" role. But his talk in these student notes of reconciling the wrathful God also suggests that there must be something more at issue than the individual's search for a principle of unity within the self. Something more dramatic is going on than merely the conflict between superficial and deeper selves, it would seem, something that Christian theology has traditionally dealt with in such terms as sin, redemption, forgiveness and reconciliation.

We shall now fast forward over ten years from these notes to *The Sickness unto Death,* a text that represents Kierkegaard's mature thought and that both discusses the inner divisions within the self in terms of sin and, in doing so, provides further pointers as to why Kierkegaard believes that the God-relationship has to be concentrated in the relationship between the believer and Christ. This does not of itself mean that the larger context provided by Kierkegaard's theology of creation is left behind, but it does mark a step beyond whatever may be contained in that context.

Guilt, sin, and forgiveness

Little imagination is needed to realize that the person who experiences the divisions of the self described by Kierkegaard in his various psychological works will experience them as distressing, and perhaps even enough to drive them to despair. Yet Kierkegaard does not limit himself to speaking of the inherent suffering or misery of life. He also describes the existence of the human being as guilty and, even more strongly, as sinful.

Although, as we have seen, *The Concept of Anxiety* reserved the topic of sin for the science of dogmatics, and Kierkegaard makes clear that sin can only be an issue for the person who has started to understand their lives in radically religious terms (more of this shortly), even from the beginning he seems to regard human existence as inherently guilty, again something that will be reflected in Heidegger's philosophy of existence. But what can this mean?

In popular English usage we are perhaps unaccustomed to drawing too sharp a distinction between the two terms, and it seems somewhat artificial when, as in the *Postscript,* Kierkegaard speaks of guilt as the "decisive expression" for Religiousness A, while reserving sin for Religiousness B, that is, a form of religiousness based on a conscious relation to the God-Man Jesus Christ. It might even seem to run against the testimony of the comparative anthropology of religion, which seems to show ideas of sin occurring in widely disparate religious contexts.

Kierkegaard's usage is not, however, entirely arbitrary, even if he can sometimes be accused of exploiting the common connotations of the two terms. The Danish term translated as guilt, *"Skyld"* (cf. the German *"Schuld"*), is not necessarily to be taken in a moral or forensic sense. Basically it means, simply, debt, so that the person described as guilty is simply a person who is in some way indebted to another. In terms of the original dependence of the creature on the Creator, then, we could speak of this too as a kind of debt in that we owe our lives to God. It is in this connection that the totalization of the guilt-consciousness of which Kierkegaard speaks in the *Postscript* can be correlated with the self-annihilation in which the creature rediscovers its creatureliness, for in this nothingness we are made entirely aware of the absoluteness of our dependence on God. Kierkegaard also speaks of this as akin to the position of humour, which, for him, involves an awareness of the utter relativity of all worldly goals, But we might also think of guilt in terms of human relationships, as in the title of one of the discourses in *Works of Love,* "Our Duty to Remain in the Debt of Love to One Another". Here the relation of debt seems to be understood in terms of obligation, and is used to flag the irreducible place of obligation in any ethical relationship. Løgstrup would presumably be satisfied. In relation to oneself, the possibility of guilt-consciousness thus seems to bring with it also the possibility of taking responsibility for my existence as a whole, for embracing *all* that I am in the relation of debt to God and neighbour. It is in this relation, although without reference to either God or neighbour, that the term comes to play such a pivotal role for Heidegger, although one might argue that an idea of "guilt/debt" so stripped of any essential relation to an Other has been stripped of the minimal condition for saying anything serious.

In none of these uses *need* the idea of guilt carry with it any sense of culpability or wrongdoing and, as I have said, Kierkegaard is emphatic that in so far as guilt belongs to Religiousness A (or, as he also calls it, the religion of immanence), it is something quite distinct from sin. Sin, as he puts it in the *Postscript,* involves a "break" (10 205/CUP1 532), that is, the self becoming something other than what it was in its original condition. Guilt, as we have seen, involves no such thing, but characterizes the original human condition from which we never move away. Yet there is a sense in which the idea of guilt does provide a foothold for the idea of sin, since it puts in place a structure of responsibility without which it would be hard to formulate any idea of sin.[26] Even if sin is seen narrowly in terms of transgressing divinely appointed laws (such as not eating from the tree of the knowledge of good and evil), such transgression can only be seen as sinful on the assumption of a relationship of responsibility towards the law-giver.[27] The slide from the one to the other can be seen in the sermon that Assessor Wilhelm sends to young A. It is a sermon from his friend, the pastor in Jutland, and it seems to hint at a more radical God-relationship than the Assessor's own. Whereas the Assessor seems to think that we *can* choose ourselves and, in doing so, lay the foundations for our constructive involvement in society, the Jutland pastor asserts that over against God we are always in the wrong. Some of his illustrations, however, seem to point more to the structure of obligation than to the forensic scenario implied by the word "wrong", and thus to guilt rather than to sin. Thus, he says, the true lover will never want to blame the beloved for any misunderstanding in their relationship. On the contrary, love proves itself to be love by wanting to be the one in the wrong. The true lover is always the first to say sorry, we might say. Far from signalling a "break" in the original constitution of the self, such wanting-to-be-in-the-wrong simply gives expression to the seriousness with which we take the natural obligation of love. But sin is something else.

One way of approaching this shift from guilt to sin is by looking at what, in *The Sickness unto Death,* is described as *potentiation*. Part 1 begins by sketching the disorder introduced into the self when the polarities that constitute its being (such as freedom and necessity or time and eternity) no longer function in creative interplay but become distorted, so that (for example) I aesthetically lose myself in the free flight of an imaginary existence and do not attend to the claims of necessity in my life. Or, if I am a *petit bourgeois* rather than a Romantic poet, I lose myself in the necessities of the daily round and decline the temptations of fancy ideas and quixotic ventures. Although some details of the anthropology of this part of *The Sickness unto Death* differ from that found in other Kierkegaardian works, the broad picture is one we are by now familiar with. All of the disorders discussed here are treated as forms of "despair". As such Kierkegaard might seem to be giving a purely psychological account and making purely psychological claims. At the beginning of Part 2, however, Kierkegaard raises the stakes. As the part title states, "Despair is Sin". However, this does not necessarily mean that everything that has been described as despair now has to be redescribed as sin. For, Kierkegaard seems to suggest, despair only becomes sin when, as he puts it, "Sin is ... with the idea of God despairingly not willing to be oneself or despairingly willing to be oneself" (15 131/SUD 77). It is, he says, this "idea of God" that "dialectically, ethically, religiously makes what lawyers called 'aggravated' despair into sin" (15 131/SUD 77). The meaning of our religious outlook, in other words, is inseparable from the level of consciousness at which we exist. Those who know nothing better may be "guilty", that is, responsible for their existence in the sense previously described, but they are not "sinners" in a strong sense.[28]

As the exposition of sin continues, Kierkegaard takes pains to distinguish the Christian view from the Socratic view. Whereas for Socrates (and, Kierkegaard believes, for the Greek view in general) sin is simply ignorance and, once knowing the Good, we could not not do it, Kierkegaard states that the Christian view involves both consciousness and volition. In knowing myself to be a sinner I know myself to be under obligation towards God ("guilty" or "indebted", as it were), but also as willing what is contrary to

God's will for me or, it may be, not willing what it is God wants me to will: knowing I should not steal, I steal, or knowing I should honour my father and mother, I pass over my obligations to them in favour of some piece of self-indulgence or other. In this passage on the difference between the Socratic and Christian understanding, Kierkegaard shows himself to be well aware of the difficulty of deciding, in any given case, what a person may or may not know and here as elsewhere he has a sharp sense for the almost infinite possibilities of human self-deception. But his key point is that it is not enough to *know* the Good, since the problem is precisely our unwillingness to do it. The issue is, of course, not just one of external duties, such as not stealing or honouring one's father and mother. As the whole discussion has been framed by the discussion of despair, it is clear that what is really at stake is our fundamental identity as persons: are we the persons God created us to be? If not, then it is no longer a matter of some natural shortcoming that might be ascribed to our finitude or to temporality (as if I could say that although I am not yet what I ought to be, I expect to become so in due course). My failure to be what I am is no longer a matter of psychology or psychological despair. As a matter of responsibility over against God, it is sin. As such, it is, Kierkegaard says, not a negation but a position. Even a sin of omission, such as failing to honour my father and mother, can be traced back to a choice, an act of will, *not* to obey. And, naturally, the more I have immersed myself in the totality of my guilt-consciousness, the more I am aware of my responsibility for all that I am, the more I will understand my very existence as sin, once this guilt-consciousness is brought into the orbit of the God-relationship.[29]

Despite his reputation as the melancholy Dane, Kierkegaard is not suggesting that this gloomy scenario is the last word on the human condition, for the God of whom this section of *The Sickness unto Death* speaks does not yet show the traits that make it necessary also to speak of God – and to give thanks to God – as redeemer. But Kierkegaard is not finished, and we should not stop him half-way! Although it is not as clearly profiled as the transition from psychological despair to sin, he now introduces a further and no less significant "potentiation" in the closing pages of the book. Under the heading "The Sin of Despairing of the Forgiveness of Sins (Offence)", he adds to the consciousness of God – or further qualifies the consciousness of God as – consciousness of Christ. As the bracketed term "offence" indicates, he once more has the deficient form of this consciousness in his sights, as when a person is offended by Christ and *will* not believe. But decisive for the relation to Christ, Kierkegaard believes, is that what is offered in Christ is precisely the forgiveness of sins. If we are not offended but believe, then we shall find forgiveness, and that, as should be clear, is not a matter just of being cleared of all charges in a forensic sense, but of finding the freedom to become who we are. And if, here, Kierkegaard speaks most about the ways in which we may be offended and *not* take to heart this offer, it is also clear that his descriptions of offence are intended to help us avoid being offended and believe. If at this point we reapply the "eye of God" motif discussed in Chapter 3, we might say that to know or to regard ourselves as being seen simply by the eye of God is to know or to regard ourselves as despairing, failed, sinful beings. But to know or to regard ourselves as if we were being seen with the eyes of Christ would be to know ourselves as accepted, healed, forgiven.

The model of faith arrived at thus far might seem somewhat simplistic and to expose itself too easily to the charge of wish fulfilment, as in Adorno's remark about the step from grief to comfort being the most banal of all transitions. We might think too of Lukács's sarcastic description of the philosophy of existence as "the Ash Wednesday of parasitic subjectivism".[30] Is Kierkegaard's tactic anything more than a somewhat refined version of the revivalist preacher's method of reducing his audience to a quivering mass of fearful sinners before holding out the promise of an answer to all their problems, if only they will believe and step forward? Even in a theological perspective, is he not in danger of simply defining God as the inverse image of human neediness?

The exigency of love

Before reaching such a conclusion we should also take note of a set of Kierkegaardian texts that offer a rather different take on the scenario set out in *The Sickness unto Death*. These are the discourses devoted to or referring to the story from Luke's gospel Chapter 7, in which Jesus is a guest in the house of one Simon the Pharisee. Suddenly an unnamed woman known locally as a notorious sinner bursts in and falls at his feet, anointing them with myrrh and cleaning them with her hair.[31] When the other guests object to Jesus accepting such a service from so sinful a person he retorts by contrasting her love with their coolness, stating that "her great love proves that her many sins have been forgiven" (Luke 7:47). Along with the Letter of James and the Sermon on the Mount, this is in fact one of the most frequently discussed portions of Scripture in Kierkegaard's religious writings, and he also uses 1 Peter 4:7, "Love shall cover a multitude of sins", as an opportunity to make further comments about the "sinful woman" of Luke 7. Significantly, some of the discourses in which she is the main focus are specifically linked by Kierkegaard to the pseudonym Anti-Climacus, the author of *The Sickness unto Death*.

The sinful woman makes her first appearance in the second of the three discourses of 1843 (that is, the second small set of discourses published by Kierkegaard). Here Kierkegaard rapidly sketches the scene depicted in Luke. He reminds us that:

> A woman could not be an invited guest, this one least of all, for the Pharisees knew that she was a sinner. If nothing else had been able to frighten her and hold her back, the proud contempt of the Pharisees, their silent ill-will, their holy indignation could well have scared her off. (4 74–5/EUD 75)

The woman is under accusation, but the love in her gives her the courage to force her way past her accusers to the feet of the Saviour, where, as Kierkegaard puts it, she is given "the grace, as it were, to weep herself out of herself and weep herself into love's repose" (4 75/EUD 76). However, as Kierkegaard goes on to ask, if love can thus overcome the guilt of one under accusation, does it follow that it will also overcome the accusation itself? Surely justice has its rights and will not be bribed by love. But love also has its right:

> for he who judges, has his demands, but he, who has his demands, he is seeking, and he "who hides the multitude of sins, is seeking love" (Proverbs 17:9); but he, who finds love, he hides the multitude of sins; for he who finds what he was seeking, he indeed hides what he was not seeking. (4 76/EUD 77)

And so Kierkegaard once more retells the story of Luke 7. This time the woman is shown bent over as she enters, bearing the weight of the multitude of her sins, the judgement of the Pharisees legible in their faces, so that all there was to see was a multitude of sins. Then, continues Kierkegaard:

> *love* discovered what the world was hiding – the love in her; and as this had not fully triumphed in her, the Saviour's love came to her aid ... and he made the love in her powerful enough to cover the multitude of sins, the love, that is, that was already there, for "her many sins were forgiven, because she loved much".
> (4 76–7/EUD 77, original emphasis)

When, six years later, Kierkegaard returns to this scenario in the three Friday Communion discourses included in *Without Authority*, it is with this element of the story, that "she loved much", that he starts, beginning in the opening prayer, whose introductory petition asks Christ to inflame the love in us that we might love Him much. So, too, when Kierkegaard comes to the exposition, that "she loved much" is once more the starting-point. His retelling of the story is more complex, more filled out with descriptive chiaroscuro than in the earlier discourse. The shame and indignity of the woman's status and the judgemental posture of the Pharisees is elaborated on and intensified. She has become the epitome of sin, venturing into the very presence of "the Holy". Even the festivity of the occasion is used to heighten the tension, as Kierkegaard contrasts the privacy of the Church's confessional with the public exposure of letting her sin be seen in the midst of such a festive gathering. That she should have to do this is not merely hard, it is "cruel" (14 195/WA 139). Nevertheless, she does it and, at the feet of the Lord, she enacts the impossibility of her situation, *doing* nothing, because she *is* nothing, and in thus *becoming nothing*, in entire self-forget-fulness, she becomes a "sign", "an image". Even Christ himself seems to regard her as nothing, speaking about her but not to her, as he tells Simon that her sins are forgiven:

> And it is almost as if the Saviour himself, for a moment, regarded her and the situation thus, as if she was not an actual person but an image … it is almost as if he turned her into an image, a parable – and yet that very thing was happening in the same moment right there. (14 197/WA 141)

Her self-forgetfulness and Christ's response transform her into "an image … a recollection" (14 198/WA 142), "an eternal image" (14 198/WA 142). And what is she an "eternal image", an icon, of? She is an eternal image both of the forgiveness of sins and of the "much love" that, as Kierkegaard writes here, are one and the same. This, more precisely, suggests to Kierkegaard that although it is true that all our sins are forgiven "in Christ" the truth of that forgiveness must be made true by each individual, and each individual can do that only by taking to heart the image of this woman and "loving much": "… by her great love she made herself – if I dare put it like this – necessary to the Saviour, for that there is forgiveness of sins, which he earned, is made true by her, who loved much" (14 199/WA 143). Kierkegaard's "if I dare put it like this" indicates that he very well knows he is close to or beyond the margin of what is permissible from within the framework of Protestant dogmatics, but this also underlines the importance that the sinful woman has for him. In the single *Upbuilding Discourse* of December 1850 (in WA), also devoted to her, he once more touches on the delicate question as to whether her love is somehow to be regarded as meriting forgiveness, only, in typically Kierkegaardian style, he does so obliquely. Referring back to Jesus' word that "her many sins are forgiven *because* she loved much", Kierkegaard comments that he presumes that *she* simply did not hear this word, or misheard it, believing him to have said that it was because *he* loved much that her many sins were forgiven, so that it was his own infinite love he was talking about (17 20/WA 157). In this way, Kierkegaard implies, the logic of love, seen from the inside, simply does not allow for the kind of talk about merit that has bothered dogmaticians. The question of "earning" forgiveness can only arise for those who are outside the orbit of love, for love regards itself as nothing, the Other as everything, and it could never arise in the heart of love to talk of merit on its own part. Similarly, in the first of the discourses of summer 1851 (in WA), where the text is again taken from Luke 7:47 ("To whom little is forgiven loves little"), although the woman is not directly mentioned, Kierkegaard expressly brushes aside the objection that he is making it sound as if love somehow earns forgiveness.

> Pay attention now and see how we are, though, not entering into the unhappy realm of merit, but how everything remains within love. When you love much, much is forgiven you – and when much is forgiven you, you love much. See here the blessed retroaction of salvation in love! First, you love much, and much is forgiven you – oh, look and see how love then increases; that so much has been forgiven you, this loves forth love once more, and you love much because much has been forgiven you!　　　　　(17 37/WA 176)

In the "eternal image" of the sinful woman weeping at the feet of the Lord, then, we have what is for Kierkegaard the perfect expression of such a virtuous circle of love begetting love in a movement that can also be described from the human side as coming to accept the forgiveness of sins. This, I believe, importantly qualifies the image of Kierkegaardian religious-ness as simply juxtaposing accounts of human despair, misery and so on with affirmations of divine blessedness, plenitude and so on. And we might also at this point remember the discourse that speaks of the good and perfect gifts of God the Creator *including* the impulse to will the good, an impulse now more forcefully characterized as love. The forgiveness of sins is not only the "answer" to despair, it is also the fruit of the love that we, as creatures, may have towards God. In terms of the history of ideas, we might say that the Kierkegaardian religious self is not only the possible ancestor of the philosophy of existence in both its secular and religious versions (which, in terms of its analysis of anxiety and despair, it surely is) but it also represents a line of a very distinctive form of religiousness that runs from Plato (especially the discourse on "eros" in *The Symposium*), through Augustine, through some strands of medieval mysticism and on into the present. This is a form of self-reflective religion that is not so much orientated by the question of belief and whether we can "know" what belief proposes as its object, but takes its cue from a desire for God that the question of belief presupposes and, in the contemporary version of Caputo's "religion without religion", outlives the weakening or even disappearance of belief. As in Caputo's own writings, the issue here is not so much whether belief is or isn't true but what kind of sense we can make of a desire for God we just can't help having. In words that Caputo takes from Augustine, the question around which such religiousness turns is simply: "What do I love when I love my God?"[32] Noting the important role Kierkegaard has played in Caputo's own intellectual development, I suggest that Kierkegaard himself, as a religious thinker, is more adequately understood as an expositor of the love of God than as a defender of the faith. Kierkegaardian subjectivity does not so much betoken a weakening of the objectivity of the contents of faith as signal that the tap-root of religious existence is not to be found in "faith" or "belief" at all.

Incarnation and history (again)

We might seem to have come a long way both from Lessing's question about the relationship between history and eternal happiness and from the question as to the genuineness of Hegel's Christology. We are, however, now in a position to come back to these questions and, I think, see them in a more adequate light.

We begin with Hegel. Whether or not Hegel himself actually believed or in any way asserted that the individual human being, Jesus of Nazareth, was God Incarnate, he does seem to have espoused the idea that a singular individual would need to have existed as the decisive moment in which the identity of the divine and the human was revealed to humankind. His starting-point was, clearly, not the historical records about Jesus, as if we were faced with this individual person and then, somehow, had to make sense of who he really was. Rather, his starting-point was his account of reason or Spirit, and the question as to what it would take for human beings to come into their own as regards existing as Spirit-in-the-world. Kierkegaard, plainly, sought to distance himself both from Right and Left versions of speculative Christology. Nevertheless, he shared one important trait with them all, namely, that he too did not begin with the historical reports and then try to see if some sort of revelation could be derived from them. He consistently avoids entering into the classical debating points that cluster around the historical claims of the text, and is especially reticent about the question of miracles. Like the Hegelians, Kierkegaard approached the question of Christology with a certain apriority. But where the Hegelian apriority concerned the needs of reason, Kierkegaard's apriority is constructed as a complex psychological modelling of the self, its divisions, its needs and its human and immortal longings for a fuller love than its immediately given human situation allows. Yet for Kierkegaard as for Hegel, the historical revelation of Jesus Christ is made understandable as the "answer" to a specific human question or complex of questions.

Does this make Kierkegaard's Christology "reasonable" and rob it of its abrasive edge, its "scandal"? Not entirely. In the first instance the model of the self that frames the Christological answer is not one in which "reason" plays the leading part. But the issue is not simply that of the substitution of a volitional for an intellectual model, since what Kierkegaard typically has in view is the repeated failure of the will, or, more precisely, the inner complexity of the will in which we choose, despairingly, not to be what we could be and yet never quite extinguish the counter-movement of love towards God and other human beings. It is a model that is relational, fractured and ambiguous. Even so, we might say, if it is not "reasonable" in a narrow sense, this model is – and must be – humanly understandable, for it is a modelling of who we ourselves are. How could we not understand it? And, rhetoric apart, what is there in this model that a non-Christian could not accept? Even if Christ is spoken of, it would seem that he does not need to be more than a symbol for the hope that keeps us from sinking down into despair and reanimates us in the quest for true selfhood and true love. In the early 1980s Cupitt claimed Kierkegaard as a forerunner of his own non-realist view of faith, according to which religious claims are not actually claims about existing states of affairs but about human aims and values. Cupitt himself focused on Kierkegaardian decisionism as characteristic of this early form of non-realism, seeing in it the substitution of radical human subjectivity for the objectivity of traditional dogma.[33] We have now seen that Kierkegaard's view of the self was more complex than that, and the idea of self-choice must also be balanced by other elements, such as the aspiration of love. Yet, up to this point in the argument, Cupitt seems right in this: what would move us to accept or reject Kierkegaard's account is not, in the first instance, its dogmatic content, but whether we find it offers a persuasive or adequate depiction of the human condition. Like Feuerbach, Kierkegaard seems to have transformed theology into anthropology. Yet his is a very different anthropology from that of materialist reductionism, for Kierkegaard's anthropology does not demand the conclusion that all religious concepts are "nothing but" misplaced materially explicable drives and needs; rather, he concludes that what is the very best in us is being able to be grateful and to speak the word of love that both answers to the divine gift and yet, in complete reciprocity, itself calls forth that same gift, making it actual. At this point anthropology itself does become inseparable from theology, but in such a way as to deflect the possibility of any direct reduction of the one to the other.

But there is a further step that Kierkegaard makes and that he makes in step with the main current of Christian doctrine. Here we come back to Lessing, and to the questions posed on the title page of *Philosophical Fragments*. Kierkegaard does seem to claim that all that he says about Christ was, in fact, uniquely found in the person, life, ministry and death of the historical individual Jesus of Nazareth. If we need the anthropological question to help us make sense of the historical record, the anthropological question does at one point touch base on historical ground. It is not the Christ-idea that Kierkegaard proclaims, but, specifically, *Jesus* Christ. On this point it seems clear that no amount of psychological preparation can itself provide grounds for making such a claim. It cannot be *proved* that all that faith looks for in Christ was, in fact, found in Jesus of Nazareth. Kierkegaard certainly offers many examples of how the story of Jesus found in the gospels fits what we would expect from a redeemer, but, not least because there was, by the nineteenth century, also the question as to textual reliability, there remains an edge of uncertainty. In this situation, the claim of faith does, finally, involve a leap. And what is this leap? It is, at its simplest, the act of judgement that *this singular man* is the one of whom it can be said, "in him our sins are forgiven".

Putting it like this moves the focus away from what is often to the fore in discussions of the Kierkegaardian "leap of faith", namely the paradoxical and absurd *content* of the Christian claim. That Kierkegaard himself emphasizes these elements in texts such as the *Philosophical Fragments* cannot be denied. However, as I have attempted to show, if we read Kierkegaard *as a whole* he does in fact create a context in which the Christian claims are meaningful, if not reasonable. In a trajectory whose coordinates are derived from the promptings of love, we can know what the point of believing in Christ would be, whether or not we find ourselves able to do so.

But, positively, this way of approaching the "leap of faith"[34] opens up links to other comments Kierkegaard makes about the category of leap. At several points he explicitly identifies it with the Aristotelian category of *kinesis* and, as such, with the transition from possibility to actuality. In these terms, then, the leap of faith is precisely the step from allowing ourselves to consider the meaning of Christ in the medium of imagination or possibility to actually affirming that "Yes, this is so." And, as the whole thrust of Kierkegaard's argument suggests, that also means saying of the imaginative depiction of the self in its manifold permutations that "Yes, this is me." To accept Christianity is not to accept nonsense or to believe six impossible things before breakfast; it is to follow through on a movement of desire that, in the judgement concerning Christ, becomes the commitment to a particular life-view that then serves as the basis for one's self-understanding and action. Kierkegaard's manifold psychological analyses may not fill in all the contours of this life-view, but they help us to see why we might be motivated to accept it and how he, at least, understands its overall shape.[35]

Implications and questions

If we have been able to track a course from Kierkegaard's anthropology through his theology of creation and so arrive at his vision of faith in Christ, the very continuity we have called upon brings with it a new problem. For if Kierkegaard's view of the self is teleologically dependent on its culmination in the relation to Christ, what happens to the self when the prospect of such a relation is no longer available? Surely the conclusion or lack of conclusion must retroactively affect every part of the whole construction of the self in Kierkegaard. If I do not have a Kierkegaardian faith in Christ, then maybe I will never be able fully to transform my anxiety into hope and joy, as he counsels. But, then again, if I do not have a Kierkegaardian faith in God in the first place, what might motivate me even to become anxious? For if what is at issue in our lives is not an eternal happiness (or, it may be, an eternal damnation), then, as Kierkegaard himself acknowledges, everything is going to appear very differently from a life in which that is, precisely, the issue.

Clearly, there are still many Christian believers in the world today. But, unlike academic philosophy in Kierkegaard's time, contemporary philosophy is largely pursued in essentially secular environments and under essentially secular conditions. The same remark could be extended to cultural life in general. And both in philosophy and in culture, we might well wonder just how much of the Christian view of the human condition can survive in the absence of its background in a consensual faith. The story often seems to go something like this: the generation who were intellectually active from the end of the Second World War through to the 1970s had already, largely, left Christianity behind, yet they retained both a broad knowledge of what Christianity itself had been and had internalized something of the moral passion of Christian belief; today, however, a younger intellectual generation is largely ignorant of even the most basic aspects of Christian doctrine, and has lost its collective memory for the kind of moral passion that even a secular existentialism was able to call upon. Whereas Nietzsche, with reference to a supposed footprint of the Buddha still to be seen in a cave in

167

India, warned that gods can outlive their deaths by many generations,[36] the half-life of Christianity in secular culture seems to be much shorter than anticipated.

But although many contemporary philosophers do not feel even the remotest need of God, it does not follow that they are incapable of conceiving what a life lived in the restless pursuit of God might look like, nor does it follow that they are incapable of considering whether there are aspects of such a life that might be humanly valuable, even when the faith that clinches it all has gone missing. Something like this was the case with the philosophy of "as if", derived from Kant. On this view we could still live in the world "as if" God existed and "as if" there were a moral world-order in which the pursuit of the Good belonged to the very structure of the world itself. I have attempted to show some of the ways in which Kierkegaard's picture of the life of the self, its self-development and its loving involvement with others, is more complex than that of Kant, although there are clearly Kantian impulses in it. Something similar to the philosophy of "as if" seems to be being suggested in Cupitt's non-realist reading of Kierkegaard. But how far we might be able to live "as if" Kierkegaardian selfhood were a real option without Kierkegaardian faith is hard to say. "Why pour so much energy into a project so palpably doomed to failure?", a critic might ask. One answer might be that it is precisely a project that gives a dignity and a value to the self and its commitments that can scarcely be paralleled in many of the secular alternatives. To live life in a Kierkegaardian way would be at least to live life seriously or, as he puts it, earnestly. As such, it might offer a means of living life less boringly or, at least, of finding it less boring. But, even if we found earnestness to be an attractive human value in itself (and, clearly, not everybody does – some claim to prefer boredom), it would still seem to be hard for such an "as if" approach to engender the same quality of earnestness as a life based on a traditional realistic belief in God. It would, at best, be a weakened earnestness. Similarly, the motivations it provided for us to love our neighbours in the Kierkegaardian way would also be weakened. We would be trying to live like that because we thought it good or admirable to live like that, not because we thought living like that was the best way of responding to the way things are. And how, within the horizons of a non-realist interpretation, could we be grateful to God for all that we have and are?

A further question now insinuates itself, a question that might be regarded as going much further than that of our psychological ability to live by Kierkegaardian values if we do not have Kierkegaardian beliefs. For this whole way of connecting beliefs and values seems to depend on a set of assumptions that belong to what Heidegger called onto-theology. According to Heidegger, the fact that the values by which we live find or strive to find legitimacy in the way things are, in Being and, finally, in God, understood as the Supreme Being, is a symptom of our having long since stepped outside the original radiance of truth-as-unconcealment and reduced our fundamental philosophical and moral commitments and beliefs to the level of utility. Whether it is a matter of calling on "Being" to provide back-up for values, or whether it is values and the moral life that are used to put into effect the demands of "Being", we have reduced what should be the matter of internal and prereflective responsiveness to a case of explanation and application. In this case, it is largely indifferent whether we are able to affirm a Kierkegaardian ontology as the basis of a Kierkegaardian lifestyle or not, for both the ontology and the lifestyle are, separately and/or together, reifications of an original possibility that has been lost or, at least, eclipsed. And Heidegger seems to have been clear in his own mind that Kierkegaard himself *did* remain trapped within the horizons of onto-theology. Indeed, he says explicitly that for all the violence of his attack on Hegel, Kierkegaard remained essentially bound to the horizons of Hegelian metaphysics.[37] Kierkegaardian faith in God is obviously not the same as Hegelian faith in reason, but in each case faith serves to ground, to justify, and, in short, to give *a reason* for holding to particular intellectual and moral commitments. Life is justified by what transcends life rather than by what simply shows itself in life, as life, as the flow of Being-in-beings.

Has Heidegger read Kierkegaard correctly at this point? Is Kierkegaardian faith something like an external buttress that, once removed, will inevitably leave what it has supported to totter and eventually to fall? Or are there aspects of Kierkegaard that are not contained within the horizons of Hegelian metaphysics (assuming Heidegger to have correctly identified these with onto-theology), and that might therefore offer another way of relating to the issues of faith and the good life than those rendered impassable by the critique of onto-theology?[38] These questions, I suggest, return us to a theme that we have already considered in another context, namely Kierkegaard's concern with the whole question of communication.

We have seen how the exigencies of moral communication moved Kierkegaard to develop a strategy of indirect communication – the "art" of ethical and ethico-religious communication – that would maieutically lead the learner to take responsibility, in freedom, for his or her own moral existence. The theological reflections of this present chapter both extend but also problematize this model, for what is to be communicated in radical Christian communication is not merely a communication concerning the self's own innate freedom but rather the self's dependence on Christ as a condition of being able to become what, according to the order of creation, it potentially is. Yet Christ himself is construed in terms of absolute paradox and the sign of contradiction. What now needs to be communicated to the anxious, expectant self is therefore something that exceeds all its possibilities of comprehension and expectation. Nevertheless, if the interpretation of Kierkegaard's own religious discourses – and especially the discourses concerning the sinful woman – is correct, then even this communicative event will be susceptible of being related to the impulse to love that Kierkegaard appears to regard as characteristic even of fallen human existence. But if, in this way, the horizon for the communication of Christ to human beings is formed solely by the incalculable exigency of love, then we would seem to be in a very different domain from that in which – as in the onto-theological discourse described by Heidegger – the God-relationship is set up as a matter of correct knowledge. Even less could it be a matter of such knowledge being predetermined to serve the interests of an absolute collective subjectivity set upon a command and control mission *vis-à-vis* its environment, which, according to Westphal, is what Heidegger perceives as the defining trait of onto-theology.[39]

But how, then, could such a communication take effect? One obvious answer would be that it might have the form of poetry, since poetry, as is well known, has a particular affinity with love. This seems promising, in that Kierkegaard too spoke of himself as a "poet of the religious", although his negative comments about the poet should alert us to the fact that any "poet of the religious" who really serves the cause of radical Christian communication will do so in a manner very different from that of any more usual poet. His will necessarily be a broken poetry, a poetry of indirections, hints, and fragments, a poetry that reflects the paradox and inner contradiction of its subject-matter. In fact, such a poet may well turn out to resemble the poet whom Heidegger regarded as supremely prophetic of the situation of post-metaphysical thinking: Friedrich Hölderlin.

As interpreted by Heidegger, Hölderlin's figuration of the destiny of a poet "in barren times" bears many of the marks of Kierkegaard's Christ: he too mediates between gods and mortals; his word is a summons to worship, to the festal union of divine and human that – as festal – is both historical, in time, yet never absorbed into the flow of secular history. Such a poetic word will, in expressions of Hölderlin's that are crucial for Heidegger's interpretation, necessarily appear as a "riddle" or an "uninterpreted sign". And, like Kierkegaard's "religious poet", Hölderlin himself can only bear the word of the gods as one who himself participates in the fate of the West, a fate in which the experience of the absence of God is a dominant moment, and which therefore calls for memory, faith and hope as the media within which the God-relationship will take place, as opposed to the Early Romantic aspiration to rediscover the divine in human creativity itself. In Heidegger's key term "*Ereignis*", the poetic word is interpreted both as an event, a happening or fate that befalls the speaker or thinker, and, simultaneously, as the act in which that event is appropriated or made one's own in language and thought. But this dynamic circularity is also what Kierkegaard seems to have in view in his account of the communication of forgiveness to the one who, in love, knows themselves to be loved by Christ. And to think in terms of Kierkegaard's idea of Christian communication of Heidegger's poetic *"Ereignis"* allows, as Cupitt's non-realist interpretation does not, a legitimate place both for the element of receptivity and for the Other-directedness of gratitude and praise.

We seem to be moving rapidly away from philosophy in any conventional sense, although if we are following Heidegger's move into a postmetaphysical way of thinking, then it is inevitable that whatever we say will probably have to take a form very different from any of the forms in which the philosophy of the last two-and-a-half thousand years has generated. Yet if, as I am suggesting, there is a significant affinity between the Heideggerian poet and Kierkegaard's conception of Christ as the communicative event of the divine presence, then that would also suggest that whatever form of theology there might be in Kierkegaard would be a theology with very different presuppositions and methods from the theology criticized by Heidegger as onto-theology.[40] All of which might, of course, merely compound the suspicion of many philosophers that what we are being offered by Kierkegaard (and, for that matter by Heidegger) is not philosophy at all but a kind of quasi-philosophical religiously toned poetry; that, far from being presented with respectable philosophical arguments, we are being targeted as the potential victims of a kind of intellectual seduction; that we are being moved rather than persuaded and being offered rhetoric rather than thought.

If this is the price to be paid, are we really willing to settle for there being no analogy to Kierkegaard's peculiar authorial strategy in the entire preceding history of philosophy? Is philosophy today to have him only on the terms of his being read as a post-onto-theological poet? For his part, Kierkegaard identified one important intellectual progenitor who was crucial not only to his own project but to the whole history of philosophy in the West: Socrates. It is therefore to Kierkegaard's view of Socrates and the implications of this for his own philosophical profile that we now, in conclusion, turn.

The Christian witness and the simple wise man of ancient times

In the very last of his works written for publication during his lifetime, the tenth number of the polemical pamphlet series called *The Moment* and dated September 1855, just weeks before his death, Kierkegaard made the following declaration: "The only analogy I have for what I am doing is Socrates. My task is the Socratic task of revising the definition of what it means to be a Christian. Therefore I do not call myself a Christian (keeping the ideal free), but I can make it plain that nobody else is either" (19 319/M 341). Both the content of this remark and its position in Kierkegaard's authorship – the last full-stop, as it were – give to it a singular pathos. But it was not just at the end of his life that Kierkegaard realized how important Socrates was to him. On the contrary, Socrates had been there from the beginning. Kierkegaard's Magister's dissertation of 1841 bore the title *The Concept of Irony, with Constant Reference to Socrates,* and Socrates would later play a conspicuous part in such key pseudonymous works as *Philosophical Fragments* (1844) and *The Sickness unto Death* (1849). Even in the more exclusively religious writings, Socrates makes regular appearances, often under the transparent incognito of "a simple wise man of ancient times". Kierkegaard's relation to Socrates was therefore both complex and varied. It was complicated further by the way in which his interpretation of Socrates was entangled both with his negative relation to Hegel and his positive evaluation of predecessors such as Hamann and Lessing. Socrates could thus variously serve Kierkegaard as the subject of a fairly conventional academic study, as a model for his own authorship, as a counter-instance to Hegel and to the Hegelian way of doing philosophy, and even as foreshadowing the essential features of a genuine witness to Christ. An introductory study such as this is not the place to go into the detail of Kierkegaard's reading of Socrates, but we both can and should see how, even in his own most violent polemics against philosophy and even in his most religious passages, Kierkegaard sought orientation from one who undeniably does belong at the core of Western philosophy itself.

It is clearly promising from Kierkegaard's point of view that there seems to be something in Socrates that is deeply alien to Hegel and Hegelianism. Even if it is conceded that there is some sort of thin conceptual continuum between the Socratic dawn of philosophy and its Hegelian zenith, Socrates' manner of relating himself to what he knows or doesn't know differs, to borrow a phrase used by Feuerbach to similar purpose, *toto caelo* from that of Hegel. Even in the texts where Socrates is most strongly distinguished from Christianity, Kierkegaard speaks of him in a way that is quite different from the way in which he speaks of Hegel and many other contemporary opponents. It is not just a matter of a kind of tenderness, fascination and even love on Kierkegaard's part but also what he claims is a difference in the kind or form of Socratic thought itself when compared with modern versions of philosophy. In this spirit, Chapter 2 of *Philosophical Fragments* opens with a eulogy over Socrates that could almost be compared with the well-known eulogy over Abraham from *Fear and Trembling*. Socrates' teaching activity, we are told, was no mere outward employment; it was a response to an inner demand no less than to demands from others, "as much autopathic as sympathetic", as Climacus puts it. To which he adds:

> That was how Socrates also understood it, and that is why he would not accept honours or distinguished positions or money for his teaching, since his judgement was as incorruptible as a dead man's. O, rare modesty, rare in our time, in which money and laurels cannot be great or glorious enough to repay the dignity of the teacher, yet in which all the gold and all the honours in the world are indeed the reward for teaching, since they are of equal worth. But our time has the positive and understands itself in the light of that. Socrates, on the other hand, lacked the positive. But look to see if that lack explains his limitations. These were in fact rooted in his zeal for the human, so that he disciplined himself with the same divine jealousy with which he disciplined others and in which he loved the divine.
>
> (6 26/ PF 23)

Growing ever more rhapsodical, Climacus finally imagines himself coming into Socrates' presence:

> And if I was a Plato in enthusiasm, and if my heart beat more loudly than Alcibiades', more than the Corybantes', when I heard Socrates, and if the passion of my admiration could not be satisfied without embracing that noble man, then Socrates would in a likelihood smile at me and say, "My dear boy, you are a treacherous lover, for

173

you are wanting to idolise me on account of my wisdom so that you would then be the one who understood me best, and be the one from whose admiring embrace I would not be able to tear myself free: are you not a seducer?" And if I did not understand him, then his cold irony would bring me to despair, as he explained to me how he owed me just as much as I owed him ... O, rare faithfulness, which seduces nobody, not even the one who uses all the arts of seduction to be seduced!   (6 27/PF 24)

This, incidentally, marks a clear shift from *The Concept of Irony,* where Kierkegaard had portrayed Socrates not merely as a seducer but as a vampire, draining his "students" of the substantial values in which they had been brought up. Now, however, Socrates is characterized by a "rare" integrity that relates not only to his indifference to worldly honours, but also to the emotional dynamics of his relation to his students. He *will* not become their beloved or their lover, because to do so would be to deprive them of the freedom in which alone they can come to realize the implicit self-knowledge that they already have. And note also that in this passage Socrates' motive is described not so much as a love of "truth" in some sort of abstract sense. It is "the human" (and quite specifically not "humanity") for which he is zealous, both in himself and in others. This is a teacher whose very inhumanity is the incognito of his humanity.[1]

It is no surprise that contemporary philosophers fare badly in comparison with Socrates. Thus, in the introduction to *Philosophical Fragments* itself, Kierkegaard speaks of "the higher lunacy's raving insanity, whose symptom is raving, convulsive raving, and the contents of this raving are the words: era, epoch, era and epoch, the system ..." (6 10/PF 6), a line of satire over some of his contemporaries' fad-like obsession with every new idea from Germany that is already found in an unfinished farce that Kierkegaard wrote as a student. Such mockery is continued in *The Concluding Unscientific Postscript* where, as elsewhere, Hegelians are the chief but not the only targets. The key features of Kierkegaard's complaints (over and above his objections to the *content* of their arguments) are implicit in what has already been quoted, but it is worth repeating them, because they offer a point-by-point contrast to the opposing virtues of Socratic philosophizing. The contemporary philosopher, then, is noisy, fond of acclamation and publicity. He believes that the truth of his ideas is proved by the fact that the present age is ready to honour them (or, rather, to honour him for having them). But this is not just a matter of simple popularity-seeking. Something more serious is going on. The real problem is that such purported philosophers believe they have guarantees for their own place in history and they believe this because they also believe they have what Kierkegaard calls a "world-historical perspective": a view of the whole that enables them not only to be spectators of history in general but also of themselves in it, thus the rhetoric of the age, the epoch, and the system. But the Socratic thinker does not have this satisfaction. *If* he does indeed have world-historical significance, then this is not something that he himself is ever able to know. Only subsequent history can decide the matter, for history is still in process and we simply do not know how the present will appear to a subsequent age. This, as Kierkegaard already pointed out in the dissertation, was the case with Socrates himself, since his undermining of the values and beliefs of the *polis* could not *at that point in time* be known to have presaged a new era of thought.

Overlooking the contingency of their historical situatedness, the speculative philosophers are also prone to overlooking the contingent reality of their own existence as individual human beings. Thus, in the *Postscript*, Kierkegaard lampoons the speculative thinker who is prepared to discuss what Christianity is but not whether there are any actual living human beings who are Christian (or who is only prepared to discuss this question in the historically general form that, for example, Denmark became a Christian country a thousand years ago and, therefore, all who have lived in Denmark since then are Christian). To which Climacus's comment is:

> As is well-known, Socrates says that if one supposes flute music then one must also suppose there to be a flautist. Consequently, if one supposes there to be such a thing as speculation, one must also suppose there to be one or more people who speculate. "And so, O valued man, O honoured speculator, to whom I may be so bold as to draw close and to speak privately: dear man! What do you think of Christianity, i.e., are you a Christian or not? The question is not whether you have gone further than it, but whether you are one ..."
>
> (9 48/CUP 51–2)

A Socrates, however, would never forget such a question, precisely because of his jealousy for the human, "the man in man", to use Bakhtin's expression.[2] Another way of stating this is to emphasize Socrates' ethical interest. Kierkegaard is thus fond of citing the story that Socrates gave up the study of the celestial bodies because it was irrelevant to the ethical situation of the human being (Pap VI B 40,3/JP 1607), not least in connection with the sudden enthusiasm for astronomy on the part of the Danish Hegelian J. L. Heiberg, an epitome of Hegelianism's ethical absent-mindedness.

The difference in style between the Hegelian/modern and the Socratic/Greek styles of philosophizing is becoming clear. Two points only need to be added. The first is that, with the exception of *The Concept of Irony*, the Socratic is always depicted by Kierkegaard as proceeding with a light touch, with an irony that is no longer vampiric but delicately humorous even when, maybe especially when, it is the heaviest of points at issue. The second is that, unlike the modern philosopher whose appetite for compendious overviews is insatiable, Socrates first stops to distinguish between what he knows and what he does not. So, in Kierkegaard's journals at least, Socrates and Hegel are brought to a head-to-head confrontation:

> The Dialectic of the Beginning
> Scene: The Underworld
> Persons: Socrates, Hegel
> Socr. is sitting by a running stream and listening to it in the cool air. Hegel is sitting at a table and reading Trendelenburg's *Logische Untersuchungen*, Part II, p. 198. He goes over to Socrates to complain.
> Socr. Should we begin by being altogether in disagreement, or should we agree on something we could call a presupposition.
> H. ...
> Socr. What do you presuppose as your starting-point?
> H. Nothing at all.
> Socr. That's quite something! So perhaps you don't start at all?
> H. I not start, I who have written 21 volumes.
> Socr. Ye gods! What a hecatomb you have offered.
> H. But I start from nothing.
> S. Is that not from something?
> H. No – on the contrary. That first makes its appearance in the conclusion of the whole, in the course of which I discuss science, world history, etc.
> Socr. How might I be able to master this difficult task for many remarkable things may well be included which would show up my stupidity. (the misuse of the rhetorical moment.) You know that I did not even allow Polos to talk for more than 5 minutes at a time, and you want to talk XXI volumes.
> (Pap VI A 145/JP 3306)

But Socrates not only offers Kierkegaard a model of exemplary philosophical style, he also has much to teach the modern theologians. In the very pages of *The Sickness unto Death* where he distinguishes between the Socratic and the Christian views of sin, Anti-Climacus (who plainly speaks for Kierkegaard here) breaks off to lament:

> Socrates, Socrates, Socrates! Oh yes, one might well call upon your name three times, nor would it be excessive to call upon it ten times

if it would help at all. People think that what the world needs is a republic and people think they need a new social order and a new religion, but nobody thinks that it is a Socrates that just this particular world that is so confused by too much knowledge needs.

(15 144–5/SUD 92)

It is not only because of the deceptive world-historical horizons of the Hegelians that we need a Socrates. Christianity itself needs such a one. This is partly because Christianity itself has been caught up in the general excitement about new eras and world history, but the problems go deeper. In a late journal entry, Kierkegaard contrasts Bernard of Clairvaux preaching crusades to the assembled thousands, thereby making the cross into a "cause", with Socrates, who worked in the opposite direction, breaking the crowd down into its constituent individuals. In this at least, Kierkegaard comments, "there is more Christianity in the Socratic approach than in that of Saint Bernard" (Pap X 5 A 133/JP 4295). If we know that Kierkegaard also described his own authorship as an attempt to detach the individual from the crowd, we can begin to see how he might have found in Socrates a prototype for his own work. The role of the Socratic in relation to Christianity is not simply negative, however. Already in *Philosophical Fragments,* Climacus declares that "between one human being and another" the Socratic way of relating teacher and learner is, in fact, the highest. Socrates thus becomes the model of the Christian pedagogue.

It is true that in relation to the situation of sin, only a God can give us the capacity for learning the truth. But this is to be taken quite literally, in that *no* one human being can presume to speak on behalf of God for another. At some points, it is true, Kierkegaard does invoke the concept of apostolic authority as the basis of Christian claims. In such cases, the apostle or priest, although also a human being, speaks in, with and under the paradoxical-transcendent determinations of divine communication itself. Even here, however, Kierkegaard emphasizes that this authority has nothing to do with those qualities that distinguish one human being from another: intelligence, sensitivity, courage and so on. Simply as a human being the apostle is as fallible as the rest of us. However, it is a moot point as to whether Kierkegaard actually believed that there was anyone still living who could claim such apostolic authority. There were plenty of ordained clergy in Denmark, of course, but given Kierkegaard's own stated view that the Christianity of the New Testament no longer existed in the Church, it is hard to see that he could consistently have conceded such apostolic authority to them.

Putting the question of the apostle to one side, the point that as between one human being and another the Socratic is the "highest" relationship we can achieve is made many times by Kierkegaard. It was, for example, central to the unfinished drafts of a series of proposed lectures on the subject of "the dialectics of communication" that we examined in Chapter 3. Here we saw how the Socratic model of communication was not only polemically distinguished from the school philosophy of speculation, but also identified as the model for all genuinely ethical communication and, therewith, the religious development of ethical communication.

The exponent of the art of Socratic ethical communication, Kierkegaard says, will be an ironist, in whom irony is "the highest seriousness":

> Seriousness lies in this: that I, as an individual relate myself to God and so to every human being – People stupidly believe that it is seriousness to have a lot of followers who would be willing if necessary to die for one. Stupidity. To help a human being as an individual to relate himself to God is seriousness. But this can only be done indirectly, since otherwise I become a hindrance to the one who is to be helped.   (Pap VIII 1 B 81 8, 23/JP 649: 274)

In the midst of Christianity's own attempt to communicate its message about the individual's God-relationship, there is thus a repetition of the basic pattern of Socratic communication. The Socratic and Christian teacher cannot *give* faith to the learner, since that remains the prerogative of God, but, Kierkegaard seems to be suggesting, he can do a number of things that are relevant to the individual's acquisition of faith: he can show the hollowness of presumptive but false forms of faith, he can help the learner to become aware of his own desire for faith, and he can draw the learner's attention to the common human situation in which the issue of faith is a matter of mutual responsibility.

Once more the issue is not simply faith: it is also one of love. The irony – Kierkegaard even speaks of the "ataraxy" (Pap VIII 1 B 81 8,24/JP 649: 274) – of the Socratic communicator is the incognito of a love that has as its goal the furtherance of the other's best interest: to realize and to be sustained in his God-relationship. Or, to put it another way, the goal of such maieutic pedagogy is to help the learner to realize that God is love and that God is love in the quite definite sense of seeking and wanting a relationship of love with the learner in his utterly individual contingency.

In the last of the meditations gathered under the title *Works of Love*, Kierkegaard (writing now in his own name) comes to the topic "The Work of Love in Praising Love". This meditation is, I suggest, crucial to the strategy of the whole work. After all, we shall only want to have love for ourselves or to practice it in relation to others if we believe that it is worth having and doing. To praise love is to give the reasons why love is to be sought and cultivated at all. It is to bear witness to love and, in the context of what is now a directly Christian text, it is to bear witness in faithful suffering to the love of God in Christ.

Kierkegaard proceeds by setting out a number of conditions that apply to anyone who is to undertake such a task. The first is that it must be done in self-denial. This sounds suitably "Christian" enough. However, Kierkegaard immediately glosses this assertion with the following comment: "If praising love is to be beneficial, one must be able to hold out over a long period in thinking one single thought" (12 343/WL 360). The thinker of such a single thought will be one who is not distracted by the multiplicity of externalities but who directs his thought inwards, "in self-deepening, so that one might discover the things that concern one's inner state, and such discovery is in the first instance very humbling" (12 344/WL 361). The resonances with what Kierkegaard has said about the Socratic thinker's concern with "the man in man" are scarcely mistakable. Nor should we imagine such a thinker's humility as being far from the Socratic spirit of the saying referred to in *Philosophical Fragments,* when Socrates declared that when he turned to examine his inner self he became bewildered and could not tell if he was a man or a monster (6 38/PF 39). The practice of thinking a single thought will train the one who is to praise love in self-denial.

But self-denial must be complemented by what Kierkegaard calls "sacrificial disinterestedness". If this can be seen as an intensification of the spirit of self-denial, it also involves attention to the situation that:

> Truth must essentially be regarded as in conflict with the world. The world has never been so good and never will become so good, that the majority will the truth or have a true idea as to what truth is, as would be required if proclaiming the truth were to meet with all-round applause.   (12 349/WL 366)

The apostle Paul is cited as an example of such sacrificial disinterestedness. But then Kierkegaard launches into a familiar lament about the present time, its absorption in the merely momentary, its conceit regarding its own discovery and possession of the truth. "Ah!" he cries out in the middle of this lament, "the time of thinkers seems to be past!" (12 350/WL 368). Note that, surprisingly, he does not say the time of "apostles" or "martyrs" or "saints", but of "thinkers" and, I suggest, it is almost invariably Socrates who provides Kierkegaard with the model of what a *thinker,* in the strongest sense of the term, should be. And, in case we are in doubt, Kierkegaard himself proceeds to draw the analogy.

> It is just as it was in the time of Socrates, in accordance with the statement of the prosecutor that "Everybody understood what was re-

quired for educating the young, there was only one who did not understand and that was Socrates". So too in our time "everybody" is wise and only here and there is there a single one who is a fool. The world is so near to having reached perfection that "everybody" is now wise, and if it wasn't for these individual weirdoes and fools, then the world would be completely perfect. (12 351/WL 368–9)

Irony, of course. While people rush around noisily admiring each other, God sits and waits in heaven, unsought and unseen.

At this point Kierkegaard places a third requirement on the one who seeks to praise God in this situation of confusion: so confused is the age that he must conceal his own role as teacher and, instead of revealing the love that motivates him, give himself out to be selfish and also depict the object of love in terms that make it appear unloving and unlovable. In case we do not immediately see why this has to be so, Kierkegaard once more appeals to the example of Socrates. It was precisely Socrates' distinction of being the ugliest man in Greece that made him the one best qualified to talk about the beautiful, since whatever he said in praise of beauty could not possibly be mistaken as a form of covert self-praise. "I think," says Kierkegaard:

> that if he had had only a beautiful nose (which he did not have, something especially conspicuous amongst the Greeks who all had beautiful noses), then he would not have spoken a single word about loving beauty. This would have been contrary to his idea, since he would have been afraid that some might think he was talking about himself or at least about his beautiful nose.
>
> (12 354/ WL 372)

So too in Christianity, what we are to love is not what we find immediately attractive or appealing, but the "neighbour", that is, the person whose only claim on us is our common humanity.

Kierkegaard's theme is Christ, and the Christian witness to the love of God revealing itself to the world in Christ. But there is an implicit reference throughout this meditation to Socrates, the one who having once seen the sun that shines in the world outside the cave, voluntarily re-entered it in order to incite others also to seek their freedom from the bonds of their collective delusions but, in doing so, exposes himself to misunderstanding, mockery and, finally, death.

But the Christian communicator who seeks to take Socrates as a model must, after all, confront the fact that he lives in a situation very different from that of Socrates. Of course, human beings remain as prone as they ever did to self-deception, to vanity and to the easy life of the crowd rather than shouldering the hard labour of individual responsibility. That is precisely why we need a Socrates. Nevertheless there are cultural changes that would make a modern Socrates very different in a number of respects from the historical original. It is possible that Kierkegaard understood his own famous practice of walking the streets of Copenhagen and engaging in conversation anyone who was willing to be cross-examined by him as an attempt more or less literally to emulate the practice of his beloved Socrates. However, this is ultimately a subordinate theme, as least as concerns the authorship itself, for the question that the authorship confronts us with is whether a *writer* could be a Socrates. Can *writing* ever be Socratic? Isn't the whole point of Socrates' way of questioning tied up with his immediate personal presence among his interlocutors? How can a book re-enact or set in motion anything like an analogue of a genuine Socratic dialogue?[3]

I have examined elsewhere some of the many ways in which Kierkegaard tries to address these questions in his literary work and to construct texts that not merely reproduce a dialogue but that set in motion a dialogue in which the reader is fully participant.[4] All I wish to add here is that Kierkegaard did not imagine himself to be the first in the field. One inspiration was J. G. Hamann, a thinker of what has been called the counter-Enlightenment, in whose *Sokratische Denkwürdigkeiten* [*Socratic Memorabilia*] Kierkegaard found a model for his own ironic and humorous mixture of flippancy and ultimate concern. He makes a clear statement as to the links he sees between Socrates, Hamann and his own project when, in words echoing what we have just read from *Works of Love*, he prefaces *The Concept of Anxiety* with the following lines, printed between the title page and the dedication:

> The age of distinction is past, the system has overwhelmed it. Whoever loves such a thing is a weirdo whose soul cleaves to something long vanished. Be that as it may, *Socrates* still remains what he was, the simple wise man with his remarkable distinction which he himself spoke of and perfected, and which only the rare *Hamann* admiringly repeated two thousand years later: "For Socrates was great in this . . . that he distinguished between what he understood and what he didn't understand." (6 102/CA 3, original emphasis)

But Hamann was not, I think, the only recent figure who offered Kierkegaard a model for a modern, literary Socrates. Also from the eighteenth century was Lessing, to whom Kierkegaard dedicates a eulogy in the course of the *Postscript*. In the course of this we find some comments about Lessing's literary style which, if we cannot say were always perfectly exemplified in Kierkegaard's own writing, provided him with an example of how a Socratic *writer* might aspire to write.

And now his style! This polemical tone, which in every moment has all the time in the world for a joke, and this in an age of ferment (for according to an old newspaper I found this was just like our own time in being an age of ferment the like of which the world had never seen). This easy-going stylistic manner, which executes a simile down to the finest detail, as if the exposition itself really mattered, as if all was peaceful and secure, perhaps despite all the printers' lads and the history of the world that everyone was expecting him to get finished. This scholarly casualness, that won't obey the norms of systematic paragraphs. This mixture of jest and seriousness, which makes it impossible for a third party to know for certain which is which – which is as it should be since the third party should know this for himself. This cunning, which might even sometimes have placed a false emphasis on what is indifferent, so that the person who understands might precisely thereby grasp what is dialectically decisive, whilst the heretics won't get anything to run away with. This manner of setting the matter forth, which entirely belongs to him individually, freshly and refreshingly making its own way and not exhaling a mosaic of catchwords and authorised tropes and contemporary expressions whose quotation marks betray the fact that the writer is in hock to the age, whereas Lessing *sub rosa* lets one know that he is following the thought. This shrewd manner of teasingly using his own "I", almost like Socrates, excusing himself from society or, rather, securing himself against it when it is a matter of the truth . . .

(9 60–61/CUP1 69)

Socrates was, historically, a once-for-all and unrepeatable historical individual. But, as Kierkegaard looks back through the history of literature and ideas and around at his own age, he sees possibilities of repeating Socrates' essential work in a variety of cultural forms and conditions, perhaps most surprisingly but not least, the task of witnessing to the love of God amid the decay of Christendom. In that task he sees, via Lessing and Hamann, a model for his own unique calling as a Christian writer. And what, then, was that calling? In the Introduction I noted the tension between the constructive element in Kierkegaard's thought, as exemplified especially in his psychology, and the more analytical motivation that led him to reflect long and hard on the boundaries dividing the various disciplines that might be presumed to have something to say about religious faith. If this latter concern seems closer to the Socratic aspect of Kierkegaard's work, perhaps even more truly Socratic – and even more truly central to his philosophical vocation – was simply the passion for tricking, teasing or arguing his readers into thinking for themselves about the values, relationships and goals that govern their lives, and, in doing so, to strip them of the self-flattering illusions to which both the age and their own inclinations made them prone. The first proposition of Kierkegaard's Master's thesis ran: "the similarity between Christ and Socrates consists precisely in their dissimilarity". But, if Christ and Socrates can here stand for the worlds of faith and philosophy respectively, Kierkegaard's own authorship might equally suggest the reflection that the dissimilarity between faith and philosophy consists precisely in their similarity.

Notes

Introduction

1. G. W. F. Hegel, *Aesthetics: Lectures on Fine Art*, T. M. Knox (trans.) (Oxford: Oxford University Press, 1975), 9ff.
2. S. Mulhall, *Inheritance and Originality: Wittgenstein, Heidegger, Kierkegaard* (Oxford: Oxford University Press, 2001), 438.
3. J.-P. Sartre, "Kierkegaard: The Singular Universal", J. Matthews (trans.), in *Between Existentialism and Marxism*, 141–69 (London: Verso, 1983).
4. See P. Tillich, *The Courage to Be* (London: Fontana, 1962).
5. The possible analogies between Kierkegaard's and Wittgenstein's philosophical style have been especially extensively explored and discussed. See, for example, Richard H. Bell (ed.), *The Grammar of the Heart: New Essays in Moral Philosophy and Theology – Thinking with Kierkegaard and Wittgenstein* (San Francisco: Harper & Row, 1988); Charles L. Creegan, *Wittgenstein and Kierkegaard: Religion, Individuality and Philosophical Method* (London: Routledge, 1989); James Conant, "Putting Two and Two Together: Kierkegaard, Wittgenstein, and the Point of View for their Work as Authors", in *Philosophy and the Grammar of Religious Belief*, T. Tessin & Mario von der Ruhr (eds), 248–331 (New York: St Martin's Press, 1995); A. Hannay, "Solitary Souls and Infinite Help", in his *Kierkegaard and Philosophy: Selected Essays*, 179–89 (London: Routledge, 2003); M. Nientied, *Kierkegaard und Wittgenstein: "Hineintäuschen in das Wahre"* (Berlin: de Gruyter, 2003); D. Z. Phillips, "Authorship and Authenticity: Kierkegaard and Wittgenstein", in his *Wittgenstein and Religion*, 200–219 (Basingstoke: Macmillan, 1993).
6. See Hannay, "Solitary Souls and Infinite Help", 7–8.
7. See, for example, references to Kierkegaard in M. McGhee, *Transformations of Mind: Philosophy as Spiritual Practice* (Cambridge: Cambridge University Press, 2000) and in M. Weston, *Philosophy, Literature and the Human Good* (London: Routledge, 2001).
8. See, for example, G. Pattison, *"Poor Paris!": Kierkegaard's Critique of the Spectacular City* (Berlin: de Gruyter, 1998); *Kierkegaard: The Aesthetic and the Religious* (London: SCM, 1999); *Kierkegaard, Religion and the Nineteenth-Century Crisis of Culture* (Cambridge: Cambridge University Press, 2002).
9. Recent work that deals with this in new and stimulating ways includes M. J. Matuštík, *Postnational Identity: Critical Theory and Existential Philosophy in Habermas, Kierkegaard, and Havel* (London: Guildford Press, 1993) and Mark Dooley, *The Politics of Exodus: Kierkegaard's Ethics of Responsibility* (New York: Fordham University Press, 2001).

10. See J. Garff, *SAK: Søren Kierkegaard* (Chicago, IL: University of Chicago Press, 2005). My own approach to biographical issues is found in G. Pattison, *Kierkegaard and the Crisis of Faith* (London: SPCK, 1997), esp. Ch. 7, "Doctor or Patient?". Also Pattison, *Kierkegaard's Upbuilding Discourses: Philosophy, Literature, Theology* (London: Routledge, 2002), esp. Ch. 7, "Building on Love's Ruins".
11. The view that we should always respect the pseudonym has been most forcefully expressed in recent years by the late Roger Poole, as in his paper "'My Wish, My Prayer': Keeping the Pseudonyms Apart. Preliminary Considerations", in *Kierkegaard Revisited*, N.-J. Cappelørn & J. Stewart (eds), 156–76 (Berlin: de Gruyter, 1997).

Chapter 1: Existence

1. Heidegger, it should be said, was well aware that Brock was Jewish, although, paradoxically, he seems to have used the smear of Jewish associations to sideline the main alternative candidate for the post. See H. Ott, *Martin Heidegger: A Political Life*, A. Blunden (trans.) (London: Collins, 1994), 190.
2. W. Brock, *An Introduction to German Philosophy* (Cambridge: Cambridge University Press, 1935), 120.
3. *Ibid.*, 117.
4. *Ibid.*, 73.
5. *Ibid.*, 86.
6. On right hand/left hand imagery see my *Kierkegaard's Upbuilding Discourses*, Ch. 1, "Kierkegaard's Right Hand", 12–33 and 150.
7. Many of the points dealt with in the discussion of logic and existence in the *Concluding Unscientific Postscript* are also dealt with elsewhere as well, for example, in the introduction to *The Concept of Anxiety* (see 6 109ff./CA 9ff.).
8. A. Trendelenburg, *Logische Untersuchungen* (Berlin, 1840)
9. G. W. F. Hegel, *The Science of Logic*, A. V. Miller (trans.) (New York: Humanity Books, 1999), 82.
10. *Ibid.*
11. *Ibid.*, 83.
12. G. W. F. Hegel, *The Phenomenology of Spirit*, A. V. Miller (trans.) (Oxford: Clarendon Press, 1977), 2.
13. For a more sympathetic view of Hegel's argument see John W. Burbidge, *Hegel on Logic and Religion* (Albany: SUNY Press, 1992), 11ff.
14. Trendelenburg, *Logische Untersuchungen*, 23.
15. *Ibid.*, 25.
16. *Ibid.*
17. *Ibid.*
18. Or, as Merold Westphal has argued "What he [Kierkegaard] seems to have in mind is something like the propositional calculus of twentieth-century symbolic logic, a system demonstrably both complete and consistent, but one whose theorems are stubbornly noncommittal about which possible facts are actual" (*Becoming a Self: A Reading of Kierkegaard's Concluding Unscientific Postscript* (West Lafayette, IN: Purdue University Press, 1996), 86–7).
19. Westphal again: "[Hegel's] system ... does purport to give us substantive knowledge about God and the world" (*ibid.*, 87).
20. Hegel, *The Science of Logic*, 69.
21. Strictly speaking, Kierkegaard never used the expression "leap of faith", which is a result of strongly interpretative translation. See A. McKinnon, "Kierkegaard and the 'Leap of Faith'", *Kierkegaardiana* 16 (1993), 107–25.

22. J. Stewart, *Kierkegaard's Relations to Hegel Reconsidered* (Cambridge: Cambridge University Press, 2003), 496.

23. Trendelenburg, *Logische Untersuchungen*, 58.

24. Louis Mackey, *Points of View: Readings of Kierkegaard* (Tallahassee, FL: Florida State University Press, 1986), 157. For a critical response to Mackey see M. G. Piety, "The Place of the World in Kierkegaard's Ethics", in *Kierkegaard: The Self in Society*, G. Pattison & S. Shakespeare (eds), 24–42 (Basingstoke: Macmillan, 1998).

25. That Kierkegaard's argument might be seen as paralleling Hegel's own argument against Kantian scepticism does not mean that Kierkegaard's argument is not anti-Hegelian, since it could also be implicitly read as saying that Hegel did not, in fact, deliver what he claimed to deliver and, by virtue of having adopted idealist presuppositions, remained within the paradigm from which he sought to escape.

26. See J. Lippitt, *Humour and Irony in Kierkegaard's Thought* (Basingstoke: Macmillan, 2000), esp. Ch. 2, "Illusion and Satire: Climacus as Satirist". Westphal is also attentive to this comic strand in Climacus's argument. See Westphal, *Becoming a Self*, e.g. 84, 86.

27. It would, I think, be possible to argue for the "empirical" moment of Kierkegaard's thought on a history of ideas basis, by showing his indebtedness to several Danish predecessors, notably F. C. Sibbern and P. M. Møller (arguably even Bishop J. P. Mynster), who particularly emphasized the claims of empirical experience against Hegelian philosophy. However, that would be somewhat of a detour in the present context.

28. It could, for example, be argued that Schelling, despite his opposition to Hegel (an opposition that, as we have seen, Kierkegaard himself took note of), falls under the strictures of Kierkegaard's view that "an existential system is impossible". The same could be said of at least some of the radical left-Hegelians such as D. F. Strauss and L. Feuerbach, who rejected Hegel's idealism but also allowed themselves to forget what Kierkegaard regarded as the necessary distinction between the individual and "humanity at large".

29. Stewart, *Kierkegaard's Relations to Hegel Reconsidered*, 452.

30. Stewart also mentions the philosopher Rasmus Nielsen. However, his role is not as crucial as that of Martensen and Heiberg.

31. Stewart, *Kierkegaard's Relations to Hegel Reconsidered*, 471.

32. Westphal, *Becoming a Self*, 89.

33. The work in question is Schopenhauer's *On the Basis of Morality* (Providence, RI: Berghahn, 1995).

34. G. Lukács, *The Young Hegel*, R. Livingstone (trans.) (London: Merlin, 1975).

35. H. Küng, *The Incarnation of God*, J. R. Stephenson (trans.) (Edinburgh: T & T Clark, 1987).

36. A. Kojève, *Introduction to the Reading of Hegel*, J. Nichols (trans.) (New York: Basic Books, 1969).

37. K. Marx, *Early Writings*, L. Colletti (ed.) (Harmondsworth: Penguin, 1974), 387, original emphasis.

38. *Ibid.*, 389.

39. See, for example, H. Marcuse, *Reason and Revolution: Hegel and the Rise of Social Theory* (New York: Humanities Press, 1968); R. Heiss, *Hegel, Kierkegaard and Marx: Three Great Philosophers Whose Ideas Changed the Course of Civilization* (New York: Dell, 1963).

40. See, elegantly, S. Agacinski, *Aparté: Conceptions and Deaths of Søren Kierkegaard*, K. Newmark (trans.) (Tallahassee, FL: Florida State University Press, 1988), "On a Thesis", 33–78; also Pattison, *Kierkegaard, Religion and the Nineteenth-Century Crisis of Culture*, Ch. 5, "Food for Thought"; Stewart, *Kierkegaard's Relations to Hegel Reconsidered*, Ch. 3, "The Ironic Thesis and Hegel's Presence in *The Concept of Irony*".

41. Speculative philosophy is not the only target of Kierkegaard's attacks in Part I. He is also

preoccupied with the theological movement inspired by the contemporary preacher, poet and historian N. F. S. Grundtvig. However, that particular polemic does not really add essentially to the philosophical thrust of Kierkegaard's argument, and I have not therefore paid attention to it here. Obviously, however, it would have its place in any historical, literary or theological interpretation of Kierkegaard's work.

42. This is not a universally held position in theology. The radical Augustinianism adopted by the theologians of the Protestant Reformation holds that human beings were so damaged by the Fall of Adam that they no longer have any capacity for receiving salvation, and can only do so if this capacity is reinstated directly by divine action as the first step of regeneration. This is, in fact, a view that Kierkegaard himself seems to have promoted in *Philosophical Fragments*. What he is doing here is rather different and, in broad theological terms, seems more typically "Catholic" rather than "Protestant".

43. As previously mentioned, this had been the matter of an extensive debate in Danish philosophy in the 1830s.

44. S. Kierkegaard, *Concluding Unscientific Postscript*, D. Swenson & W. Lowrie (trans.), (Princeton, NJ: Princeton University Press, 1941), 279.

45. See especially my *Kierkegaard: The Aesthetic and the Religious* (London: SCM Press, 1999), Ch. 3, "The Dialectics of Communication", and *Kierkegaard's Upbuilding Discourses*.

46. The most substantive picture of the Kierkegaard–Schelling relationship is found in the articles collected in J. Hennigfeld & J. Stewart (eds), *Kierkegaard und Schelling: Freiheit, Angst und Wirklichkeit* (Berlin: de Gruyter, 2003). This volume concludes with important essays in English as well as in German.

Chapter 2: Anxiety

1. That being said, the introduction in *The Concept of Anxiety* does deal with some of the issues about logic and actuality that are also discussed in the *Postscript* and, as we shall see, the dialectic of possibility and actuality also plays an important part in *The Concept of Anxiety*.

2. Psychology was, for example, an important part of the thought of F. C. Sibbern, one of Kierkegaard's philosophy professors, and of Bishop J. P. Mynster, the theologian with whom he had a long and complex relationship.

3. "Dogmatics" means the systematic presentation of Christian doctrine, which, across Protestant Europe, was a regular part of university studies in Kierkegaard's time. "Theology" is a broader term, since it also comprises, for example, biblical studies. However, I shall follow general usage and occasionally use "theology" in the narrower sense of "dogmatics".

4. See Roger Poole, *Kierkegaard: The Indirect Communication* (Charlottesville, VA: University of Virginia Press, 1993), 100.

5. F. Nietzsche, *The Birth of Tragedy and The Genealogy of Morals*, F. Golffing (trans.) (New York: Doubleday Anchor, 1956), 178.

6. I am aware that I am making some very broad generalizations here that concern matters of intense scientific and public debate. However, my point is not to insist that this is how the differences between infants and adults or between animals and human beings are to be understood, but rather to characterize a long-held popular wisdom, what Heidegger might have called the point of view of average everydayness, for the purpose of clarifying Kierkegaard's starting-point.

7. S. T. Coleridge, *Opus Maximum: Collected Works*, T. McFarland & N. Halmi (eds) (Princeton, NJ: Princeton University Press, 2002), 73. See also his *Essay on Faith*.

8. Obviously one cannot indicate the nuances of a real-life situation in such a sketch, and

much will always depend on tone of voice, previous experience, total context and so on.

9. See Paul Tillich, *Systematic Theology* (one-volume edition) (Welwyn: James Nisbet, 1968), II, 45ff. ("Creation and Fall").

10. See J.-P. Sartre, *Being and Nothingness*, H. Barnes (trans.) (London: Methuen, 1958), 29.

11. I. Kant, "Religion within the Boundaries of Mere Reason", in *Religion and Rational Theology*, A. Wood & G. Giovanni (trans.), 39–215 (Cambridge: Cambridge University Press, 1996), 78. Kierkegaard's whole discussion here could bear close comparison with Part 1 of Kant's "Religion within the Boundaries of Mere Reason".

12. Erik H. Erikson, *Childhood and Society* (Harmondsworth: Penguin, 1965).

13. For the connection between anxiety and sexuality (or what Kierkegaard calls "the consequence of the relationship of generation") see 6 154–63/CA 62–73.

14. I have developed this point more fully in, for example, my *"Poor Paris!"*, 38–42, and in several of the essays in my *Kierkegaard, Religion and the Nineteenth-Century Crisis of Culture*.

15. S. Kierkegaard, *Purity of Heart*, Douglas V. Steere (trans.) (New York: Harper and Row, 1956).

16. The Kantian resonances of Kierkegaard's analysis in this text have been commented on several times. See, for example, Ronald Green, *Kierkegaard and Kant: The Hidden Debt* (Albany, NY: SUNY Press, 1992); J. Walker, *To Will One Thing: Reflections on Kierkegaard's Purity of Heart* (Montreal: McGill-Queen's Unviersity Press, 1972), and, most recently, Ulrich Knappe, *Theory and Practice in Kant and Kierkegaard* (Berlin: de Gruyter, 2004).

17. F. Nietzsche, *Thus Spoke Zarathustra*, R. J. Hollingdale (trans.) (Harmondsworth: Penguin, 1969), 160 (from the section "On Redemption").

18. The name has been glossed as "the fellowship of buried lives".

19. See, for example, the section entitled "The Unhappiest Man" in *Either/Or 1* and the sixth of the *Christian Discourses*.

20. It is not at this point relevant to investigate whether or not Kierkegaard is correct in his comment about Aristotle.

21. This distinction between "representation" (Danish *Forestilling*, cf. German *Vorstellung*), places Kierkegaard in a long-running discourse to which both Hegel and Heidegger are important contributors.

22. For a full discussion of this reference see N. N. Eriksen, *Kierkegaard's Category of Repetition: A Reconstruction*, Kierkegaard Monograph Series 5 (Berlin: de Gruyter, 2000), 69ff. Apart from the light it throws on the idea of the moment, Eriksen's discussion highlights the value of checking Kierkegaard's literary allusions, allusions that are often missed by readers naturally unfamiliar with literature that, in its time, was well known to Kierkegaard's readers.

23. F. D. E. Schleiermacher, *On Religion: Speeches to its Cultured Despisers*, R. Crouter (trans.) (Cambridge: Cambridge University Press, 1996), 112ff.

24. It is in this context that we can also read the long interlude in *Philosophical Fragments*, in which Kierkegaard discusses the question as to whether the past is more necessary than the future and concludes that it is not.

25. It is relevant to note Kierkegaard's concern here with the distinction between the human being and the animal, a motif that is also found in his description of the Fall.

26. Sartre, *Being and Nothingness*, 29.

27. M. Heidegger, *Being and Time*, J. Macquarrie & E. Robinson (trans.) (Oxford: Blackwell, 1962), 61–2, original emphasis (German edn, 37–8). Macquarrie and Robinson give the page numbers of the first German edition in the margins; hereafter references to this German edition are given in the text as "SZ".

28. Fans of Kierkegaard should not feel too bad about this since many other thinkers extensively studied by Heidegger in the preparation of *Being and Time* are only dealt with in

the text of *Being and Time* itself obliquely, *en passant* or not at all.

29. See Mark C. Taylor, *Journeys to Selfhood: Hegel and Kierkegaard* (Berkeley, CA: University of California Press, 1980), 5.

30. A. Come, *Kierkegaard as Theologian: Recovering My Self* (Montreal: McGill-Queen's University Press, 1997), 21.

31. Jörg Disse, *Kierkegaard's Phenomenology of the Experience of Freedom* (Freiburg: Karl Alber, 1991).

32. Calvin Schrag's *Existence and Freedom: Towards an Ontology of Human Finitude* (Evanston, IL: Northwestern University Press, 1961) is also still worth reading in this connection.

33. A. Grøn, *Subjektivitet og Negativitet: Kierkegaard* (Copenhagen: Gyldendal, 1997), 48.

34. We might also ask whether this is even a good portrait of Kierkegaard's own practice. He does, after all, make frequent use of the "literary repertoire", as in the reference to Ingeborg's glance and, given both the extent to which and the manner in which he plunders his own past for illustrations, he might well be accused of poetizing "half-dead reminiscences".

35. John D. Caputo, "Kierkegaard, Heidegger and the Foundering of Metaphysics", in *International Kierkegaard Commentary: Fear and Trembling and Repetition*, Robert L. Perkins (ed.), 201–24 (Macon, GA: Mercer University Press, 1993), 224.

Chapter 3: The good

1. This is a slightly freer translation than I have usually allowed myself, but I think that it accurately captures Wilhelm's idea.

2. Mikhail Bakhtin, quoted in G. Morson & C. Emerson, *Mikhail Bakhtin: Creation of a Prosaics* (Stanford, CA: Stanford University Press, 1990), 31.

3. A. MacIntyre, *After Virtue* (London: Duckworth, 1981, 1985), 42, original emphasis.

4. MacIntyre, incidentally, also rejects aspects of Kierkegaard's criticism of the aesthetic, arguing that one *can* choose the aesthetic with ethical seriousness. His example is that of the generation who, having experienced the horrors of the First World War, gave themselves over to lives of deliberate frivolity in the 1920s as a kind of ethical dissociation from the culture that had allowed the perpetration of such horrors. The example does not seem well chosen. The phenomenon was, in itself, far more complex than MacIntyre describes and it is not hard to find testimonies (such as that of the theologian Paul Tillich) that acknowledge the returning soldiers' "aesthetic" indulgence in sex, drugs, jazz and every latest fad of avant-gardism. But is also possible to see in such "aestheticism" a phase in a larger and deeper search for reorientation. It need not be lacking in compassion to say of such traumatized young men that if they did not in some way come out on the other side of their "aesthetic" indulgence, then they had succumbed to despair. In the context of another form of war trauma, there are many relevant reflections in V. E. Frankl, *The Doctor and the Soul: From Psychotherapy to Logotherapy* (Harmondsworth: Penguin, 1973).

5. MacIntyre, *After Virtue*, 41.

6. A. MacIntyre, "Once More on Kierkegaard", in *Kierkegaard after MacIntyre: Essays on Freedom, Narrative and Virtue*, J. Davenport and A. Rudd (eds), 339–55 (Chicago, IL: Open Court, 2001), 344.

7. See Chapter 2, note 14.

8. I. Kant, *Groundwork of the Metaphysics of Morals,* in *Practical Philosophy: The Cambridge Edition of the Works of Immanuel Kant*, M. J. Gregor (trans.) (Cambridge: Cambridge University Press, 1996), 67.

9. *Ibid.*, 69.

10. Walker, *To Will One Thing*, 4. The Kantian ambience of *Purity of Heart* has also been discussed by, among others, Ulrich Knappe (see "Kant and Kierkegaard on the Failure of the Unity of the Self", *Kierkegaardiana* 22 (2002), 155–71). Anthony Rudd rejects this "Kantian" approach on the grounds that, despite its low-key vocabulary (using "the Good" where we might expect "God" or "the Eternal"), the argument of *Purity of Heart* is determined by the conviction that "the will can only become single and thus 'pure', if it is directed to a higher power wholly other than what it is": that is, that it is, in Kantian terms, heteronomously determined. See A. Rudd, *Kierkegaard and the Limits of the Ethical* (Oxford: Oxford University Press, 1993), 137. However, this begs the question as to whether there may not be ways of conceptualizing this "higher power" non-heteronomously.

11. It is, of course, open to question whether the simple contest between "subjective" and "objective" points of view is more than a very rough and in some ways misleading way of stating the case. Walker is alert to the dangers of using these terms in simplistic, blanket ways; see *To Will One Thing*, 15–17. See also the short but characteristically insightful section "Objective/Subjective" in E. Mooney, *Selves in Discord and Resolve: Kierkegaard's Moral–Religious Psychology from Either/Or to Sickness unto Death* (London: Routledge, 1996), 80–81.

12. D. Edmonds & J. Eidinow, *Wittgenstein's Poker* (London: Faber, 2001), 2.

13. Mackey, *Points of View*, p. 40.

14. *Ibid.*, 62ff.; also Mulhall, *Inheritance and Originality*, 354ff. and John Lippitt, *Routledge Philosophy Guidebook to Kierkegaard and Fear and Trembling* (London: Routledge, 2003), 160ff.

15. On the role of the concept of attunement in Kierkegaard's writings about literature see my "Søren Kierkegaard: A Theater Critic of the Heiberg School", in *Kierkegaard and his Contemporaries: The Culture of Golden Age Denmark*, J. Stewart (ed.), 319–30 (Berlin: de Gruyter, 2003).

16. For a wonderful commentary on these and, more generally, on what she calls Kierkegaard's "Fictitious Stories", both in *Fear and Trembling* and elsewhere, see Jolita Pons, *Stealing a Gift: Kierkegaard's Pseudonyms and the Bible* (New York: Fordham University Press, 2004).

17. Including Lippitt, *Routledge Philosophy Guidebook*, 11. Note that the customary Anglo-American practice of writing "Johannes de Silentio" implies that "de Silentio" is some kind of surname (like "de Tocqueville"), but Kierkegaard does not do this: "de silentio" is printed on the original title page in bold Latin script following a Gothic script "Johannes", clearly showing that, however we are to understand it, it is *not* a surname.

18. C. Rogers, *On Becoming a Person: A Therapist's View of Psychotherapy* (London: Constable, 1961), 177–8, original emphasis. Rogers insists that such a person will also be better able to accept others and, in general, is to be regarded as "a positive ... constructive ... realistic ... trustworthy" member of society. Nietzsche, of course, would say something similar of the Superman.

19. See, for example, J. Kellenberger, *Kierkegaard and Nietzsche: Faith and Eternal Acceptance* (Basingstoke: Macmillan, 1997). Kellenberger by no means conflates the two, and is clear about the ultimate difference between them, but he brings them into the closest proximity, since it is just this proximity that makes the difference meaningful. See also B. Zelechow, "*Fear and Trembling* and *Joyful Wisdom* – The Same Book; A Look at Metaphoric Communication", *History of European Ideas* 12(1) (1990), 93–104.

20. L. Chestov, *Kierkegaard et la philosophie existentielle* (Paris: Vrin, 1972). Shestov also criticizes Nietzsche himself in similar terms. Nietzsche's recourse to eternal recurrence, he argues, is the manifestation of a last-minute loss of nerve in face of the absoluteness of the once-off uniqueness characteristic of a truly free life. However, whereas Brandes' criticism is directed precisely against the religious element in Kierkegaard, Shestov is

arguing for a view of religious faith that is a willed return to the "beyond good and evil" of Edenic innocence.

21. Quoted in A. Nagy, "Abraham the Communist", in Pattison & Shakespeare, *Kierkegaard: The Self in Society*, 196–220, esp. 207.
22. *Ibid.*, 208.
23. *Ibid.*, 208–9.
24. For a discussion of the alternative views that Abraham did not really expect to lose Isaac and that he did, see Lippitt, *Routledge Philosophy Guidebook*, 66ff.
25. Mooney, *Selves in Discord and Resolve*, 51.
26. *Ibid.*
27. E. Mooney, *Knights of Faith and Resignation* (Albany, NY: SUNY Press, 1991), 85.
28. *Ibid.*
29. J. Derrida, *The Gift of Death*, D. Wills (trans.) (Chicago, IL: University of Chicago Press, 1995), 68.
30. *Ibid.*
31. Lippitt, *Routledge Philosophy Guidebook*, 159.
32. M. Buber, "The Question to the Single One", in *Between Man and Man*, R. G. Smith (trans.), 60–108 (London: Collins, 1947), 60.
33. *Ibid.*, 63.
34. *Ibid.*, 62.
35. In T. W. Adorno, *Kierkegaard: Konstruktion des Ästhetischen, Mit einer Beilage* (Frankfurt: Suhrkamp, 1962), 270. See Guide to further reading for details of English translation.
36. A saying associated with the early Church theologian Tertullian, and reaffirmed in some texts by Kierkegaard.
37. *Ibid.*, 271.
38. A distinction taken up and systematized in Anders Nygren's *Agape and Eros: A Study in the Christian Idea of Love*, A. G. Herbert (trans.) (London: SPCK, 1932), in which Nygren contrasts the preferential and ultimately self-gratifying love designated as "eros" with the other-regarding love known as "agape".
39. K. E. Løgstrup, *Den etiske fordring* (Copenhagen: Gyldendal, 1991), 260.
40. See especially Jamie Ferreira, *Love's Grateful Striving: A Commentary on Kierkegaard's Works of Love* (Oxford: Oxford University Press, 2001).
41. *Ibid.*, 78–83.
42. Ferreira thinks not, and repeatedly emphasizes that in taking "God" as the middle term of the love relationship, Kierkegaard is actually strengthening the force of our obligation to love the actual human beings with whom we have to do in the world. See especially *ibid.*, 71–6.
43. Perhaps one could go further and, with Dostoevsky, imagine a situation like that of Sonia Marmeladova in *Crime and Punishment*, who prostitutes herself to support a family impoverished by her father's drunkenness.
44. This, it seems to me, is one of the central ideas of Amy Laura Hall's study *Kierkegaard and the Treachery of Love* (Cambridge: Cambridge University Press, 2002). Hall uses *Works of Love* as a key to reading a number of the early pseudonymous works.
45. See Pattison, *Kierkegaard's Upbuilding Discourses*, Chapter 4.
46. Don Cupitt, *After God: The Future of Religion* (New York: Basic Books, 1997), 83.
47. Cupitt also specifically links this with Kierkegaard's idea of remembering the dead, and using the memory of the dead to guide us in our daily choices.
48. Perhaps there is an intermediate state here to which Kierkegaard has not paid sufficient attention, something we might call comradeship, as perhaps in the Australian idea of a "mate": a relationship marked by preference but also imposing moral obligations. To be a "mate" you have to act like one, and not just turn up when your "mate" is buying the drinks.

49. See, for example, Nietzsche, "Of the Bestowing Virtue", in *Thus Spake Zarathustra*, 103–4.
50. J. Walker, *Kierkegaard: The Descent into God* (Montreal: McGill-Queen's University Press, 1972), 130.
51. Kant, "Religion within the Boundaries of Mere Reason", 78, original emphasis.
52. *Ibid.*, 79, original emphasis.
53. Some years ago Thomas Oden gathered many of these into a collection he entitled *The Parables of Kierkegaard* (Princeton, NJ: Princeton University Press, 1978).
54. See M. Thust, "Das Marionettentheateer Sören Kierkegaards", *Zeitwende* 1 (1925), 18–38.
55. See E. Mooney, "Moriah in Tivoli: Introducing the Spectacular *Fear and Trembling!*", in *Kierkegaard Studies Yearbook 2002*, N.-J. Cappelørn, H. Deuser & J. Stewart (eds), 203–26 (Berlin: de Gruyter, 2002), 209.

Chapter 4: The infinite qualitative difference and the absolute paradox

1. K. Barth, *The Letter to the Romans* (Oxford: Oxford University Press, 1968), 10.
2. See Chestov, *Kierkegaard et la philosophie existentielle*.
3. See E. M. Cioran, *Tears and Saints* (Chicago, IL: University of Chicago Press, 1995).
4. The relationship between the picture presented by the upbuilding discourses and Religiousness A is not, however, one of simple identity, although there are significant overlaps. Climacus's model is, broadly speaking, not as fleshed out as that of the discourses and has a more abstract, hypothetical character, in keeping with his own claim merely to be observing the process of becoming a Christian from the outside, and not as a believer.
5. See, for example, the classic expression of this view in Edward, Lord Herbert of Cherbury, *The Antient Religion of the Gentiles and Causes of their Errors Consider'd* (London, 1705).
6. See Pap IV C 29/JP 30373.
7. One could perhaps translate "*Forklaring*" as "clarification", thus drawing attention to the underlying metaphorics of illumination that permeate this discussion.
8. M. Theunissen, "Die Erbauliche im Gedanken an den Tod: Traditionale Elemente, innovative Ideen und unausgeschöpfte Potentiale in Kierkegaards Rede *An einem Grabe*", in *Kierkegaard Studies Yearbook 2000*, N.-J. Cappelørn & J. Stewart (eds), 40–73 (Berlin: de Gruyter, 2000; English translation forthcoming in *IKC: TDIO*).
9. *Ibid.*, 46–63.
10. Adorno, *Kierkegaard: Konstruktion des Ästhetischen*, 253.
11. In this connection it is worth adding that in a discourse of 1848 devoted to the question of resurrection, Kierkegaard insists that resurrection is to be understood entirely in terms of the self being under judgement and that not a word must be said about survival or the afterlife. See "The Resurrection of the Body is at Hand – of the Just and of the Unjust", in *Christian Discourses*.
12. For an anthology of key texts see Alan Schrift, *The Logic of the Gift: Towards an Ethic of Generosity* (London: Routledge, 1997). For the theological implications of the debate see the essays collected in John D. Caputo & Michael J. Scanlon (eds), *God, the Gift and Postmodernism* (Bloomington, IN: Indiana University Press, 1999). See also John Milbank, "Only Theology can Overcome Metaphysics", in his *The Word made Strange* (Oxford: Blackwell, 1997). See also "The Lord Gave, the Lord Takes Away, Blessed be the Name of the Lord", in *Eighteen Upbuilding Discourses*.
13. Derrida would seem to be supported by the Sermon on the Mount; see Matthew 6:3.

See also Luke 14:12–14.

14. Job 1:21. See the discourse of this title in *Eighteen Upbuilding Discourses*.

15. See J.-L. Marion, *God Without Being*, T. A. Carlson (trans.) (Chicago, IL: University of Chicago Press, 1991) and *Reduction and Givenness: Investigations of Husserl, Heidegger and Phenomenology* (Evanston, IL: Northwestern University Press, 1998).

16. For an exceptionally insightful discussion of this, see Pons, *Stealing a Gift*.

17. Barth, *The Letter to the Romans*, 49.

18. *Ibid.*, 50.

19. See Augustine, "The Usefulness of Belief", John S. Burleigh (ed. and trans.), in *St Augustine: Early Writings*, 284–323 (London: SCM Press, 1953).

20. D. F. Strauss, *The Life of Jesus Critically Examined*, M. Evans (George Eliot) (trans.) (London: SCM Press, 1973), 776.

21. *Ibid.*, 781.

22. G. W. F. Hegel, *Lectures on the Philosophy of Religion* (one-volume edition), Peter C. Hodgson (ed.) (Berkeley, CA: University of California Press, 1988), 454.

23. *Ibid.*, 455, original emphasis. This would also seem to anticipate Sartre's previously discussed notion of Christian existence as "the universal singular".

24. These arguments were, interestingly enough, repeated in the late-nineteenth and early twentieth centuries by debates between the personalist wing of British Idealism, as represented by A. S. Pringle-Pattison, and Hegelians such as Bradley, Bosanquet and McTaggart. From Pringle-Pattison's perspective the lack of a personal God in their systems made it impossible for them to secure the ideal of human personality to which some of them at least were committed. Divine personality was the precondition of human personality. See, for example, A. S. Pringle-Pattison, *The Idea of God in the Light of Recent Philosophy* (Oxford: Clarendon Press, 1917). Note also Hannay's reference to "personality" as a possible foothold for philosophical engagement with Kierkegaard – a concept that, for Hannay himself, is associated with John Macmurray, a direct inheritor of the personalist tradition represented by Pringle-Pattison (see Hannay, *Kierkegaard and Philosophy*, 7–8).

25. *Søren Kierkegaards Skrifter,* vol. 18 (Copenhagen: Gad, 2001), 331.

26. The ease of moving from one to the other can be indicated by the way in which the traditional Scottish version of the Lord's Prayer has "forgive us our debts" where the contemporary English translation has "forgive us our sins".

27. Of course, some religious traditions, including the Hebrew Bible, seem to know of unwitting sins, as when a person transgresses some ritual law by, for example, accidentally eating a forbidden food. But even here the "sin", although not the result of a deliberate act of defiant freedom, is what it is only within the structure of responsibility that binds the individual, his community and God.

28. Whether there are any extant human beings – especially within the once Christian Western world – who are so completely devoid of knowledge of the God-relationship as to be able to claim innocence is, of course, a whole further discussion. And already the claim to be innocent might, in a Kierkegaardian perspective, be regarded as suspicious!

29. This might once more be seen in relation to Derrida's supposition that I am always inevitably sacrificing one obligation for another.

30. See G. Lukács, *The Destruction of Reason* (London: Merlin, 1980).

31. She is often identified – without any good textual basis – in Christian tradition with Mary Magdalene and both are also often identified with Mary, the sister of Lazarus and Martha.

32. See John D. Caputo, *On Religion* (London: Routledge, 2001).

33. See the references to Kierkegaard in Don Cupitt, *Taking Leave of God* (London: SCM Press, 1982).

34. Note the caveat in Chapter 1, note 19.

35. I am not arguing here that Kierkegaard's account of the Christian life-view *is* the Christian life-view *tout court*. That would, certainly, require an intra-theological discussion going well beyond the remit of this introductory study. What I am emphasizing is that, like the Hegelians, he moves the ground of debate from the argument about the objectivity of dogmatic claims to what offers the best account of the human situation as we know it.

36. F. Nietzsche, *Die Fröhliche Wissenschaft,* aphorism 108, in his *Werke II*, K. Schlechta (ed.) (Frankfurt: Ullstein, 1969), 389.

37. M. Heidegger, *Beiträge zur Philosophie: Vom Ereignis* (Frankfurt: Vittorio Klostermann, 1989), 233.

38. One may, of course, choose simply to reject Heidegger's critique of onto-theology. Thoroughly to investigate what is to be said for and against this from either a philosophical or a theological viewpoint would go way beyond the scope of this book. My discussion here simply assumes that a contemporary reading of Kierkegaard within the continental tradition of philosophy will want to show itself not to be contained within the Heideggerian critique.

39. Merold Westphal, *Overcoming Onto-Theology* (New York: Fordham University Press, 2001), 11ff. Westphal insists that Kierkegaardian faith, so far from being hit by the Heideggerian critique of onto-theology, shares many of its underlying motivations.

40. It might also invite the reflection that, as Karl Löwith argued many years ago, the later Heidegger is no less theological and, indeed, no less Kierkegardian, than the early Heidegger. See K. Löwith, *Heidegger: Denker in dürftiger Zeit*, in *Sämtliche Schriften* vol. 8 (Stuttgart: J. B. Metzger, 1984), 156.

Epilogue: The Christian witness and the simple wise man of ancient times

1. However, one should add that although Socrates is generally the supreme example of this in Kierkegaard's authorship, he is also typical of Greek philosophy as a whole in this respect. The genuinely Greek thinkers, Kierkegaard insists, never forgot that what they were concerned about was the actual, existing human being.

2. M. Bakhtin, quoting Dostoevsky, in *Problems of Dostoevsky's Poetics*, C. Emerson (trans.) (Minneapolis, MN: University of Minnesota Press, 1984), 60ff.

3. See M. Heidegger, *What is Called Thinking?*, J. Glenn Gary & F. Wieck (trans.) (New York: Harper & Row, 1968), 17. Here Heidegger emphasizes that there is an intrinsic connection between Socrates' status as the "purest thinker of the West" and the fact that he wrote nothing.

4. See Pattison, *Kierkegaard's Upbuilding Discourses*.

Guide to further reading

This guide does not include all the books or articles referred to in the text, details of which will be found in the relevant footnotes. It does include a number of titles that are useful for the study of Kierkegaard that have not been discussed in the body of the book.

Works by Søren Kierkegaard

Works in Danish

1909–48. *Papirer*, vols I–XI iii, P. A. Heiber, V. Kuhr & R. Torsting (eds). Copenhagen: Gyldendal.

1962. *Samlede Vaerker* (20 volumes), 3rd edition, A. B. Drachmann, J. L. Heiberg & H. O. Lange (eds), P. Rohde (rev.). Copenhagen: Gyldendal.

1997– . *Søren Kierkegaards Skrifter*, N.-J. Cappelørn, J. Garff, J. Kondrup *et al.* (eds). Copenhagen: Gad.

Works in English

1967–78. *Søren Kierkegaard's Journals and Papers* (7 volumes, including index), H. V. Hong & E. H. Hong (ed. and trans.). Bloomington, IN: Indiana University Press.

1978–2002. *Kierkegaard's Writings* (26 volumes, including index), H. V. Hong & E. H. Hong (eds). Princeton, NJ: Princeton University Press.

1985. *Fear and Trembling*, A. Hannay (trans.). Harmondsworth: Penguin.

1989. *The Sickness unto Death*, A. Hannay (trans.). Harmondsworth: Penguin.

1992. *Either/or: A Fragment of Life* (abridged), A. Hannay (trans.). Harmondsworth: Penguin.

1996. *Papers and Journals: A Selection*, A. Hannay (trans.). Harmondsworth: Penguin.

2001. *A Literary Review*, A. Hannay (trans.). Harmondsworth: Penguin.

Series

Cappelørn, N.-J. & H. Deuser (eds) (& J. Stewart from 2000) 1996– . *Kierkegaard Studies Yearbook*. Berlin: de Gruyter.

Cappelørn, N.-J. *et al.* 1997– . *Kierkegaard Monograph Series*. Berlin: de Gruyter.

Perkins, R. L. (ed.) 1984– . *International Kierkegaard Commentary*. Macon, GA: Mercer University Press. (Each volume comments on a volume of *Kierkegaard's Writings*.)
1955– . *Kierkegaardiana*. Copenhagen: Reitzel.

Biographical and historical background

Garff, J. 2005. *Søren Aabye Kierkegaard*, B. Kirmmse (trans.). Chicago, IL: University of Chicago Press.
Hannay, A. 2001. *Kierkegaard. A Biography*. Cambridge: Cambridge University Press.
Kirmmse, B. H. 1990. *Kierkegaard in Golden Age Denmark*. Bloomington, IN: Indiana University Press.
Kirmmse, B. H. 1996. *Encounters with Kierkegaard*. Princeton, NJ: Princeton University Press.
Tudvad, P. 2004. *Kierkegaards København [Kierkegaard's Copenhagen]*. Copenhagen: Politiken.

General

Adorno, T. 1962. *Kierkegaard: Konstruktion des Ästhetischen, Mit einer Beilage*. Frankfurt: Suhrkamp. Translated as *Kierkegaard: Construction of the Aesthetic*, R. Hullot-Kentnor (trans.) (Minneapolis, MN: University of Minnesota Press, 1989).
Agacinski, S. 1988. *Aparté: Conceptions and Deaths of Søren Kierkegaard*, K. Newmark (trans.). Tallahassee, FL: Florida State University Press.
Connell, G. 1985. *To Be One Thing: Personal Unity in Kierkegaard's Thought*. Macon, GA: Mercer University Press.
Davenport, J. J. & A. Rudd (eds) 2001. *Kierkegaard after MacIntyre: Essays on Freedom, Narrative and Virtue*. Chicago, IL: Open Court.
Derrida, J. 1995. *The Gift of Death*, D. Wills (trans.). Chicago, IL: University of Chicago Press.
Dooley, M. 2001. *The Politics of Exodus: Kierkegaard's Ethics of Responsibility*. New York: Fordham University Press.
Evans, C. S. 1992. *Passionate Reason: Making Sense of Kierkegaard's Philosophical Fragments*. Bloomington, IN: Indiana University Press.
Fenves, P. 1993. *"Chatter": Language and History in Kierkegaard*. Stanford, CA: Stanford University Press.
Ferreira, M. J. 1991. *Transforming Vision: Imagination and Will in Kierkegaardian Faith*. Oxford: Oxford University Press.
Ferreira, M. J. 2001. *Love's Grateful Striving: A Commentary on Kierkegaard's* Works of Love. Oxford: Oxford University Press.
Ferguson, H. 1995. *Melancholy and the Critique of Modernity: Kierkegaard's Religious Psychology*. London: Routledge.
Hall, A. L. 1992. *Kierkegaard and the Treachery of Love*. Cambridge: Cambridge University Press.
Hannay, A. 1982. *Kierkegaard*. London: Routledge & Kegan Paul.
Hannay, A. 2003. *Kierkegaard and Philosophy: Selected Essays*. London: Routledge.
Hannay, A. & G. Marion (eds) 1998. *The Cambridge Companion to Kierkegaard*. Cambridge: Cambridge University Press.
Jegstrup, E. (ed.) 2004. *The New Kierkegaard*. Bloomington, IN: Indiana University Press.
Law, D. 1993. *Kierkegaard as Negative Theologian*. Oxford: Clarendon Press.
Léon, C. & S. Walsh 1997. *Feminist Interpretations of Kierkegaard*. University Park, PA: Pennsylvania State University Press.

Lippitt, J. 2000. *Humour and Irony in Kierkegaard's Thought*. Basingstoke: Macmillan.

Lippitt, J. 2003. *Kierkegaard and Fear and Trembling*. London: Routledge.

Malik, H. C. 1997. *Receiving Søren Kierkegaard: The Early Impact and Transmission of his Thought*. Washington, DC: Catholic University Press of America.

Matuštík, M. J. & M. Westphal (eds) 1995. *Kierkegaard in Post/Modernity*. Bloomington, IN: Indiana University Press.

Mooney, E. 1991. *Knights of Faith and Resignation: Reading Kierkegaard's Fear and Trembling*. Albany, NY: SUNY Press.

Mooney, E. 1996. *Selves in Discord and Resolve: Kierkegaard's Moral-Religious Psychology from Either/Or to Sickness unto Death*. New York: Routledge.

Mulhall, S. 2001. *Inheritance and Originality: Wittgenstein, Heidegger, Kierkegaard*. Oxford: Clarendon Press.

Pattison, G. 1998. *Kierkegaard: The Aesthetic and the Religious*. London: SCM.

Pattison, G. 1999. *"Poor Paris!": Kierkegaard's Critique of the Spectacular City*. Berlin: de Gruyter.

Pattison, G. 2002. *Kierkegaard, Religion, and the Nineteenth-Century Crisis of Culture*. Cambridge: Cambridge University Press.

Pattison, G. 2002. *Kierkegaard's Upbuilding Discourses: Philosophy, Literature, Theology*. London: Routledge.

Pattison, G. & S. Shakespeare (eds) 1998. *Kierkegaard: The Self in Society*. Basingstoke: Macmillan.

Pons, J. 2004. *Stealing a Gift: Kierkegaard's Pseudonyms and the Bible*. New York: Fordham University Press.

Poole, R. 1993. *Kierkegaard: The Indirect Communication*. Charlottesville, VA: University of Virginia Press.

Rae, M. 1997. *Kierkegaard's Vision of the Incarnation: By Faith Transformed*. Oxford: Clarendon Press.

Rée, J. & J. Chamberlain (eds) 1998. *Kierkegaard: A Critical Reader*. Oxford: Blackwell.

Rudd, A. 1993. *Kierkegaard and the Limits of the Ethical*. Oxford: Clarendon Press.

Shakespeare, S. 2001. *Kierkegaard, Language and the Reality of God*. Aldershot: Ashgate.

Smith, J. H. (ed.) 1981. *Kierkegaard's Truth: The Disclosure of the Self*. New Haven, CT: Yale University Press.

Walker, J. 1972. *To Will One Thing: Reflections on Kierkegaard's* Purity of Heart. Montreal: McGill-Queen's University Press.

Walker, J. 1985. *Kierkegaard: The Descent into God*. Montreal: McGill-Queen's University Press.

Weston, M. 1994. *Kierkegaard and Continental Philosophy: An Introduction*. London: Routledge.

Westphal, M. 1992. *Kierkegaard's Critique of Religion and Society*. University Park, PA: Pennsylvania State University Press.

Westphal, M. 1996. *Becoming a Self: A Reading of Kierkegaard's Concluding Unscientific Postscript*. West Lafayette, IN: Purdue University Press.

Index